Jewish Foreign Trade Officials on Trial

Jewish Foreign Trade Officials on Trial

In Gheorghiu-Dej's Romania 1960–1964

Veronica Rozenberg

LEXINGTON BOOKS
Lanham • Boulder • New York • London

Published by Lexington Books
An imprint of The Rowman & Littlefield Publishing Group, Inc.
4501 Forbes Boulevard, Suite 200, Lanham, Maryland 20706
www.rowman.com

86-90 Paul Street, London EC2A 4NE, United Kingdom

British Library Cataloguing in Publication Information Available

Library of Congress Cataloging-in-Publication Data

Names: Rozenberg, Veronica, author.
Title: Jewish foreign trade officials on trial : in Gheorghiu-Dej's Romania 1960–1964 / Veronica Rozenberg.
Description: Lanham : Lexington Books, an imprint of the Rowman & Littlefield Publishing Group, Inc., [2022] | Includes bibliographical references. | Summary: "This book describes a series of six staged economic trials conducted by the Romanian state against Jewish key officials between 1960-1964. Rozenberg places these trials in the context of the Romanian State's overall treatment of Jews and the strengthening of Gheorghiu-Dej's policy of national communism"— Provided by publisher.
Identifiers: LCCN 2021047199 (print) | LCCN 2021047200 (ebook) | ISBN 9781793652843 (cloth) | ISBN 9781793652850 (epub)
Subjects: LCSH: Trials (Political crimes and offenses)—Romania—History—20th century. | Romania—Officials and employees—History—20th century. | Jews—Legal status, laws, etc.—Romania—History—20th century. | Jews—Romania—Economic conditions—History—20th century. | Romania—Ethnic relations—History—20th century. | Foreign trade regulation—Romania—History—20th century. | Gheorghiu-Dej, Gheorghe.
Classification: LCC KKR40.P64 R69 2022 (print) | LCC KKR40.P64 (ebook) | DDC 345.4980231—dc23/eng/20211105
LC record available at https://lccn.loc.gov/2021047199
LC ebook record available at https://lccn.loc.gov/2021047200

I dedicate this book to my parents, Malvina and Adalbert Rosinger, whose lives were not crowned with joy and happiness, but who always knew how to face the vicissitudes of life with dignity and courage.

Veronica Rozenberg (Rosinger), July 2021

Epigraph

"And what do you say now?" asked the uncle, who had forgotten all the hurry and excitement with the letter and still seemed to have read it once.

"Yes, uncle," said K., "it's true."

"True?" Cried the uncle. "What is true? How can it be true? What kind of trial? But not a criminal case??"

"One Criminal trial," replied K.

"And you're sitting here quietly with a criminal trial around your neck?" cried the uncle, whose voice got louder and louder.

"The calmer I am, the better it is for the outcome," said K. tired, "don't fear anything."

"That can't calm me down!" shouted his uncle, "Josef, dear Josef, think of you, of your relatives, of our good name! You have been our honor so far; you must not become our disgrace. I don't like the way you're behaving," he said, looking at K. with his head tilted.

"I don't like it, no accused man who is innocent and still healthy behaves like that."

Franz Kafka, *The Trial*[1]

---

1 Franz Kafka, "Der Prozeß," p.32, Accessed on August 12, http://www.digbib.org/Franz_Kafka_1883/Der_Prozess_.pdf. The translation from German to English was done by the author of the book and edited by Ms. Deena Lari.

Contents

Foreword

A Daughter's Remarkable Victory

Arthur House

With the election of President Jimmy Carter in November 1976, national security observers questioned whether the new president, with little foreign affairs experience, could deliver on his promises to engage peace in the Middle East.

Right after the election, Senator Abraham Ribicoff, Democrat of Connecticut, chaired a Senate delegation with Senator Howard Baker, Republican of Tennessee, as vice chair meet with the Israeli leadership, and with certain Arab countries. Fortunately for me, the chairman was allowed to bring a note-taker and report writer.

Senator Ribicoff was famous in Israel as a prominent Jewish American and former member of President Kennedy's cabinet. Less well known was that in addition to chairing a major Senate committee (Governmental Affairs), he chaired the Finance Committee's Subcommittee on International Trade.

A major function of the latter was to review annual applications of Soviet satellite countries seeking trade status the same as "the most favored nation" (actually "normal status" would be more appropriate) and not be charged extra trade tariffs imposed on communist countries. To gain such status each year, Romania and its cohorts had to comply with the Jackson-Vanik amendment that required demonstrated freedom of emigration for dissident groups, especially Jews.

The delegation's arrival in Israel was a major news event. The King David Hotel in Jerusalem buzzed with activity as journalists sought interviews with the Senators, and others hoped to make contact for a wide range of reasons. Security kept distance between the Senators and those who sought contact.

Senator Ribicoff's wife, Casey, selected a few messages from those left at the front desk addressed to the Senator. She asked me to check them out.

Veronica (Rosinger) Rozenberg was in the hotel lobby, weary from camping there for a few days. She had a memorable face: attractive and tired, personable but driven. I was to learn that Veronica was the most patiently tenacious woman I had ever met.

Her story was striking, but all the setting had already been familiar to the International Trade Committee. She had been able to reach Israel, but her parents, Adalbert and Malvina Rosinger, were forbidden to leave Romania, because of Kafkaesque reasons regarding her father's previous governmental position in the Romanian Foreign trade. The Romanian state had imposed debts on Adalbert, claiming his work undermined the national economy and inventing national security reasons to prevent him from leaving.

The result was that her parents were forced to remain in Romania while she was allowed to emigrate to Israel.

Veronica had taken a bus to Jerusalem. When she left King David, I promised I would look into the case when we returned to Washington. She refused my offer of a meal at the hotel or bus fare home. She was wary. Her eyes showed the skepticism of one who had seen empty promises and bureaucratic indifference.

In the Senate, I established a case docket and included her parents in the committee's annual list for Romanian emigration permission. Veronica and I established and sustained correspondence despite no signs of progress.

Romanian President Ceausescu played an unusual role among the Soviet countries at the time, sometimes setting a relatively independent course in foreign relations that the Soviets tolerated because of his tough control over internal dissent. Most favored nation trading status was important to him. When he and Foreign Affairs Minister George Macovescu visited the United States in April 1978, President Carter invited Senator Ribicoff to participate in one of the most important working sessions at the time

Enter again the tenacious Veronica on her mission. She wrote me a letter, which I received just before President Ceausescu's arrival and included with it a personal letter from her to Ceausescu asking for her parents' release. Would I ask Senator Ribicoff to give it to Ceausescu?

The Senator liked the idea, admired Veronica's spunk and put the letter in his pocket. Later, he told me that during his meeting, Ceausescu had touted his government's compliance with Jackson-Vanik freedom-to-emigrate provisions, and the Senator countered to say they still were not adequate—and here was a letter describing a specific case to which he should pay personal attention.

Ceausescu issued Decree 131 two months later, on June 8, cancelling Veronica's father's phony debts, enabling him to emigrate to Israel and providing relief to others, including some who were not Jewish. The relief and joy of family reunion ended far too soon by her father's death. But Veronica's persistence was rewarded and created memories that will last forever.

Adalbert and Malvina shared much sorrow during their lives; however,they were blessed with a very loving and devoted daughter.

The Washington Post wrote that the Ribicoff-Baker delegation paved the way to the Camp David Peace Accords. Rozenberg's book with compelling style and a gifted pen tells a story far afield from that historic moment but tied to the same Senate delegation.

She gives voice to imprisoned souls seeking dignity in the face of harsh authoritarian bureaucracy. It's the triumph of a skilled and tenacious daughter.

Arthur House met Veronica Rozenberg when he was an aide to U.S. Senator Abraham Ribicoff. His subsequent career included work for the director of National Intelligence and in the private sector. He most recently was chief cybersecurity risk officer for the State of Connecticut. He is currently an adjunct professor at the University of Connecticut.

Acknowledgments

This volume, dedicated to my parents, Adalbert and Malvina Rosinger, is meant to bring to light the torture to which my father, Adalbert Rosinger, was subjected, along with other Foreign Trade officials during the 60s in communist Romania. The publication of this book is primarily the outcome of the complex doctoral dissertation in Hebrew that I completed in 2016 at the Department of Jewish History of the University of Haifa. For this, I thank the professors who were my supervisors, Ms. Minna Rosen, today Professor Emeritus at the University of Haifa, and Prof. Rafi Vago of Tel Aviv University.

My decision to embark on the challenging journey of translating my Romanian book into English was largely due to the influence of the multifaceted scholar, Prof. Michael Finkenthal, to whom I am most grateful. Without his advice, I probably would never have thought of translating the doctoral dissertation, which had already been turned into a book for Romanian readers, into English, in order to bring these sad and practically ignored events in Romanian history to a much broader audience. These events took place in the 1960s and they left a dark shadow on the life of a group of people who had served the country selflessly for over a decade.

For access to the rich documentation necessary to complete this book, in its first Romanian version, I would like to express my gratitude to Ms. Alina Pavelescu, deputy director of the Bucharest National Archives, Ms. Florica Dobre, former director of the National Council for the Study of the Securitate Archives (CNSAS) research department, and the other researchers of CNSAS who helped me locate the relevant documents amid the huge quantity of material in their care. These are Mr. Silviu Moldovan, the current director of the research department at CNSAS, Miss Alina Ilinca, Mr. George Vişan, and the entire team of workers of the Archives from Popeşti Leordeni, where the CNSAS documents are stored. Special thanks go to Mr. Valentin Fuşcan, historian at the Archives of Bucharest, who supported me in finding one of the most important documents I was looking for, and also to Ms. Mihaela Vişan, the director of the Economic Archives within the National Archives of Romania. I would also like to thank the people from the Chamber of Commerce and Industry of Romania, Ms. Ioana Oprea and Mr. Ovidiu Silaghi, who were kind and prompt in granting me the necessary copyright to use the photos of foreign trade companies.

Special and heartfelt thanks go to Professor Vladimir Tismaneanu of the University of Maryland, for being consistently available to answer my questions and for granting me a meeting in Washington, even prior to the completion of my thesis. Thanks to Ms. Oana Axinia Soare and Mr. Cosmin Budeanca, researchers at Institutul de Investigare a Crimelor Comunismului şi Memoria Exilului Românesc (IICCMER) and to Dr. Raluca Grosescu, today affiliated with Imre Kertezs College in Jena, both of them also offered their help. I also thank Mr. Adrian Cioflânca, director of the Center for the Study of Jewish History in Romania, Ms. Lya Benjamin a notable historian of the same Center and especially Ms. Germina Nagâţ of CNSAS, who offered me some accepted English translations of Romanian terms used in the Securitate documents.

My gratitude also goes to a considerable number of professors at various universities around the world, journalists, historians, and people of culture, who have offered me help through benevolent, professional, and timely responses to a wide range of queries, arising from the research and aimed at finalizing the first manuscript. I would like to mention the special assistance offered by Professor Emeritus Peter Solomon of Toronto, Canada, who had a special contribution in my understanding of criminal justice issues and terminology. Warm thanks go to the entire staff of the library of the University of Haifa, where I found an intellectual shelter without which it would not have been easy to produce this volume.

Special thanks are due to Ms. Deena Lari, for helping me with some of the translation, but mostly for editing the English translation of my book, first published in Romanian, which now, will be published thanks to the special kindness and interest of the publishing team at Rowman & Littlefield and Lexington Books.

Ms. Deena Lari, although she did not know much about this complicated subject, coming from a world completely different from the one depicted in the book, proved an exemplary capacity to penetrate and understand the gloomy realities that Romanian communism imposed on the country's population, under Gheorghiu-Dej's leadership.

I would also like to thank my friends who specialize in English, with whom I have sometimes consulted on certain special expressions whose origin was in Romanian, and who have helped me to give them the most appropriate translation in English, Ms. Mariana Segal and Ms. Marina Zaharopol.

In regard with the book cover, I would like to thank my friend Dr. Amalia Reisenthel, who helped me in the conceiving and creating its first versions and especially the graphic designer Ms. Cristina Barsony, who brought it into its final shape.

My thanks also go, of course, to my family: my husband, Jacov, my son, Igal, and especially my son, Eyal, who sometimes took an active part in producing the more concise adaptation of my written narrative. The book ultimately remains a tribute to my parents, Malvina and Adalbert Rosinger.

And last but not least, I am very grateful to Lexington Publishing House, and thank them from the bottom of my heart for agreeing to publish this book. Special thanks to Ms. Becca Beurer, managing editor at Rowman & Littlefield and Lexington Books, who has consistently responded with special attention and understanding to the questions I asked her in various situations, referring to multiple aspects, some complicated and others completely new, all raised by the publishing of this English volume. I also thank Mr. Carter Moran, acquisition editor at Lexington Publishing House, who offered his helpful advice in the technical aspects of the publishing process, and I thank the reviewer of my book, who provided a positive and encouraging review, contributing to the enrichment of the final version of my manuscript.

With the hope that this book will serve as an opening to a field as convoluted as it is unknown.

Introduction

> Lastly, I did not then know what I know today, that the past is not an archive, a warehouse where, either today, or tomorrow, or the day after, you could find the same things, just older, dustier, yet in essence the same. The past lives, is alive, participates in the present, influences and changes it in response to the things that happen to us. Similarly, the present changes the past and this mutual influence makes important memories to pale, to lose their vitality, while others gain new and unexpected sense. From nothing, they become essential events.
>
> Octavian Paler,[1] "Reflection in a broken mirror"[2]

The book focuses on secret legal proceedings that took place in Romania toward the end of Gheorghe Gheorghiu-Dej's[3] rule. These were lawsuits filed against a group of 27 high-level Jewish functionaries, who had been active in Romanian Foreign Trade for over a decade, as officials employed in several state-owned import-export companies.

The relationship between law and history is reflected in the way court proceedings and legal theories of the past are presented in their historical context. Some researchers believe that both law and history engage with the restoration of facts and the unveiling of additional meaning and importance of past events.

A grasp of the complex relationship between law and history is essential for understanding the events that characterized this late Stalinist period in Romania, and in that context, this book will pursue the goal of shedding light on a page of micro-history, characterizing the last period of Gheorghe Gheorghiu-Dej's leadership.

To best understand the nature of these legal proceedings, I will refer to the specifics of Romanian politics, both at the time of the trials and in the immediately preceding period.[4] Using primary sources, I will present a historic scan of a series of archival documents, which refer to events revealing the party officials' intentions and persistent activity aimed at fabricating a case against Jewish Foreign Trade functionaries and bringing them to trial.[5] The case was built little by little, in a step-by-step process with an eye toward the future proceedings, which would lead to the staged trials of the Foreign Trade officials, which took place between 1960 and 1964. The steps from suspicion to prosecution, from surveillance to arrest and investigation, culminated in the arraignment[6] before the military court. In this way, the Jewish high-level officials turned from the founders and those who carried on the Romanian Foreign Trade at its beginnings into criminals who were blamed for having tried to deceive the Romanian state. The Foreign Trade trials have never been researched before, and their existence was hidden from the eyes of their contemporaries. As the reasons given for these proceedings fall within the economic realm, I will refer to them as economic trials.

Since accusations of fabricated economic crimes were used to bring a predetermined group of people to trial, I call them "economic staged trials." Although such trials are usually referred to as "show trials" in literature, the Foreign Trade economic trials in Romania were conducted in complete secrecy, without the knowledge of the press or of anyone other than those convicted and their families.[7]

These trials brought back the typology of Stalin totalitarianism, which had dramatically shaped the history of the communist regimes in Eastern Europe after World War II, to the political scene of Romania. Through their timing, human typology, and especially their economic character, these trials stand out as unique in the political tapestry of the mid-1960s' Eastern European bloc.

For its relevance to the success of this project, I will further refer to the historical and political context that allowed the necessary research.

The apparently deficient management of Romania in recent history can be attributed to two main determining factors, among others. The first is the evolution of the communist regime in Romania, and the second is the way in which this regime was overthrown, through a sort of popular revolution that broke out sequentially in only a few of the country's cities and was violently repressed by the army and the Securitate forces.[8]

The research for this book involved by accessing previously locked primary sources,[9] which was made possible only because of radical changes in Romanian politics and legislatures after the fall of the communist regime in December 1989. Following those events, the abuses and atrocities committed by the Communist Parties became subjects of intense public scrutiny.

However, unlike that of the other countries in the Eastern European bloc, Romania's transition has been problematic and from certain points of view has not yet been successfully completed.

One of the consequences of these large-scale investigations was the release of communist and governmental records to both vested historians and the interested public. For instance, as a result of the promulgation of Law no. 187 / 07.12.1999[10] regarding the access to one's own file and the disclosure of the Securitate as the Romania's political police, the National Council for the Study of the Securitate Archives (CNSAS) organization was established.[11]

State's permission for the former victims and their descendants to access the information was much more dramatic.[12] The material that was actually released to the former victims of secret surveillance was only a very limited percentage of the huge volume of documents in the possession of the Securitate archives. The official reason invoked for this policy was that part of the files should be protected from the public eye as "state secrets."[13]

Several files that I requested during the long period of my research were never received, and there was no logical explanation for this. Consequently, there were pieces of information that I may have missed. In my opinion, this was due to the Securitate's opposition to releasing all the existing material for public scrutiny, a position that was supported by the government or the president of Romania.

The release of the archives was one of the first steps taken by the post-1989 transitional government in Romania, and it was meant to be followed by more aggressive, extensive steps. Just to review some of the laws that followed the change of the political regime in Romania, and which can be considered as expressions of the implementation of transitional justice, I would mention, for example, Law 118/1990 for the compensation of the people persecuted by the communist regime, or other laws relating to the return of property: Laws 112/1995, 10/2001, and 247/2005.[14]

Yet, this project stopped shortly after its start, and no more progress was made in the decades following the fall of the communist regime.[15] Political changes within the state, namely the transition from a totalitarian regime to a democratic one, could have met with success if all the measures required by the transitional justice had been implemented as planned.[16]

When one form of government is replaced by another, one would expect a consequential improvement in political, legal, and economic procedures that would benefit the citizens of the country. This is often intertwined with the idea of the trial and punishment of the perpetrators of the previous regime's crimes and misdeeds.

Transitional Justice refers to the complex set of legal and juridical measures meant to ensure the smooth transition from a totalitarian system to a democratic one. Among others, this compendium includes the revisiting of past injustices, the reevaluation or cancellation of past sentences and, if applicable, financial retribution to those found entitled to it. De facto, these measures were intended to correct and make amends for the injustices and abuses perpetrated by the communist totalitarian system in this case, on its victims. This phase can be considered completed when the political transfer from violence and repression to sociopolitical stability has taken place. In essence, the civil society works to ease the transition from violent repression to civic dialogue, from distrust to equitable human relations while contributing to laying the foundations of a government and of a legal system based on equity and fairness.

This would have been particularly important and necessary as the country's historical treatment of its minorities was both abysmal and fraught with oppressive relapses.

During the Romanian "gulag" period, for example, most of the detainees were citizens considered by the communist regime to be potential enemies of the state. Some were incarcerated for petty crimes; some were completely innocent. Most often, they represented the social classes deemed—quite arbitrarily—by the communist regime as "enemies of the people." Similarly to Soviet ideological patterns, some of those placed in this category were previous sympathizers of the system who, for various reasons, were later seen as its enemies. Another part were the ethnic minorities.

During the leadership of Gheorghe Gheorghiu-Dej in Romania, this policy was applied in similar ways. With the help of the Securitate[17] and the army branches that had remained loyal to the regime, these so-called enemies of the people were dealt with harshly. Those who held positions in the economic, political, and social sectors were arrested and sent to jail with heavy sentences. Among them, the high-ranking Jewish officials working for the Foreign Trade Ministry constituted a specific, distinct category.

METHODOLOGY

For the desired depth and accuracy of this work, primary sources were of utmost importance. Unfortunately, relevant oral testimonies could not be obtained as most of the defendants of the staged economic trials had passed away. Additionally, these historical witnesses, with just one exception, left no written documents detailing their ordeal at the hands of the communist regime. Consequently, the great majority of the primary sources were those found in various Romanian archives. Very few of them could be located in other archives, either in the Open Society Archive in Budapest[18] or even fewer in the Israeli State Archives.[19] According to the late historian Florin Constantiniu,[20] one of the most problematic aspects of the existing primary sources was the fact that they were written, almost exclusively, by those in charge of the trials themselves, and thus, in part, by the accusers or those who represented their interests.

From 2006 to 2013, I visited several administrative organizations in order to retrieve information relevant to the 1960–1964 economic trials. One of the sources I would have expected to consult was the archive of the Romanian Ministry of Justice, but unfortunately, there was no trace there of any of the trials this document analyzes. I suppose that the reason was that the entire judicial procedure was totally controlled by the former Romanian Securitate. Without success, I also approached other institutions: the National Police Department, the Department of Penitentiary, the Aiud Penitentiary, various ministries which had connections to the former Romanian Foreign Trade Ministry, and also the archives of the Ministry of Foreign Affairs and many others.

Ultimately, my main source for documentation was the CNSAS,[21] founded in 1999, with the goal of providing free access of the local and foreign public to individual records and files created by the Securitate during the communist regime. This archive was originally created to house all the records and files previously held by the Securitate.[22]

The second source in order of importance was the National Archives of Romania,[23] which made a series of important documents from the communist period available. I made use of its two archival sections: first, the one hosting the PCR archive, a voluminous collection of documents detailing the activity of the party during the years, second, the one hosting all other relevant documents, including the economic records relevant to my research. I was hoping to find decisions and orders showing a decision of PCR leaders to place functionaries of the Foreign Trade Ministry under surveillance but found no such documents. I was also hoping to find concrete written documents showing the party's intention to eliminate certain high-level functionaries employed in the Foreign Trade State Enterprises or in the Foreign Trade Ministry. The period I was interested in was post 1958, which had been a key year for significant party decisions. In the end, the only relevant document on this subject was located at the Bucharest Municipal Archives, a branch of the National Archives.

This unique document states the clear intention of the PCR to eliminate high-level Jewish functionaries from their respective positions. The first time I heard about this document was when I had the opportunity to read my father, Adalbert Rosinger's memoirs. The document was issued by the Ministry of Commerce,[24] as the written protocol during one of its October 1958 working sessions, which marked the beginning of the purging of Jewish functionaries from the same ministry and its affiliated enterprises. I also partly studied the archives of the Ministry of Foreign Affairs.

Unfortunately, many institutions associated with the now existing Foreign Trade Ministry, whose functionaries were involved in these trials, did not keep relevant records (other than payroll). The Românoexport company ("Intreprinderea Românoexport") is still active today, yet in a much-diminished role, as compared to its pre-1989 activities. It now functions as a joint-stock company. After contacting CNSAS as early as 2002, I was given access to the Românoexport trial file labeled as P179. Later, all the files of the six Foreign Trade trials were transferred from the former Securitate archives to CNSAS. The procedure included a restructuring process that resulted in change of pagination, archival change of the registration number, and adding an explanatory page at the beginning. Still, I must confess that several files (like surveillance files or personal files regarding part of the involved persons) requested during the long period of time my research took place were not received, and this happened without any logical explanation. Consequently, there were pieces of information that I have seemingly missed, because of unknown reasons, which in my opinion were a consequence of the Securitate opposition to forward all the possessed material for public documentation.

Having access to these documents, through visits to Romania during my research, allowed me to relive the experiences of the defendants in these trials, many of whom I knew personally. I felt that I was one of them, experiencing the investigations firsthand, or pacing within the confines of the small cells, walking along the long corridors of the Malmaison barracks,[25] or sitting in the courtrooms of the Regional Military Courthouse in Bucharest.

This was the space where the spectacle of the Românoexport trial, representing the case study of this book, was staged behind closed doors, from June 9th to July 9th, 1964.

Bringing to light the plight of the defendants in these trials is one of the main goals of the study which had led to my original Romanian book. Through its English translation, I hope not only to make available to a much larger audience their tragic personal and professional stories but also to showcase the legal and historical abuses, in the last part of Gheorghiu-Dej's leadership, as a micro-history page in the overall history of the communist regime in Romania.

NOTES

1. Octavian Paler (1926–2007) was a Romanian journalist and author. Between 1944 and 1977, he held important leadership positions with political clout, but was later scrutinized by the Romanian Securitate, due to his pro-Western views and his critique of the Romanian Communist Party (in Romanian, "Partidul Comunist Român," henceforth PCR) and its secretary, President Nicolae Ceaușescu. After

the fall of the totalitarian regime in 1989, Paler maintained his anti-communist position as an important member of the emergent civic society. Together with the philosopher Gabriel Liiceanu and the poet Ana Blandiana, he founded the Group for Social Dialogue ("Grupul de Dialog Social"). Accessed October 24, 2020, www.gds.ong.ro.

2. Octavian Paler, Autoportret într-o oglindă spartă (Iaşi: Polirom, 2010). http://dezvoltarepersonala2012.blogspot.co.il/2012/02/avem-timp.html.

3. Gheorghe Gheorghiu-Dej (1901–1965) was the first secretary of the PCR (ultimately "Romanian Workers' Party," PMR) from 1944 to 1954 and from 1955 to 1965. Under his rule, Romania was considered one of the Soviet Union's most loyal satellite states, though Gheorghiu-Dej was partially unnerved by the rapid De-Stalinization policy initiated by Nikita Khrushchev in 1956. Gheorghiu-Dej stepped up measures for rapidly increasing trade relations between Romania and the Western countries. However, at the same time his government was accused of human rights violations within the country.

4. See chapter 1 of this book.

5. The details will be found in chapter 3.

6. The English term "arraignment" is used for the Romanian expression of "trimitere în judecată," signifying the procedural activity carried out by the prosecutor after receiving the indictment conclusions file from the investigating body (Securitate in our case), following the termination of the criminal investigation. The information is translated from the internet dictionary accessed on February 14, 2021. https://legeaz.net/dictionar-juridic/trimitere-in-judecata.

7. A. Andreescu., L. Nastasă, A. Varga, & Centrul de Resurse pentru Diversitate Etnoculturală, *Minorităţi etnoculturale: mărturii documentare: evreii din România (1945–1965)* (Cluj: Centrul de Resurse pentru Diversitate Etnoculturală, 2003), 665 (item # 250), henceforth, Andreescu, *Minorităţi Etnoculturale.*

8. Raluca Grosescu, Raluca Ursachi, *Justiţia penală de tranziţie - De la Nürnberg la postcomunismul românesc* (Iaşi: Polirom, 2009), 112–113 (in English : *Transitional criminal justice - From Nuremberg to Romanian post-communism*).

9. In the study of history as an academic discipline, primary sources are constituted by any artifacts, documents, or diaries, manuscripts, recordings, or any other informative sources for the period studied. They are distinguished from secondary sources, which generally refer, cite, comment, or build upon these primary sources.

10. The law responsible for this access is known as the Law 187/07.12.1999 and, after its passing, was announced in the Official Monitor, Romania's national publication for legal matters, henceforth, MO, passed in no. 603 / 09.12.1999, Accessed June 22, 2021, http://legislatie.resurse-pentru-democratie.org/legea/187-1999.php

11. The National Council for the Study of the Securitate Archives, henceforth CNSAS, in Romanian Consiliul Naţional pentru Studiul Arhivelor Securităţii, Accessed July 12, 2021, cnsas.ro

12. Lavinia Stan, *Transitional Justice in Post Communist Romania: The Politics of Memory* (Cambridge: Cambridge University Press, 2012), 58, henceforth Stan, *Transitional Justice in Post Communist Romania.*

13. Ibidem.

14. For instance, the Laws 112/1995, 10/2001, and 247/2005. These laws, enacted by the Romanian parliament as restitution laws, stipulated that buildings and lands that were forcibly taken by the state, organizations, or official persons or nationalized between 6/03/1945 and 22/12/1989 should be returned under the same conditions. For situations where return is not possible, corrective action will be taken, according to the value of the expropriated property.

15. After the revolution in December 1989, the leadership was taken over by the State President Ion Iliescu, and that of the government by Petre Roman, among the ministers who held important functions during the previous communist time. The evidence most representative of Romania's inability to lead the transition to completion was the fact that unlike all the other former communist countries of Eastern European bloc, in Romania to this day, a law of lustration has been rejected by majority vote, by Decision no. 308 of March 28, 2012.

16. The term "Transitional Justice" was coined in 1995, as a result of the publication of Neil J. Kritz (ed.), *Transitional Justice: How Emerging Democracies Reckon with Former Regimes* (Washington, DC: US Institute of Peace Press, 1995). The term was developed later by Prof. Ruti Teitel, Professor of Comparative Law, University of New York in her homonymous book *Transitional Justice* (London: Oxford Univ. Press, 2000).

17. It was the popular term used for the Departamentul Securității Statului (Department of State Security), the secret police agency of the Socialist Republic of Romania, henceforth Securitate.

18. Also known as OSA, the archive contains the materials broadcasted by the Free Europe radio station during the communist period, in the Eastern European bloc, accessed July 20, 2021, http://www.osaarchivum.org.

19. In Hebrew, Ginzah Hamedina, it is located in Jerusalem, Accessed July 20, 2021, https://www.archives.gov.il/en/.

20. Florin Constantiniu (1933–2012) was a well-known Romanian historian. Among his important books can be named, *O Istorie Sinceră a Poporului Român* (Bucureşti: Univers Enciclopedic, 2002) (in English, A Sincere History of the Romanian People), which had seen several reprints.

21. For more information, please see, http://www.cnsas.ro. Accessed December 1, 2019. All the references to the CNSAS Archives will be mentioned as ACNSAS, Pxxx/Ixxx/Rxxx, vol. YY, pp. aa–bb, where P-penal, I- informant, and R- network are the types of files, xxx or xxxxx their numbers, YY the volume number of the xxx file, and aa–bb the page range. The letter v will be added where the intention is to refer to the verso of the same page.

22. Presently, the accepted Romanian acronym for the former Securitate department remained SRI, Serviciul Roman de Informaţii, or the Romanian Intelligence Service.

23. In Romanian, Arhivele Naţionale ale României, Bucharest. All the references to the ANR Archives will be mentioned as ANR, Fond XXXX, YYY Section, File AA/BBBB, pp. aa–bb. The letter v will be added where the intention is to refer to the verso of the same page. Accessed July 15, 2021, http://arhivelenationale.ro/site/en/first-page/

24. The Ministry of Foreign Trade (in Romanian, Ministerul Comerţului Exterior, MCE) was at times a part of the Ministry of Commerce, together with the Ministry of Internal Trade, but at times it had an independent status, as a separate ministry, the MCE, as it happened during the economic trials.

25. "Locuri in Bucureşti" (in English, "Places in Bucharest"). Accessed October 24, 2020. https://armyuser.blogspot.com/2009/06/cazarma-malmaison.html.

Chapter 1

Romania's Post–World War II Sociopolitical Context

ROMANIA ON ITS WAY TO COMMUNISM

This chapter presents a brief historical overview of Romania between the two world wars. As the only Eastern European country with Latin origins, Romania prided itself in preserving and upholding this heritage which made it unique in the region.

Romania after World War I

Like all of the other Eastern European countries, after the end of World War I, Romania went through major geopolitical changes. As a result of the 1919 Versailles and the 1920 Trianon peace treaties, Romania regained some of its historical territories (Bessarabia, Bucovina, and Transylvania), where a large population of Romanians lived. In addition to the population increase, the reannexation of these territories also brought about abundant natural resources, which would later support the economic growth of the country. Romania became a unitary state when the two principalities of Wallachia (Ţara Românească) and Moldova merged in 1859, and soon afterward, in 1877, the newly formed statal entity gained its independence from the Ottoman Empire.

In 1918, Transylvania and Bucovina, more advanced economically and culturally and previously under Austro-Hungarian rule, were added to the national territory and helped foster rapid economic, social, and political growth.

It is usually believed that "geopolitics are determined by the relationships between political power and the geographic space,"[1] yet in the case of Romania post-World War I, none of the promises of the acquired territories took form in the political and economic arena. Despite annexing new territories and the fact that Greater Romania had a great economic headstart, the new country failed to experience the growth that could have been expected.

Later, during the interwar period (1929–1933) and after the global economic crisis, Romania experienced a time of moderate economic growth, with state-run protectionist economic practices. It might be reminded that following the depression in these years, in 1938, Romania achieved record growth compared with both the preceding period and the years immediately following. Lucreţiu Pătrăşcanu[2] noted that, despite these developments, Romania's political presence was not as established as those of the other countries in Eastern Europe.

Romania's internal political activity before World War I was very limited.[3] The country was a constitutional monarchy, and the right to vote was income-based. As such, the majority of the population, comprising peasants and blue-collar workers, had limited political power. It is worth mentioning here that according to an opinion launched by other scholars, "proposals for and against reforming the countryside were tied up with the definitions of the peasantry as the repository of the national spirit."[4]

The political parties active at the time included the Conservative Party (representing landowners)[5] and the Liberal Party (representing industry owners and bankers). For these two parties, the Romanian Parliament was the background against which political games and frequent changes of power took place, with King Carol I[6] having the last word. After the end of World War I, the Conservative Party saw a sharp decline following the implementation of the 1921 Agrarian Reform when most of the landowners lost their vast properties.

The 1919 Versailles Treaty[7] sparked numerous changes in the Romanian political arena at the time, and the most important ones are detailed here.

- Although these changes fulfilled nationalist dreams, they also brought tremendous problems of reorganization and unification. While it facilitated and supported its national aspirations, it also highlighted the large presence of the minorities (almost 30% of the entire population).[8] The task of unifying the administrative, fiscal, juridical, and religious apparatuses proved arduous because now, Romania's population contained 28% national minorities as compared to only 8% in the prewar times, all making claims and looking towards outside powers.[9] Therefore, those concerned about urban ethnic imbalances sought to encourage Romanians' social advancement into elite status, as well as to raise their cultural level and thereby encourage the minorities to assimilate.[10]
    - Addressing the national minorities[11] in the country's territory was an imperative for interwar governments. As such, it required a specific

political restructuring as well as a "cultural offensive"[12] to secure absolute control over its new territories.

  - The soul and essence of the Romanian people continued to be wrapped in the strong influence of Eastern Orthodoxy. Partisans of a peasant-based, ahistorical national essence objected strenuously, for instance, to proposals for industrializing Romania.[13]
  - This situation was partially responsible for the rise of the Legion of Archangel Michael.[14] Founded on July 24, 1927, by Corneliu Zelea Codreanu, it preached a radical nationalistic ideology with fascist inclinations and clear anti-Semitic tendencies that later translated into a radical nationalist political party. The latter exhibited the same characteristics, its nationalistic ideology and anti-Semitic policies came to be known as clerical fascism.[15] The Legion of Archangel Michael's ideology was built on popular and Christian Orthodox beliefs deeply imbedded in the general population's psyche, making it easy to manipulate popular sentiments.
- Numerous revolutionary events in the area, that is, the liberal-revolutionary movements in Europe, the 1917 Russian revolution, and the 1919 Hungarian revolution impacted the political activities of the country. Namely, they forced Ferdinand I,[16] the Romanian monarch at the time, and the country's leading parties to take action and implement sociopolitical measures for long-term reforms, among them are
  - changing the voting system, from one based on income to one universally available (June 1917) and
  - finalizing a new Constitution (March 1923).

Yet, despite these important internal measures, the constant changes of political power within the Romanian government, primarily between the National Peasants' Party (PNT)[17] and the National Liberal Party (PNL),[18] prevented lasting stability from taking root.

Additionally, as a consequence of the global economic crisis from 1929 to 1933, the living conditions quickly deteriorated in the country, and this, in turn, fueled nationalistic and anti-Semitic tendencies. The Legion of Archangel Michael transitioned into political activity under the name the Iron Guard in 1930 and played an important role in the internal political arena up until the first stages of World War II. The party went through several changes. It dissolved in 1933 and was replaced two years later by "All for the Country."[19] The latter, in particular, exercised considerable influence during the 1937 elections and had a substantial presence in the anti-Semitic Goga-Cuza government[20] (17% or, 66 out of 387 total seats).[21] In the interwar period, the Goga-Cuza government was the second overtly anti-Semitic government in Europe, after the Nazi party already in power in Germany.

> An association between "Jew" and "Bolshevik" exacerbated the problems Jews now faced in Romania and augmented the currents of antisemitism already flowing prior to World War I.[22]

Close inspection of the convergence of factors that facilitated the rise to power of nationalistic and fascist movements in Romania reveals that the external events alone, numerous though they might have been, could not have won over the local population so quickly, despite the fact that both Italian fascism and the German socio-nationalistic ideologies were being adopted on the continent. However, the local conditions were more than ripe for such ideas and their accompanying practices to appear and quickly gain traction.[23]

For example, in an interview for *The New York Times*, Professor Alexandru C. Cuza,[24] a minister at the time,[25] expressed his desire that "every single Jew shall pack up his baggage and leave Romania."[26] In the same year, 1938, under Carol II,[27] the monarchy took a turn toward the dictatorial end of the political spectrum, and the Iron Guard was expelled from the political arena, despite having played a crucial role in the king's return to Romania in 1930.

Analyzing this specific period of the twentieth century:

> In both Romania and the other countries of the Eastern European bloc, the belief that Western style democracies could be transplanted in areas with vastly different histories and social structures than those where democracy was the norm (Western Europe or North America), failed.[28]

The Socialist Movement in Romania

Inception and Key Players

At the end of the nineteenth century and the beginning of the twentieth century, Romania was primarily an agrarian society whose economy was in the hands of its landowners and the emergent urban bourgeoisie. The slow modernization and late emergence of an industrial proletariat with a politically active inclination were among the reasons for the delayed and rather pale leftist movement in Romania.[29] Nevertheless, the industrial development ultimately saw the emergence and political participation of the new socioeconomic class, that of the factory workers. This class was quickly influenced by socialist thinking, either through Romanian intellectuals educated in the West, or through Russians and Serbian refugees, escaping the wrath of tsarist authorities. Among them, Constantin Dobrogeanu-Gherea[30] is considered one of the key influencers and facilitators for the Marxist and Socialist ideology on Romanian soil. He was the one who asserted: "The nation is a sentimental ideological Utopian fantasy that does not exist."[31]

It can be said that such ideas reflected the internationalism of the socialist movement at the time, and its propagating of the ideology for the dismantling of the Nation, by upholding the rights of its minority communities.[32]

An interesting idea Gherea expressed was the recognition of the need to follow legal channels in order to achieve the political and economic objective of the emancipation of the working class.[33]

The Social Democratic Workers' Party of Romania,[34] modeled after the German Social-Democratic Party,[35] was founded on March 31, 1893. It dissolved shortly afterward due to lack of funding and differences of ideas (1899).

The General Commission of Trade Unions in Romania[36] was founded in 1906 with the goal of putting socialist ideas into practice and promote the rights of the workers.

The Romanian Social Democratic Party[37] was founded on January 31, 1910, and among its members, only a few were Jews. During World War I, when Romania remained neutral, this party maintained a pacificist agenda and worked toward enacting political changes and creating a local democracy based on socialist principles. On December 11, 1918, the party changed its name to the Socialist Party and, similar to its Soviet Bolshevik counterpart, adopted a Mission Statement.[38] According to this document, the political power had to belong to the people who would, in time, create a new political regime, the dictatorship of the working class.

In March 1919, after the founding of the Third Communist International, that is, the Comintern,[39] members of the Socialist Party had to decide either to support it by joining or to oppose it. Consequently, this internal conflict later resulted in the splitting of the Socialist Party into two distinct groups. In 1921, one of the factions became the future PCR[40] and the other continued as the Social Democratic Party.[41] During the interwar period, the latter worked to consolidate its power around economic and political objectives and improve the living and working conditions of the workers without necessarily aiming to also change the political status quo in the country.

The Evolution of PCR

PCR was formed as a result of the ideological rift between the traditionalist and moderate social-democrats, the radical communists, and the extremists, who were ready and eager to follow Moscow's most radical directives to achieve their ultimate goals. When it comes to these goals, the Bolshevik party exerted substantial effort to bring the Comintern members under its direct jurisdiction and control.

Initially, some of the PCR leaders believed in the importance and the role of Bolshevik principles in the institution of a new type of political regime in

Romania. Yet, as they soon found themselves trapped in Stalin's harsh prisons, their attitudes and beliefs regarding the moral qualities of the doctrine quickly changed. Shortly after its inception, the PCR failed to increase its presence and influence. One of the things responsible for this situation was the fact that it propagated ideas that were in direct opposition to the wishes of the Romanian people. One of these ideas was the separation of Bessarabia from the newly reunited Romanian state.

An even more important element for the future of Romanian national ideology was the position taken by the Communist International between 1922 and 1928, when it openly supported minority struggles for national liberation even where these jeopardized the integrity of already constituted existing sovereign states.[42]

This set of ideas was strongly encouraged by the Soviet Union that framed it as "autodeterminare," for example the right of Bessarabia to become an autonomous region. In truth, the Soviet Union opposed Romania's control over it, despite the fact that most of its citizens shared the same ethnic, cultural, and linguistic origin with their neighbors, the Romanians.

> Romania itself was labeled an imperialist creation and an oppressor of its newly acquired minorities. Because of this challenge to the country's political integrity, the government banned the newly formed Romanian Communist Party and its potential contributions to defining the national soul.[43]

PCR's political activities resulted in it being made illegal in 1924, shortly after its founding. Under the Communist Internationale's requirements, it continued its existence, but not without internal strife, ideological conflicts, and leadership replacements.

In 1931, after the PCR's 5th Congress, a new leader emerged from its ranks. By trade, a railroad electrician, Gheorghe Gheorghiu (later, he added the suffix Dej,[44] to his name)[45] was active and arrested during the railway workers' strike at the "Griviţa Roşie" factory in 1933. As a result of these events and his implication in the trial that followed, Gheorghiu-Dej became the de facto leader of the workers.[46]

Shortly after the beginning of World War II, this period, characterized by dictatorial tendencies on King Carol II's part and exacerbation of nationalist policies, ended in several key events. Although Romania generally maintained its neutrality in the war, the king's policies favored German interests, and this resulted in a direct collaboration between 1940 and 1943. In 1940, in an unfortunate move, Ion Antonescu was named through the Royal Decree signed by Mihai I. Antonescu as the head of the state and as prime minister of the country.[47] He would be the one who would later force King Carol II to give up the crown in favor of his son, the future king Michael I.[48] Antonescu took firm control of the situation and instituted a fascist dictatorship and, in the same year, Romania entered the war, alongside the Axis powers.

In 1944, when Germany's impending defeat became apparent, King Michael I, in collaboration with several leading parties, including the National Liberal Party, the National Peasants' Party, and PCR, removed Antonescu from power and, soon after, Romania joined the Allied Forces. The PCR, which, until then, had a modest membership of a little more than a thousand, started to expand its numbers through general mobilizations. Its membership grew from 250,000 in 1945, to 600,000 in 1948.[49]

The increase of PCR's political power and influence was facilitated by the Soviets' occupation, their close collaboration and the continuous presence of Soviet party members in Romania, which continued even after 1944. The latter played a major part in the implementation of drastic measures to suppress the freedom of the local population.[50]

ROMANIA: STAGES AND EVENTS

A People's Republic under Gheorghiu-Dej's Leadership

After its political legalization in 1944, the PCR quickly gained political power and, by 1947, it managed to assure its political supremacy in the country. Consequently, in the same year, the monarchy was abolished and King Michael I was sent into exile. This was the year when the Romanian People's Republic was declared. In the same year, the Social-Democratic Party and the Communist Party merged as the Romanian Workers' Party.[51] In order for the new party to maintain its political supremacy, the Patriotic Guards[52] and the information services were established and were given an increasingly prominent role by Romania's party leadership in the following years. Emil Bodnăraş,[53] one of the key players in these political machinations, had an important role not only in the FLP but also in the establishment of the "auxiliary services."[54] The latter worked to cover the presence and the actions of Soviet agents who had infiltrated the Romanian Police and the Securitate, once the Ministry of Internal Affairs was taken over by the Romanian communists.

By 1948, the PMR had gained effective control of all political institutions in the country. The elections scheduled for March 28 of the same year were meant to establish a parliamentary system in service of the communist regime and its new constitution.[55] The new parliament, called the Great National Assembly,[56] had only one party, the PMR, which, after 1946, was responsible for the establishment of the totalitarian regime. During this period, two distinct groups vied for political power: the "Muscovite" faction, which included Emil Bodnăraş, Vasile Luca, and Ana Pauker, and the "Local" faction, centered around ex-innmates from Doftana, a famous prison for political activists in the interwar period. Among the latter, Gheorghe Gheorghiu-Dej figured prominently.

Between 1944 and 1947, several state-based organizations were founded to support the radical changes envisioned by the PMR. First, on August 30, 1948, the Ministry of the Interior[57] headed by Teohari Georgescu was established. Georgescu, appointed as minister, reorganized the "Miliţia" system. The secret police was founded as a special department of MAI, known as the Securitate.[58] The official name of this department was the DGSP's Security. In April 1949, the whole legal system was replaced by a new one, and changes were incorporated into the country's system of government and its economic policy. Because of this new legislation, the prison system and later associated work colonies were made fully subordinate to the new regime in 1949 by their transfer from the jurisdiction of the Ministry of Justice to that of the Ministry of Internal Affairs.[59]

Within this new political system, the three operating branches, the legislative authority (Council of Ministers[60]), the juridical authority (the judges and the prosecution), and the executive authority (the government) were de facto in service of the PMR. The New Criminal Code, introduced in 1948, boasted methods to deal with "dangerous actions against society." These actions were not yet categorized as crimes but as felonies.[61] A network of "control and surveillance" developed with thousands of people under surveillance, some not even affiliated with the Communist Party. Gradually, as the political system veered toward dictatorship, this network perfected its intimidating and repressive mechanisms.

Many of those judged and convicted by the new juridical system were sent to labor camps like the Danube-Black Sea Canal[62] or to other work camps. Among them, a majority were farmers and clerks who had refused to adopt the communist ideology. To describe their stance, a new vocabulary was developed, which included terms like "deviation from the party line," "enemy of the people," "anti-revolutionary propaganda," "sabotage," and "agitation."[63] After firing army leaders, nationalizing privately own land, and confiscating privately held capital, the party set its sights on the Jewish population. The latter was considered a poisonous weapon serving Anglo-American capitalism and undermining the emergent communist society.

Between 1953 and 1954, several trials took place in Bucharest and Timişoara, against Jews, identified as Zionists, which were documented by Romanian-Jewish historians who had relocated to Israel. Some of them had been themselves implicated in these trials.[64] The new 1952 Constitution stated that the Romanian Workers' Party would be leading the political and social order of the country, unchallenged.

The eliminations of several top leaders of the Communist Parties in the early fifties, which took place in almost all the countries of the communist bloc, were largely dictated by Stalin's ambitions, obsessively pursuing the destruction of the "enemy from within," anyone who was possibly harboring "Zionist," "Titoist" inclinations, or other potentially imaginary opponents. Although in almost all the states that became People's Republics, the circumstances in which the staged trials took place were diverse, the abuse of power exercised by Stalin involved not only the removal of Jews who had survived in local administration and politics but also the elimination from the political scene of supposed political opponents, who held political positions.

Unlike in other countries, in Romania, eliminations were not incited by Stalin's decrees but by Gheorghiu-Dej's desire for absolute power and his requests to do away with anybody who could rise against him. In Romania, in particular, this struggle was almost exclusively an expression of personal conflicts in the process of climbing to the top of the power pyramid.

Around the same period, a political schism took place and, as a result, the group of politicians known as "right sympathizers"[65] was also eliminated. Initially, the staging of a trial similar to other trials that took place in Czechoslovakia, Hungary, or Bulgaria was planned in order to facilitate the elimination of the triumvirate. Yet, in Bucharest, this show-trial ended differently.[66] In his dealings, Gheorghiu-Dej benefited from the support of Stalin, who considered him a loyal follower of Kremlin policies and an autonomous local leader who could be trusted.

Consequently, Alexandru Drăghici[67] was appointed to the position of Minister of Interior instead of Teohari Georgescu. His advent solidified the PMR's political clout and that of his leader, Gheorghiu-Dej. The latter was preoccupied with eliminating Lucreţiu Pătrăşcanu, one of his stronger rivals. Lucreţiu Pătrăşcanu was one of the few early Romanian communists with a solid reputation, as both a genuine Marxist and a patriot.

The investigation against the latter, imprisoned in 1948, was prolonged and lasted for six years. At its conclusion in 1954, Lucreţiu Pătrăşcanu was sentenced to death. It was one of the heinous crimes committed by the Georghiu-Dej government, for which it never assumed responsibility.[68] More such purgings took place, targeting highly placed functionaries, mostly Jews, who worked in Militia, Army, public administration, economics, and cultural institutions.[69] To lend some legitimacy to these purgings, those marked as "enemies of the people" were involved in staged trials, judged by military courts. One example of such trials was the Danube-Black Sea Canal trial, when a military court was temporarily relocated to Poarta Alba,[70] and another one was the Zionists' trials.[71]

A good way to understand the constitution and function of the Romanian totalitarian regime is to imagine a pyramid with the Securitate at the top and the representatives of the Militia and the Prosecution at its base. The economic centralization followed similar patterns and was instituted through forced collectivization and industrialization. The State Planning Committee (CSP) was founded in 1948 to oversee the implementation of measures in all industrial sectors and the management thereof. Initially, Romania's economy was geared toward the development of industrial branches selected by the Soviet Union as potential producers of goods toward war reparations. This operation materialized in the formation of the Sovroms.[72] Despite this added economic burden, the Romanian economy at the beginning of the 1950s experienced impressive growth, which rivaled that of industrialized Western countries.[73]

Consequences of Khrushchev's Secret Speech

In March 1953, after Stalin's death and subsequent internal struggles, Nikita Sergeyevich Khrushchev[74] emerged as the party's leader. At his request, a certain level of liberalization was allowed in the economics sector. A similar trend was followed in Romania, aiming to improve the living standards of the population and expand economic markets. Yet, the party's internal purging continued through the PMR's Second Congress, December 23–28, 1955.[75] As a direct consequence, the construction of the Danube-Black Sea Canal, which had claimed thousands of victims, was stopped in 1955. For a brief period, respite could be felt in economic and cultural endeavors and amends were made to diminish the impact of mass terror conducted by the communist regime. To regain public trust, the party initiated several amnesty cases for political prisoners in 1955. Some of those released were later rearrested in 1956 and 1957 following the Hungarian uprising.

After this brief period of change, 1956 was an important year. It culminated with Khrushchev's famous "Secret Speech," during the Communist Party of the Soviet Union[76] XXth Congress, on February 25, 1956, in a session that Gheorghiu-Dej attended himself. It is believed that Khrushchev was convinced that, after unveiling the errors of the Stalinist regime to the members of the Eastern Bloc in the audience, his plan would gain quick traction. Yet, while this speech was intended to start a process of de-Stalinization in all participating communist countries, Romania veered sharply away from such a possible course.

While "Khrushchev's Thaw"[77] rolled like a wildfire through the rest of the Eastern Bloc countries, Romania under Gheorghe Gheorghiu-Dej experienced but a flicker out of the light that was expected. With great tenacity, the Romanian leader continued on the repressive path he had started prior to the speech. Numerous party members in high positions were eliminated.[78]

> In this oppressive political system, the Securitate fulfilled its mission as intended: it used illegal, unpredictable, and vague measures against innocent people, measures which were forbidden by the norms of accepted law.[79]

The implementation of the de-Stalinization process could have revealed the criminal deeds of the Gheorghiu-Dej's regime illegitimate attitudes of the past politics, shaking his leadership from the very foundation and undermining his absolute rule. Its elimination would have been a sine qua non condition in achieving a significant change in Romania's future policy, as "the Secret speech" had portended.

In Gheorghiu-Dej' Romania, it would have been impossible to adopt steps toward de-Stalinization, for the leader of the party and his acolytes would never have admitted the crimes that had been committed in their names.

The Failed Thaw

Khrushchev's famous speech was not the only important event of 1956. The same year saw the rise of popular revolts with long-lasting effects in Poland[80] and Hungary.[81] The Hungarian revolt started on October 23, 1956, and shook the foundations of the local Communist Party and greatly influenced the politics of Gheorghe Gheorghiu-Dej. The Romanian leader and his associates were terrified by the quick demise that a political system could experience at the hands of resisting citizens and quickly stopped the already slow-moving "thawing" of the country. With the complete support of the party, the Securitate enacted measures aimed to prevent the repetition of the Hungarian events in Romania.

> The main lesson Gheorghiu-Dej learned by observing and monitoring the Hungarian Events, was that the future of the communist rule in Romania depended on the ability to quickly suppress any popular resistance.[82]

As such, soon after the Hungarian revolt, the methods of suppression and oppression in the country increased. After 1958, Romania requested the withdrawal of the Soviet forces from its territory, partly in recognition of the part it had played in suppressing the Hungarian uprising. The country's strategic placement in the geopolitical arena of the communist bloc contributed to this request being granted by Khrushchev. Besides ensuring the retreat of the Soviet troops, this request also aimed to open Romania toward the West.[83] After the Soviet forces' departure, Gheorghiu-Dej continued to make use of measures taken against those perceived as "the enemies" of the state in an effort to prove that he had absolute control of the local population. What followed could be characterized as a "tightening of the screw" or a closing of the circle around those seen as hostile to the communist ideology. Through the implementation of his draconian measures against the scientists, writers, and intellectuals of the time, Gheorghiu-Dej aimed to show Moscow that he was an absolute ruler in full control of the population. These actions increased after 1958. Among those targeted by these actions were also the Jewish functionaries at the Ministry of the Foreign Trade who would later be involved in the staged economic trials. In fact, despite the PMR's official discourse, anti-Semitic attitudes were implemented in the actions of the party.

Based on the evidence available, the author could not pinpoint the precise moment when the fate of these functionaries was decided by the PMR leadership. Yet, from these same documents, it is impossible not to sense their intentional marginalization and further exclusion from positions of influence in the Romanian economy. Next, I will detail the aggressivity of this campaign initiated from the highest PMR ranks, yet hidden from the public eye.

CHANGES IN GHEORGHIU-DEJ'S POLITICS AFTER 1956

New Directions in Gheorghiu-Dej's Politics

> Dej is guilty of two crimes committed against the Romanian people. First, he prevented the normal course of history, using crime to prevent the ascension of his possible successor;[85] second, he did not prevent the abnormal course of history and allowed a criminal to succeed him.[86]
>
> Victor Frunză, *Istoria Stalinismului*[84]

As already mentioned, Gheorghiu-Dej was deeply affected by the Hungarian revolt and its serious consequences for the local Communist Party. After Khrushchev's tanks restored the "public order," that is, the dictatorship, it was not surprising that the measures he took to prevent their repeat on Romanian soil were drastic and immediate.[87] More precisely, he and the party leadership came up with two distinct courses of action in the domestic realm of the country: first, promote specific elements of national communism, elements that came to characterize the latter part of Gheorghiu-Dej's reign, and second, increase the power and influence of the Securitate over the daily life of the general population. In this context, the Securitate was the means used by the PMR to establish national communism as a political aim in itself.

Gheorghiu-Dej's Take on National Communism

At the end of 1960s, Romania's politics, which had been Stalinist in practice, gradually changed. Under Gheorghiu-Dej's leadership, and influenced by international circumstances, it took the form of a policy known in history as national communism.[88] In practice, this ideology manifested at least in two different ways: first, in the political arena, as a distancing from the Soviet Union and its political, military, and economic relationships, and, second, in the ethnic makeup of the economy, through gradual, consistent removal of Jewish ethnics (as well as other ethnic groups) from the economic (industry and commerce) and the cultural sectors.[89]

If in the beginning, Romanian national communism focused on bringing about a gradual abandonment of its subordination to Moscow, concurrently, it started asserting its autonomy and national identity on multiple levels, economic, sociopolitical, and cultural.[90] The PMR leaders banked on the population's affinity for these changes and acted on it.

> They knew that the national feelings of the people and also their anti-Soviet sentiments would outweigh the antipathy which they themselves inspired. They relied on the idea of national pride and reaped a useful harvest.[91]

Peter Zwick,[92] analyzing this phenomenon, assessed that Romania was the site on which national communism was taken to the extreme. As such, in the 1960s, and toward the end of Gheorghe-Dej's leadership,[93] this ideology took the form of radical nationalism.[94] Concomitantly, the country distanced itself from the Soviet Union in two distinct steps: first, it removed Soviet troops, advisers, and ammunition from the country's territory and second, between 1962 and 1963,[95] it implemented a policy of economic independence against the integrationist politics of the Council for Mutual Economic Assistance (CMEA).[96]

In the literature of the field, the political model used by Gheorghiu-Dej and his PMR associates is known as the "model of Stalinist nationalism."[97] After the success in bringing about the withdrawal of Soviet troops in 1958, 1964 was another milestone that marked Romania's independence in the Eastern European arena. It was the year of the promotion of the Declaration of Independence.[98] During CMEA session, through its representative, Alexandru Bârlădeanu,[99] Romania rejected the Valev program[100] and clearly stated its rejection of Moscow's plans to keep it predominantly agrarian. Instead, it would adopt PCR's plans for the development of specific industries, increased economic self-sufficiency, and economic trade with the West. As a member of the Warsaw Pact, Romania also actualized its creed with the necessary separation from Moscow's economic and political control[101] in the area. To achieve these goals, two things were necessary: one, the support of the population from within, and two, the support of the Western countries, from outside.

Still active on Gheorghu-Dej's agenda at this time was the need to deal with the presence of several ethnic minority groups in Romania that were perceived as problematic. National Communism tendencies, manifested in the politics carried out by Gheorghiu-Dej, shaped not only the country's foreign policy but also its internal policies. For the latter, it meant that those "undesirables" serving higher functions in the economic sector would be removed by any means. These methods included the staged economic trials, through which the Jewish officials belonging to various Foreign Trade professions were accused of severe crimes against the Romanian state. Upon Gheorghiu-Dej's death, on March 19, 1965, the sentences of the six trials detailed in this volume had already been established by the Military Court of Bucharest.

PCR's Politics versus Romania's Ethnic Minorities: The Jews

> He persecuted the national minorites under the guise of protecting their rights.
>
> The Report of the Presidential Committee for the Analysis of Communist Dictatorship in Romania.[102]

In the beginning, the communist regime forbade any anti-Semitic propaganda, any expression of chauvinism. This political stance was made public in laws, yet its prohibition by law didn't mean its disappearance. Merely smothered, this attitude was referred to as a sleeping, sedated monster, whose awakening was imminent. The communist regime used it for its own purposes while officially condemning it. During this period, many of the Jews whispered among themselves: "shhh, speak softly, the monster could spring to life at any moment."[103]

Even after the popular people's democracies[104] were established in Eastern Europe, a lack of consensus vis-a-vis the Jewish problem prevailed.[105] In România, a year after the new Republic was formed, this problem appeared in a PMR plan to address the minorities' presence in the country. This plan was known as the "December 12, 1948, PMR Resolution on the national problem"[106] and denounced the minorities' "collective guilt" and the imperative that their interests should be subordinated to the priorities of the proletariat, or the working class.[107] The mere presence of this document shows the difficulties PMR experienced dealing with the local non-Romanian groups, in particular, the Jews, the Hungarians, and the Germans. The document denounced the still active Zionist groups in Romania but did not offer any practical advice on how to integrate the Jewish population in the new economy or discuss its emigration.[108] In itself, the Jewish problem remained a puzzle even for the Westerners entertaining leftist sympathies: many had hoped that with the institution of a radically new sociopolitical system, the Jews would benefit from equal rights. Unfortunately, the experience gained during the communist period in Eastern Europe, proved exactly the opposite.

For many Jews, the communist ideology held great hope, and its precepts looked capable of delivering universal "absolution," very much like a new religion would. According to its promises, the Jewish identity, which had brought so much pain and oppression over the centuries, should have been not only accepted but also should have ceased to be a reason for hatred. The problem raised by Fejtő concerned many of those who were engaged in the struggle for the implementation of communist ideals. Many of its proponents fell prey to its promises and substituted religious idols with new figures, those belonging to the Marxism-Leninism Parthenon: Marx, Engels, and Lenin. In the late 1970s, when most of its followers had been disappointed with its practices, one of the victims of the economic trials noted:

> In the socialist countries, nationality problems, like the Jewish problem, are declared solved, "fundamentally, by constitution." In the leaders' eyes, these were theoretical problems, mere words on paper. In reality, during the Party meetings and in different newspapers and magazines, the Jews were expected to praise the system and the "majestic" ways through which it solved these problems. Meanwhile, it was common knowledge that antisemitism was alive and well and served the interests of the ruling party. How else could the massive Jewish emigration be explained in Eastern Europe during this time? It was far superior to those undertaken during Horty's, Antonescu's, and Hitler's time, and it took great numbers towards Israel and other free countries. The divorce between Jews and the Marxist-Leninist regimes was final.[109]

Rosinger's words illustrate that, in the 1960s, the situation mentioned by Fejtő a decade earlier had remained the same. During this period, the Securitate spies embedded in the American Embassy in Bucharest obtained reports regarding Romania and the participants in the Warsaw Pact. The reports contain information regarding the attitude of the two-decade-old communist system vis-a-vis its Jewish citizens.[110] If, after World War II and the communization of the Bucharest political system, Jews still held important functions in administration, industry, trade, medicine, and culture, at the end of the 1950s and the beginning of the 1960s, their presence in these fields was greatly diminished due not only to emigration but also to the purges that followed the intensified nationalist politics in Bucharest, after the Hungarian revolution.

The Jews of Romania continued to belong to one of the following two groups: one, those whose main goal was to leave for the Promised Land,[111] and two, those who, during the interwar period, identified with the vision of the communist ideology and believed in its implementation. Among the latter, some joined the ranks of the PMR, and some were its non-affiliated supporters, yet, especially after the tragic war events and subsequent events in Romania and Transnistria, all realized the disparity between promise and reality.

While the PMR's emigration policy does not constitute the topic of this book, it should be mentioned that, as long as they were allowed to work and maintain a decent living standard, most of the Jews belonging to the second group still chose to stay in Romania. When their harassment increased, however, and they were either fired or excluded from leadership positions, the number of Jews requesting to emigrate increased dramatically. The Romanian authorities increasingly doubted the loyalty of those who had decided to stay.

The Jews were not the only oppressed minority in communist Romania. The nationalist politics of Gheorghiu-Dej also affected the German and the Magyar (Hungarian) minorities. They, too, were subjected to similar, yet somewhat different, degrading practices.

To return to the topic of anti-Semitism, in communist Romania, its presence was like a smothered, yet not extinguished, dangerous fire. Its expression was somewhat subtler than in the previous regimes, including those preceding Antonescu's fascist regime and continuing after 1944, when the communists took power.

> The Romanian anti-semitism is rooted in both the Romanian inner conflict of the self at war with itself and the refusal to take responsibility for one's actions and their consequences.[112]

Anti-Semitism manifested as overt hatred against this ethnic group or as overt acts of aggression against Jewish institutions like cemeteries or synagogues. The anti-Semitism in Romania had no ideological basis, at least not an official one. As such, the anti-Semitism manifested during the communist regime could be characterized as an anti-Semitism determined by the specific Romanian circumstances.[113]

While not an integral part of the initial communist ideology, anti-Semitism became an integral part of it in the second decade of the regime. To make it so, the PMR needed the support of the general population, malcontent with the fact that many Jews still held positions of power and consequence in the state. The witch hunt that started between 1952 and1953 intensified after 1956 when Securitate agents searched for "spies or enemies" of the working class among their ranks.

The purge of Jews[114] during the years following the 1956 events was concurrent with the consolidation of policies against the opponents of the political regime. While the Zionists' and the Canal trials had been public, other cases were carried out in secret, as per the PCR's order. Such trials, started after lengthy periods of surveillance and investigation, were initiated at the request of the party. Their execution, however, became possible only after the Securitate was granted absolute operational powers. The trials analyzed further in this volume, and which took place at the beginning of the 1960s, were all "staged" by the Securitate and resulted in the removal of a great number of Jews working at the MCE.

CONCLUSION

To sum up, the ideological and political characteristics of the communist system during its first two decades were: extreme intolerance, rigidity, and continuous exercise of pressure on the population. To these, Gheorghiu-Dej added fundamentally Stalinist concepts and practices to impose his dictatorship in the country. His "National Communism" and "Political Autonomy" programs caused great trauma to the general population and brought about the destruction of the local economy.[115] Ubiquitous, the Securitate was the tool of choice used to repress and terrorize the people. Under Gheorghiu-Dej, it was responsible for the elimination of all those opposing his rule.[116] Instead of functioning as a servant of the people and keeper of their individual liberties (as apparently its name implied), the Securitate was responsible for their almost blind submission to the totalitarian communist system.

Researchers of the policy pursued by Gheorghiu-Dej in the international geopolitical context of the time considered its most significant results to be the weakening of Soviet hegemony in Eastern Europe during the 1960s. Additionally, his vetoing of the latter's integrationist economic policies prevented Soviet policentrism[117] and greatly reduced its clout in the international political arena.[118] Yet, despite the fact that Gheorghiu-Dej managed to stop Soviet influence in Romania, his internal politics were characterized by a "tightening of the screw" and the terrorization of the population, which lasted for the entire duration of his leadership. From 1962 to 1964, a slight liberalization could be noted manifesting as the series of decrees freeing political prisoners imprisoned for their crimes against "national security." At this time, the great majority of the MCE functionaries had already been judged or sent to prison. Following the year 1967, at the celebration of twenty years since the proclamation of the Romanian People's Republic, a larger amnesty was passed by N. Ceausescu, the then president of Romania. This amnesty contributed to the liberation of most of the prisoners, because at that time, they had already done most of their sentence, while the last ones were to be liberated after reaching the age of 60, in 1968 or 1969. Even released, they had never been rehabilitated, and all of them continued to pay on account of their presumptive debts of millions of lei.[119]

The sequel of this book will strive to give a coherent and documented explanation of the bitter reality of those times.

NOTES

1. Oyvind Osterud, "The Uses and Abuses of Geopolitics," *Journal of Peace Research*, (Thousand Oaks, CA: SAGE Publications, 2, 1998), 191.

2. Lucreţiu Pătrăşcanu (1894–1954) was a Romanian communist politician, member of the PCR, known for his activities as a lawyer, a sociologist, and an economist. Having disagreed with Stalinist tenets and representing a threatening figure for the Romanian party leader Gheorghiu-Dej, he was imprisoned and executed in 1954, without a proper trial.

3. Lucreţiu Pătrăşcanu, *Sous trois dictatures* (Paris: J. Vitiano, 1946), 98, henceforth Pătrăşcanu, *Sous trois dictatures.*

4. Katherine Verdery, *National Ideology under Socialism Identity and Cultural Politics in Ceausescu's Romania* (Berkeley: University of California Press, 1991), 45, henceforth Verdery, National Ideology.

5. The Conservative Party remained on the political scene of Romania between 1932 (after its reappearance as a new variant of the old Conservative Party [1880]) until it was dissolved in 1938.

6. Carol I (1866–1914) born Prince Karl of Hohenzollern-Sigmaringen, was the first foreign monarch of Romania. After Alexandru Ioan Cuza's resignation by a coup d'etat, he was elected Ruling Prince (Domnitor) of the Romanian United Principalities on April 20, 1866. Two months after Carol's election, the Romanian parliament adopted the first Romanian constitution. In May 1877, Carol proclaimed Romania an independent and sovereign state, which would be recognized by the Treaty of Berlin one year later, at the end of the war against the Ottoman Empire. Carol became King Carol I of Romania in 1881.

7. Signed on June 28, 1919, at Versailles Palace, this treaty ended World War I and the armed conflict between Germany and the Allied Powers.

8. Irina Livezeanu, *Cultural Politics in Greater Romania. Regionalism, Nation Building and Ethnic Struggle, 1918–1930* (Ithaca, NY: Cornell University Press, 1995), 10, henceforth Livezeanu, *Cultural Politics in Greater Romania.*

9. Verdery, *National Ideology*, 59.

10. Andrew C. Janos, "Modernization and decay in historical perspective: The case of Romania," In *Social change in Romania, 1860–1940*, ed. Kenneth Jowitt (Berkeley: University of California, Institute of International Studies, 1978), 72–116.

11. Romania was one of the last European countries to emancipate its Jewish population. Their situation was changed after the passing of a May 22, 1919, decree (The Official Gazette of Romania, published on May 28, 1919), which was later made into law by Article 133 included in the 1923 Constitution when the Romanian citizenship of the Jews was officially legislated.

12. Livezeanu, *Cultural Politics in Greater Romania,* 34. The term of cultural offensive used in Livezeanu's book is mentioned as part of the National Liberal Party's aggressive cultural policies for describing their program of national unification by means of the school.

13. Verdery, *National Ideology*, 45.

14. The movement had a paramilitary character and was modeled on the nationalist-fascist organizations in Germany. It had a secretive, mystic, violent character and targeted primarily communists, Jews, and Masons.

15. This ideology, supported by the Romanian fascist movement Iron Guard combines fascist ideology with a religious conception that church can dominate the political, social, and cultural life of the peoples.

16. King Ferdinand I (1865–1927) was the king of Romania between 1922 and 1927, successor to Carol I.

17. In Romanian, "Partidul Național Țărănesc." It was founded in 1926, achieving a fusion of the Romanian National Party (PNR), a conservative-regionalist group whose center was in Transylvania, and the Peasants' Party (in Romanian Partidul Țărănist, PȚ), which had merged with the left-leaning agrarian movement in the Old Kingdom and Bessarabia. Iuliu Maniu was the party leader.

During the World War II, it activated as an underground organization, supporting the Allied Powers. Its activity was banned by the communists after 1947. Its main leaders Iuliu Maniu and Ion Mihalache died in the communist prisons. Accessed July 18, 2021, pntcd.ro/istoria-pntcd/.

18. In Romanian, "Partidul Național Liberal." It was a major active party, in the Kingdom of Romania, between 1875 and the World War II. It was founded officially on May 24, 1875, when a group of liberals, among whom were Ion. C. Brătianu, Mihail Kogalniceanu, and others, laid the foundations of the political formation that would mark the history of modern Romania. Brătianu was its first leader. The interwar period was a prolific one for Romania and for the liberals, who promoted the agrarian reform, the unitary administrative organization, a new electoral legislation and measures to restore the economy. After the communists' coming into power, the PNL stopped its activity in 1947. Many of the liberal leaders died in communist prisons, paying with their lives for faith in democratic principles and liberal values, while others were forced into exile. Accessed July 18, 2021, pnl.ro.

19. In Romanian "Totul pentru țară."

20. William I. Brustein, *Roots of Hate* (Cambridge, UK: Cambridge University Press, 2003), 4.

21. Kurt W. Treptow, "Alegerile din decembrie 1937 şi instaurarea dictaturii regale," *Romania și al doilea Razboi Mondial* (Iaşi: Centrul de Studii Româneşti, 1996), 42–43.

22. Verdery, *National Ideology*, 61.

23. Pătrăşcanu, *Sous Trois Dictatures*, 61.

24. Alexandru C. Cuza, a Romanian politician with an openly anti-Semitic attitude, professor at Iasi University receiving several doctorates (political sciences, economy, and law). He founded the Christian National Defense League in 1923, a party which later merged with Octavian Goga's National Agrarian Party, thus laying the foundations of the National Christian Party.

25. At the time of this declaration, Romania was led by Octavian Goga's short-term government (12/1937–02/1938), among whose ministers, Alexandru C. Cuza held the position of minister of state.

26. *New York Times*, January 21, 1938, Accessed February 10, 2020. https://timesmachine.nytimes.com/timesmachine/1938/01/22/issue.html.

27. Carol II (1893–1953) reigned as King of Romania from June 8, 1930, until his abdication on September 6, 1940. He was the eldest son of Ferdinand I and became crown prince upon the death of his grand-uncle, King Carol I in 1914. He was also the first of the Hohenzollern kings of Romania to be born in the country (both of his predecessors were born and grew up in Germany and only came to Romania as adults). Carol spoke Romanian as his first language and was the first member of the Romanian royal family to be raised in the Orthodox faith.

28. Antony Polonsky, *The Little Dictators* (London: Routledge & Kegan Paul, 1975), XI.

29. Vladimir Tismăneanu, *Stalinism pentru Eternitate, O istorie politică a comunismului românesc* (Bucureşti: Ed. Polirom, 2005), 61 (in English: Stalinism for all Seasons: A Political History of Romanian Communism), henceforth, Tismăneanu, "*Stalinism pentru Eternitate.*"

30. Constantin Dobrogeanu-Gherea (1855–1920) born Solomon Katz, in Ucraine, Ekaterinoslav area.

31. C. Dobrogeanu–Gherea, *Opere Complete, vol 2* (Bucureşti: Ed. Politică, 1976), 134.

32. Verdery, *National Ideology*, 69 (in English: *Complete Works*).

33. Tismăneanu, "Stalinism pentru Eternitate," 62.

34. In Romanian, "Partidul Social Democrat al Muncitorilor din România," PSDMR from now on.

35. In Romanian, "Partidul Social Democrat German."

36. In Romanian, Comisia Generală a Sindicatelor din România.

37. In Romanian, "Partidul Social Democrat Român," henceforth PSDR.

38. In Romanian, "Declarație de principii."

39. The Comintern was founded by V.I. Lenin in 1919 and continued to exist until 1943. The purpose of the Comintern was to continue the tradition of the two internationals founded by Karl Marx in order to fight by any means (including armed forces) against the international bourgeoisie.

40. The party was outlawed in 1924, while a small group of people continued to illegally activate being totally under Comintern control. After 1944, the PCR emerged again, and with the support of Soviet troops, King Michael forced to abdicate and the Romania Peoples' Republic was established on December 30, 1947. Starting

with 1948, the party switched its name to the Romanian Workers' Party (Partidul Muncitoresc Român).

41. In Romanian, "Partidul Social Democrat," henceforth PSD.

42. Verdery, "*National Ideology*," 60.

43. Ibidem.

44. Dej is a small town situated in Transylvania, Romania's Western province.

45. The name Gheorghiu-Dej will be used in this book.

46. Ghita Ionescu, *Communism in Romania, 1944–1962* (Connecticut: Greenwood Press, 1976), 45, henceforth Ionescu, *Communism*.

47. Lya Benjamin, *Evreii din România între anii 1940–1944 Vol I Legislația Antievreiască* (București: Hasefer, 1993).

48. King Michael I (1921–2017) was the last king of Romania. He reigned as a regent between 1927 and 1930 and as a monarch between 1940 and 1947. King Michael I was forced to abdicate on December 30, 1947.

49. D. Chirot, "Social Change in Communist Romania," *Social Forces* 57, no. 2, Special Issue (December 1978): 457–499.

50. These measures were implemented with the aid of the Allied Control Commissions ("Comisiile de control ale aliaţilor") stationed in the country after World War II. Part of the peace treaties at the end of the war, these commissions monitored the economic, social, and political activities of the defeated countries.

51. In Romanian, "Partidul Muncitoresc Român." This name was preserved between 1948 and 1964 until it officially returned to its old one, PCR, on July 24, 1965, under the leadership of Nicolae Ceaușescu, the new secretary general after Gheorghiu-Dej's death in March 1965.

The party name, will be henceforth referred to as either PMR or PCR, interchangeably.

52. In Romanian, "Formaţiunile de Luptă Patriotică" (henceforth FLP).

53. Emil Bodnăraş (1904–1976) was the son of a Ukrainian father and a German mother. He was an artillery officer who, after some conflict with the Romanian Royal Hous, defected and became a Soviet agent. In 1935, he returned to Romania and became a key figure in Gheorghiu-Dej's political faction. Between 1945 and 1947, he led surveillance operations for the Secret Services.

54. Gabriel Catalan, "Scurtă Istorie a Securităţii," Accessed December 25, 2019. https://gabrielcatalan.wordpress.com/2013/09/24/scurta-istorie-a-securitatii.

55. On April 13, 1948, the Great National Assembly (in Romanian, Marea Adunare Naţională), henceforth MAN, voted for a new constitution, which legalized the power of PMR in the country.

56. MAN was the Romanian People's Republic legislative body before 1965, and the Socialist Republic of Romania's after this date.

57. In Romanian Ministerul Afacerilor Interne, henceforth MAI.

58. Its name was the "General Directorate of People's Security, in Romanian, "Direcţia Generală a Securităţii Poporului" (henceforth DGSP), more commonly known as the Securitate. It was founded on August 30, 1948, by Decree 221/30 issued by the Presidium of the MAN. A short history of the Intelligence Institutions in Romania is briefly presented in appendix II.

59. Monica Ciobanu, *Repression, Resistance and Collaboration in Stalinist Romania 1944–1964, Post-communist Remembering* (London: Routledge, 2020), 3+11 of chapter I. The structure of the Ministry of Internal Affairs is briefly explained in appendix II. In Romanian, it is called Ministerul Afacerilor Interne (MAI).

60. In Romanian, Consiliul de Ministri.

61. Ionescu, *Communism*, 172. Chapter 2 of this book classifies the criminal offenses according to their gravity.

62. In Romanian "Canalul Dunărea-Marea Neagră." This project was not completed during Gheorghiu-Dej' leadeship, but later, during that of Nicolae Ceauşescu's.

63. In Romanian, "abatere de la linia de partid," "duşmanul poporului," "propaganda antirevoluţionară," "sabotaj," and "agitație."

64. For example, the Romanian-Israeli historian Theodore Wexler Lavi.

65. The name refers to a triumvirate of three political figures at the time, Vasile Luca, Ana Pauker who arrived in Romania together with the Soviet army, and the third member, appointed as Interior Minister, Teohari Gerogescu.

66. Ana Pauker was accused of cosmopolitanism, "anti-partisan" activities, of sabotaging the collectivization of agriculture and sympathizing with legionaries, foreign agents and Zionists. In February 1953, she was subjected to a series of interrogations for a political trial but, a month and a half after Stalin's death, she was released from prison and kept several years under house arrest. Vasile Luca was arrested on August 14, 1952, investigated until the fall of 1954 and prosecuted for undermining the national economy and the working class. He was sentenced to death, but his sentence was changed to life-long forced labor in 1954.Teohari Georgescu was accused on February 18, 1952, but did not serve his sentence.

67. Alexandru Drăghici (1913–1993), CCPCR member (CCPCR was the PCR Central Commitee), minister of the interior between 1952 and 1965, was one of the most avid supporters of the communist agenda and the leader of its executive branch, the Securitate.

68. Sorin Toma, *Privind inapoi—din amintirile unui fost jurnalist comunist* (Bucharest: Compania, 2004), 259, henceforth Toma, *Privind înapoi.* In English, *Looking back—from the memories of a former communist journalist.* Sorin Toma (1914–2016) was the chief editor of "Scânteia" (in English, The Spark) between 1947 and 1949. This was the official party newspaper during the whole period of Communist Romania. He was trusted by the party leadership apparatus then in power.

69. Dan Pavel, "Banalizarea Răului în Istorie," *Sfera Politicii* 60 (May 1998): 31, quoted in Marcela Pineles' manuscript, 45. This document is now in the author's possession.

70. Victor Frunză, *Istoria Stalinismului în România* (Bucureşti: Humanitas, 1990), 378–379, henceforth Frunză, *Istoria Stalinismului* (in English, Victor Frunză, The History of Stalinism in Romania). The small town Poarta Albă is situated on the Bucureşti-Constanța train route.

71. During the years 1953–1954, a series of anti-Zionist trials were held in Military Courts. The defendants were forced by repressive measures to give false

testimonies, and they were accused of activity against socialism and the Romanian people.

72. The Sovroms were a mix of Romanian-Soviet cooperatives, founded in 1945, whose primary goal was to ensure Romania's war reparations repayment to the Soviet Union. They functioned until 1956.

73. Andrea C. Tsantis, & Roy Pepper, *România, The Industrialization of an Agrarian Economy under Socialist Planning* (Report of a Mission sent to România by the World Bank) (Washington, DC: World Bank, 1979).

74. Nikita Sergeyevich Khrushchev (1894–1971) held the position of First Secretary of the Soviet Union Communist Party, between 1953 and 1964, and also that of Premier of the Council of Ministers of the Soviet Union, between 1958 and 1964.

75. Frunză, *Istoria Stalinismului*, 425–426.

76. In Romanian, Partidul Comunist al Uniunii Sovietice, henceforth PCUS.

77. The term "thaw" was coined by Ilya Ehrenburg (1891–1967) in his novel bearing the same name, *The Thaw* (1954). This name was used to characterize Khrushchev's policy after his Secret Speech.

78. During the Central Committee Plenary-meeting from June 28 to July 2, 1957, Iosif Chişinevski and Miron Constantinescu were released from their political functions.

79. Marius Oprea, *Banalitatea Răului, o istorie a securității in documente* (Iaşi: Polirom, 2002), 12, henceforth Oprea, Banalitatea Răului.

80. A series of events that started with the workers' strike in Poznań and culminated with Wladislaw Gomulka's ascent to the leadership of the Polish United Workers' Party.

81. A series of events that started with a students' revolt against the Bolshevik leader Mátyás Rákos on October 23, 1956, and escalated to a full-scale revolution whose suppression required the intervention of the Soviet military forces who, between November 10 and 11, massacred the participants in great numbers.

82. Dennis Deletant, *Teroarea Comunistă în România* (Iasi: Polirom, 2001), 208, henceforth Deletant, *Teroarea Comunistă.*

83. Ibid. 210.

84. Frunză, Istoria Stalinismului, 461.

85. The reference is to Lucreţiu Pătrăşcanu.

86. The reference is to Nicolae Ceauşescu.

87. Adrian Cioroianu, "Atuurile lui Gheorghiu-Dej," *Dosarele Istoriei* An II 8, nr.3, (1997), 25.

88. Toma, *Privind înapoi,* 264.

89. Ibid., 264.

90. George Schöpflin, "Romanian Nationalism," *Survey* 20, no. 2–3 (1974): 77–104.

91. Ghita Ionescu, *The Breakup of the Soviet Empire in Eastern Europe* (London: Penguin Book, 1965) 130, henceforth Ionescu, The Breakup of the Soviet Empire.

92. Peter Zwick was a historian and researcher at The Office of Global Education, California.

93. Gheorghe Gheorghiu-Dej died of a severe disease on March 19, 1965.

94. Peter Zwick, *National Communism* (Boulder, CO: Westview Press, 1983), 116.

95. Ionescu, *The Breakup of the Soviet Empire*, 128–130.

96. CMEA was an economic organization active between 1949 and 1991. Led by the Soviet Union, it comprised the countries of the Eastern Bloc along with a number of socialist states elsewhere in the world.

97. Vladimir Tismăneanu, *Fantoma lui Gheorghiu Dej* (Bucureşti : Humanitas, 2008), 159.

98. Declaration presented by Bârlădeanu at CMEA in April 1964, regarding Romania's opposition to Valev's economic plan.

99. Alexandru Bârlădeanu (1911–1997) was a Romanian politician and economist of Bessarabean origin. He was a member of the PCR Central Committee, served as Senate president, as a deputy minister, and then as full minister of the MCE, 1948–1954. Between 1959 and 1964, he was the Romanian representative at CMEA, where he presented the country's Declaration of Independence. After the fall of the Communist regime, he served as Senate president.

100. Emil Borisovici Valev was an economist and a professor at the University of Moscow. He is the one who elaborated an economic program according to which independent national territories would be subsumed to a greater unit known as the Danube Complex. According to this plan, România was to have its national land divided according to Moscow's decisions on economic politics in the area. PCR opposed Valev's Program categorically.

101. Ghiţă Ionescu, "Communist Rumania and Nonalignment (April 1964-March 1965)," *Slavic Review*, 24, no. 2 (1965): 241–257.

102. *The Report of the Presidential Commission for the Study of the Communist Dictatorship in Romania*, 2006, 19. "He" refers to Gheorghiu-Dej, as the book is limited to the years of Gheorghiu-Dej's leadership. Accessed on August 1, 2021.

https://www.wilsoncenter.org/sites/default/files/media/documents/article/RAPORT%20FINAL_%20CADCR.pdf, 19, henceforth *The Presidential Comission Report*.

103. Toma, *Privind înapoi*, 215.

104. A governmental regime whose ideology, inspired by Marxism-Leninism, appeared and was used in the satellite states of the Soviet Union, which tried to exercise the Marxist principle of democracy. This system of government was based on the total power of the single party and a centralized state economy.

105. Francois Fejtő, *Les Juifs et l'antisemitisme dans les pays communistes* (Paris : Plon, 1960), henceforth Fejtő, *Les Juifs et l'antisemitisme*. Francois Fejtő (1909–2008) was a Hungarian journalist and political scientist who lived in France and whose expertise was Eastern Europe.

106. In Romanian, "Rezoluţia din 12 decembrie 1948 a PMR privind problema naţională."

107. ANIC, fond CC al PCR - Cancelarie, dosar nr. 230/1949, 1–12, quoted in *The Presidential Comission Report*, 527.

108. Liviu Rotman, "Evreii din România până la 1965," In *Istoria evreilor din România, 5th part*, ed. Raphael Vago (Tel Aviv: Goren Goldstein Center for investigating the Diaspora Jews, 1965), henceforth Rotman, Evreii din România până la 1965.

109. Adalbert Rosinger, *Cartea neagră a Comerțului Exterior românesc*, Chapter 6. Rosinger was one of the main defendants convicted in the Românoexport trial. The manuscript was written between 1979 and 1980, shortly before Rosinger's death in September 1981. It is in the possession of the author. It contains 12 written chapters and an expanded summary of all the originally planned chapters, 36 in number, which remained unfinished, following his death. In English, *The Black Box of Romanian Foreign Trade,* henceforth Rosinger, *Cartea neagră.*

110. Marius Oprea, "Evreii din România, o minoritate care dispare," *Observatorul Cultural,* 101, no. 2 (2012). Accessed on October 25, 2020. http://www.observatorcultural.ro/Evreii-din-România-o-minoritate-care-dispare*articleID_264-articles_details.html

111. Some of these Jews were later defendants in the Zionist trials previously mentioned.

112. Alina Tudor Pavelescu, "Avatarurile antisemitismului românesc," *Sfera Politicii*, 60 (May 1998): 24–25, Accessed on October 25, 2020. http://www.sferapoliticii.ro/sfera/pdf-1/Sfera_60.pdf.

113. This concept occurred as part of my numerous conversations and correspondence with Mrs.Lya Benjamin, researcher at the Institute for the Romanian Jews History (CSIER), in Bucharest. She defined this type of anti-Semitism as dependent on circumstances, ergo, circumstantial.

114. Titu Simon, *Pacepa quo vadis, Din Culisele Serviciilor Secrete Româneşti* (Bucureşti: Odeon, 1992).

115. Vladimir Tismăneanu, "The Ambiguity of Romanian National Communism," *Telos* 60 (Summer, 1984): 73.

116. Larisa Muşat, "Terorismul de Stat din România," in *De ce trebuie condamnat comunismul*, ed. Marius Oprea, C. Budeancă, S. Cucerai, A. Muraru, and R. Grosescu (Iaşi: Polirom, 2006), 30.

117. Doctrine by virtue of which the Communist Parties could simultaneously have several management centers, this definition uses the online Explanatory Dictionary of the Romanian Language.

118. George Gross, "Rumania: The fruits of Autonomy," *Problems of Communism* 15 (January–February 1966), 27.

119. Romanian currency at the time.

Chapter 2

Political Trials as Repression Mechanisms in Communist Countries

Political trials represent Gordian knots.[1] While a court may cut through the issues with a rule în a sharp decision—the defendant may be convicted or acquitted—the dilemmas of responsibility, morality, representation or legitimacy remains.

Ron Christenson, *Political Trials*, 7[2]

LEGAL TERMINOLOGY, INTRODUCTION, AND DEFINITIONS

Legal Terminology

This chapter will introduce a series of legal terms, some of which will be detailed here. Some others will be detailed separately.[3] Criminal Law is a legal branch that deals with antisocial behavior and the society's response to it, as well as the punishments imposed on those who break the rules. It also aims to preserve the state's sovereignty, its independence, unity, and indivisibility. Additionally, it aims to preserve the individual's self-determination, freedom, and private property. Lastly, it aims to do all this while preserving social order and important social values. As such, Criminal Law represents an extension of the state's power vis-à-vis individual rights. It is based on a series of rules and laws that define social life, the legal system, and its applications. As I am speaking about Romania, which is a country whose Law system is the Civil Law (also named the Continental Law) there are two distinct areas, called the Criminal Law (or Substantive Criminal Law) and the Criminal Procedure Law.

The former refers to the laws dealing with the rights, the obligations, and the types of punishment of lawbreakers. It decides what constitutes illegal behavior and the state's position vis-à-vis each particular case. The sum of all these definitions and laws constitutes the Criminal or Penal Code, and the document that dictates its usage is called the Code of Criminal Procedure.[4] Substantive Criminal Law takes into account the laws that refer to rights, but also to obligations, and types of penalties imposed on those who violate them. Substantive Criminal Law also defines what type of behavior is illegal and what punishment is prescribed by the state for each individual case. The three categories of offenses included in the Criminal Code are, from the slightest to the gravest, misdemeanor, felony, and crime. I will use the term "offense," generally, and one of the precise terms mentioned earlier, when discussing each specific example.

The Political Trial as a Tool of the Regime

The definition of the political trial has been central to academic debates from as far back as World War II. Yet, no unanimously accepted definition or concept has resulted from them. Topical studies showed the difficulty of building a theoretical framework when it comes to both democratic and totalitarian regimes. A comprehensive theoretical model valid for both political systems was never properly published. The historians who researched totalitarian regimes have a different perspective from those who studied political trials through the lens of liberal theory and jurisprudence. The latter consider individual freedom and civil rights fundamental values of state politics. A theoretical analysis of the trials that took place in Eastern Europe, similar to that of trials in the Western world, has not yet been done, and the literature dealing with these trials consists mainly of memoirs and presentations of local cases in the various countries, which had belonged to the Eastern European bloc.[5]

Political science researchers have primarily focused on Western-based political trials. They interpreted them through the prism of the three branches of government: legislative, executive, and judicial, which are inherent parts of the political system in power.[6]

Among the three branches, the judicial branch is the weakest link in the decision-making process and the governing of the country.[7] Legislators create the theoretical part of the law, whereas the state observes its application through its executive branch. In themselves, political trials could be analyzed from different perspectives, from defense to prosecution. For example, a trial considered by the prosecution political could be construed as such in a fraud case, especially when the fraud was committed against a state-own institution. Another example is a trial considered political by the defense where the offense is violation of the public order. In this case, the defendant could claim that the police tried to prevent a public demonstration, thus violating the freedom of expression.

There are major differences between the ways that liberal and totalitarian regimes engage with political trials:

The liberal democratic system allows for an ideological dispute between the defendant and the government. As such, political trials should not be common occurrences in these states. Yet, specialized literature shows that they happen there, too.[8] For the defendant, these societies facilitate methods of proving one's innocence, known as procedural protections.[9]

In totalitarian states, political trials are generally equated with show trials. This term was coined in the Soviet Union in the 1930s during the "Moscow Trials." Later, after World War II, on Stalin's orders, Eastern European leaders used the legal system to eliminate individuals no longer considered useful to the state's interests. Their elimination from state and party leadership roles took the form of such show trials. Several totalitarian regimes have also used political trials as a public platform to present the fate of the accused, which have often already been decided, in advance. That is why this kind of trials was also called "conceptual trials," since the development of the proceedings was conceptualized in advance. In itself, the term "show trial" does not directly correspond to all the political trials of Eastern Europe. Linguistically speaking, the term has a pejorative meaning. In Romanian, the term that best describes this phenomenon is "staged trial," or "proces înscenat" in Romanian.

Show trials are political in nature and are used by the ruling power's propaganda units to manipulate public opinion, via public court trials. Not all staged trials were show trials or public trials. Some were carried out in secret (as our economic trials) and did not allow media participation. These trials aimed to divest unwanted individuals of their political, social, and economic functions. In terms of meaning, a differentiation can be made between a criminal trial and a political trial the same way a differentiation can be made between a political trial and a show trial. A specific inclusion relationship exists between the three types of trials (criminal, political, and staged) and it functions as follows:

Inclusion Relationship:

As in Set Theory, or Group Theory, an inclusion relationship
is denoted by the symbol

"$\subset$." Group A is included in Group B (graphically $A \subset B$) if and only if every element of Group A is also an element of Group B. The phrase that sums up this relationship in Group A is included in Group B. When applying this relationship to our case studies, the formula reads as follows:

$$\text{Staged Trials} \subset \text{Political Trials} \subset \text{Criminal Trials}$$

More precisely, this means that every staged trial is also a political trial, and the latter is, in turn, also a criminal trial. In the case of the economic trials analyzed in this book, they were staged and consequently political. They were used by the communist authorities to promote their own political agenda,[10] namely the removal of the Jews from the economic sector. After the PCR initiated legal action against them, it was the Securitate that carried out the orders.

The totalitarian nature of a political regime is not a necessary and sufficient condition for the existence of show trials. Yet, most of the time, this type of trial proceedings took place in totalitarian states. Barbara Falk argues that many of the political trials took place during the Cold War,[11] and the ruling powers in both Western and Eastern European countries used them to cement their rule and mold the masses. Falk believes that, regardless of their distinct political context, these trials shared similar traits. They showcased the countries' internal conflicts, but also, as international relationships go, the tension between East and West.[12] Moreover, they show that the law in liberal societies cannot be considered totally free of political influences.[13]

Current studies show that the staged trials that took place in satellite Soviet states were not directly influenced by the tense international relationships of the time. In these particular countries, the positions of members of the government were strengthened by the consolidation of the political arena from several parties to just one. During this period, the Communist Parties had already taken control, by legal means or fixed elections, in most Eastern European countries. Based on the Soviet model, these trials had two main objectives: first, to consolidate the position of the Communist Party as the governing body and, second, to eliminate those members perceived as dangerous to the goals of the ruling party. The trials, which initially aimed to distance some of the opposing leaders from positions of influence, escalated to their physical removal.

In essence, these staged trials, regardless of whether their cause was Soviet Stalinist influence, or the goal of eliminating opposing political leaders, were used in the political struggle for absolute power. For example, in Romania, these conflicts were not anchored in divergent political opinions but, rather, in deeply embedded personal rivalries and the fear of losing power. This type of trial mimicked those used by Stalin in the Soviet Union, replicating them later in most Eastern European countries after World War II.

The Stalinist trials could be characterized as aiming to eliminate the "political enemy" as most of the accused were close to Lenin and Stalin and held leadership positions in the political system. It is likely that most of them were designated as enemies of the people rather arbitrarily, based on Stalin's personal beliefs. In the satellite countries, the trials that dealt with those perceived as political opponents became a part of daily reality.

At first glance, it seemed that in those states that subscribed to the Universal Declaration of Human Rights[14] after the end of World War II, the principles of legalism made their way into communist legislation. Under these conditions, in order to carry out an arrest, it is imperative to have a legal reason for doing so, and this reason should be in the form of a judge's arrest order. This law principle is called habeas corpus.[15] According to it, a person can be arrested only when there is evidence to justify his arrest. In its original form, this principle was not observed in Communist Romania. In the 1952 Constitution, in effect during the economic trials, the arrest order could be issued not only by a judge but by a prosecutor as well.[16]

The present book focuses on economic trials. Although this is not a legal term, I use it because in the analyzed trials, the accusations took the guise of economic offenses. The main goal of so many trials in the Soviet satellite states was the elimination of individuals considered a threat to the leaders in power. The trials were used as "educational" opportunities by those initiating them: to "reeducate" those going through them and to deliver important lessons for those hearing about them later.[17] The court was the stage where such proceedings took place, as a metaphorical battle between Good and Evil. It was the place where the inequality between the two parties was most evident and the rigging of the process clear.

But this is not all concerning the political trials. For close to half a century there was no open political confrontation between the accused and the accusing parties in the Eastern European countries. The reality of the interaction in the trials was that of a monologue of the prosecution. The accused were never heard. As already mentioned, any political trial is first of all a criminal trial that requires the presence of two things to grant it viability: the factual element (*Actus Reus*) and the element of intent (*Mens Rea*) of the criminal act. Yet, even if this requirement was a sine qua non condition of the trial, this was not observed by the communist authorities. As such, the law was broken in the communist states as it was, sometimes, in liberal states, too.

According to Kirchheimer's political justice theory, the goal of such political trials was the elimination of political enemies,[18] but they also served an instructional and cautionary purpose.

Political Trials in Eastern European Countries

The staged trials constitute a distinct chapter in the history of Eastern European communist countries after they became totalitarian regimes[19] in the aftermath of World War II. They became public knowledge starting with key events in 1920s' Soviet Union, like the 1928 political trials at Sahti (Donbas)[20] and the 1930 Industrial Party trial.[21] Another well-known trial, involving Kirov's assassin and his accomplices, took place after Kirov's[22] death and had a significant impact on the political scene of the union.[23] Soon after these trials, there followed a purge of many Soviet leaders from the communist elite. Their arrest, trials, and sentencing to death are known as the Great Terror. The trials carried out between 1936 and 1938 became known as the "Moscow Trials."[24] The Soviet Union show trials[25] were another example of the infamous misuses of justice by the Stalinist regime.

This type of trial was imported by the popular democracies of Eastern Europe after World War II. Some of the communist leaders who were key in the emergence of these countries were singled out, followed, and arrested between 1949 and 1954. After the communist takeover, many communist leaders became the victims of trials staged in the vein of "The Great Purge." Although the majority of those involved were Jewish, their elimination was not motivated only by their ethnicity, but by the power struggle in those respective countries: "Political leaders like Rajk,[26] Kostov[27] or Slansky,[28] served as the scapegoats during the time that popular resistance to Kremlin politics started to intensify."[29] Kostov, Rajk, and Slansky's elimination served as an example for similar endeavors in the Soviet satellite states. After the Nuremberg trials, in the beginning of the 1950s, a series of trials followed, considered by some historians to be show trials.

> The Show trials were an effective intimidation tool used by the Stalinist regime and were, in different versions, later introduced in the satellite countries. If, in the 1930's, the victims were chosen first and the scenarios incriminating them built later, in the 1950's, incriminating concepts and scenarios came first and the accused to be judged and sentenced to death were affixed later.[30]

Hodos categorizes the staged trials of the 1950s as being a phenomenon specific to the Eastern European countries. He also believes that they were precipitated by three international events: the intensification of the Cold War, Stalin's increasing paranoia toward the end of his life, and the falling-out between the Soviet Union and Iosip Broz Tito's Yugoslavia. While the accused during "The Great Purge" were accused of Trotskyism,[31] the ones accused after World War II were found guilty of Titoism.[32] After Kostov's death sentence and the elimination of the "Swedish Group" in the Rajk trial in Hungary, the witch hunt[33] continued until Stalin's death in 1953.

The most publicized trial was that of the first secretary of the Czech Communist Party, Rudolf Slansky, and his group in November of 1952. The fourteen Czech and Slovakian leaders were accused of being in the service of Great Britain and Zionism. Eleven of them were condemned to death and three of them to life imprisonment. Among the latter there were two Israelis, Shimon Orenstein[34] and Mordechai Oren,[35] who were later released. Arthur London was another survivor of the Slansky trial, an experience he detailed in a book.[36] The fact that political trials also took place in liberal regimes shows that the political regime in itself is not a solid indicator of the democratic mechanisms that are usually associated with liberal societies.

As it stands, political trials, regardless of their location, are the clear expression of the leading power. When taking place in a totalitarian regime, the political trial was that much more the embodiment of an oppressive authority that acted under the guise of a righteous state.[37]

ECONOMIC TRIALS IN SOCIALIST STATES

The Relationship between Economic and Political Trials

The term "economic trial" will be used to denote the further analyzed trials in which the accusations were linked to offenses of an economic nature. These types of offenses include the mismanagement of contracts and offers and premeditated actions that led the prosecution to press charges of undermining the Romanian economy. According to the Criminal Code, offenses of an economic nature that involve property come under the heading of "common law."[38] These offenses are of a civil nature and require the payment of incurred debt to the damaged party. They have nothing to do with the Common Law, characterizing the Anglo-Saxon legislation. In totalitarian regimes, thus in communist countries, too, economic offenses pass for political offenses, or acts against the state. In liberal societies, most, if not all, economic offenses are not considered political crimes.

Contrary to this view, in most communist countries, an economic crime was also considered a crime against the state, by virtue of the fact that it was a crime against its property. Economic crimes involving large amounts of money have the potential to affect the country's economy, but this is not necessarily enough to consider them political crimes.[39] In socialist countries, due to the management of the socialist economy, economic crimes were crimes against the state and were consequently considered political crimes.

Economic Trials in the Soviet Union

If in the period 1945–1961 almost all the trials that took place in the socialist camp countries, with one single exception in Czechoslovakia,[40] could be classified as political and not economic trials, the Soviet Union was the single country in which the years 1960–1964 were marked by a series of economic trials that were among the events that led to significant changes in the legislation.

The following chapters will present some aspects of the policy pursued by N. S. Khrushchev[41] during the aforementioned period, and the steps taken to change the Soviet law and the Criminal Code, in particular with an eye to economic crimes. Next, two main points will be followed:

a. If all the trials that took place in the Communist bloc during the 1950s are considered to have been initiated under the direct influence of Stalin, the economic trials in Romania were initiated in a different context, a decade later, remaining unique in the way they were organized and the effects they had.
b. During the period of the economic trials in Romania, a series of economic trials took place in the Soviet Union, as well. There were, however, significant differences between the two countries in the foundations of the judicial policies and in the punitive measures applied for the acts categorized by both countries as economic crimes.

Legislative Changes under Khrushchev

- Background

Economic development and the consolidation of the Soviet Union's position in the international arena have been noted as important topics throughout Khrushchev's term as party secretary. Despite the various measures taken under his leadership, both in the areas of economic planning and its implementation, over time they became new forms of control and repression exercised over the population.

Following the civil war and the revolution of 1917, V. I. Lenin[42] had instituted a program aimed at promoting a new economy. The program known as NEP[43] aimed to combine a minimum private free market economy with the maintenance of state ownership over heavy industry, agricultural land and natural resources, transport, and the media. This program included some freedoms, allowing farmers to sell their products on the market according to the laws of supply and demand, while the townspeople were given the opportunity to set up and manage some trade and produce goods in small workshops. On the one hand, the system provided a solution for the population, which was hostile to the communist regime in its beginnings due to the disappearance of the private sector, and on the other hand, prevented the collapse of the Russian economy with the onset of the nationalization process. Furthermore, the official top-priority objective of the Soviet economy, in all branches, was the development of grandiose industrial projects, mostly heavy industry for the army, with much less investment in the production of consumer goods. Consequently, at the end of the 1930s, the lowering of the population's standard of living gave rise to a phenomenon that would help the population survive economically—the illegal production of neglected consumer goods and the organization of a clandestine "black market" for the sale and purchase of these products.

- The Second Economy

This type of economy, which developed in those years, was named the "Second Economy." Its main products were primarily the consumer goods that were increasingly missing from the free market. These items were procured by means of the existing infrastructure of the formal economy, owned and operated by the state. In any normal national economy, both public needs and private needs are addressed in order to ensure the supply of individual needs as much as possible.[44] As a result of the expansion of the Second Economy, as an illegal phenomenon, any private initiative began to be considered by the authorities as an economic crime. The evolution of the Second Economy intensified after World War II, when the eruption of consumerism increased in inverse proportion to the waning concerns of war. Toward the end of the 1940s, with the rise of anti-Semitism in the Soviet Union, the number of Jews who lost their jobs increased. In order to continue to ensure their economic survival, many of these unemployed Jews engaged in Second Economy activities as an alternative.[45] Under Khrushchev's leadership, the government made great efforts to reduce the phenomena involved in the development of the Second Economy, while emphasizing the prominent role of Jews in its illegal practice. Khrushchev, aware of the Second Economy's existence, considered to be a "serious structural disease" of the Soviet system, was also aware of the negative role the party apparatus had played in opposing any private initiatives, especially in terms of economic development. However, Khrushchev did not have the understanding and courage to detect other economic and social factors that could have been responsible for what was happening. He operated as a strict reformer, but the reforms initiated were essentially aimed at changing the form and not the content.[46]

The political leadership of the party, which should have faced the economic problems, sought the liquidation of the Second Economy in order to ensure effective political control over the entire existing economy. For this purpose, Soviet leaders needed both the definition and the practical application of clear and relevant legislative measures, as well as stable laws, specifying, on the one hand, the rights and obligations of citizens and, on the other, those of the economic enterprises.

To this end, shortly after the 20th Congress of the party, both the Criminal and the Civil Code were replaced, together with the corresponding Procedures Codes.

Starting in 1961, Khrushchev launched increasingly ambitious initiatives in the economy in order to catch up with the West and the United States, especially in the field of agricultural products (cereals, meat, and milk). A program aimed at achieving objectives by implementing rules over a seven-year period failed miserably, as the agricultural sector was unable to comply with the requirements.

Party officials who were responsible for what happened hid the truth and created the impression that the objectives had been met. Khrushchev, who was among the initiators of the ineffective plan, was the one who reacted harshly, increasing the severity of the penalties prescribed by law on the whole, and specifically including new Criminal legislation referring to economic crimes.[47]

Khrushchev, without resorting to the methods of his predecessor Stalin, whom he himself had condemned in his "secret speech," returned at least partially to the latter's orientation, using the aid mechanisms provided by the KGB.[48] Khrushchev had staged, through the recently modified mechanisms of economic justice, a whole range of economic trials in all the republics of the Soviet Union. Many of the staged trials were presented and documented in Evgenia Evel'son' book.[49]

Following all these events, a new Criminal Code was formulated during Khrushchev's time, in the Russian Soviet Federative Socialist Republic and later in the other republics of the Soviet Union.

Starting in 1960, new versions of the Criminal Code and the Code of Criminal Procedure were also developed. The initiative to change the legislation was a direct consequence of the difficult economic situation in the Soviet Union. This led to additional punishments, specified in the New Criminal Code, and, as will be explained later, also gave the authorities more power to decide upon and implement more severe punishments, including the most serious of all, the death penalty. The decision on the escalation of punitive measures had a clear purpose, namely to discourage the population from continuing to commit crimes that were considered to be economic ones and officially defined by the authorities as such.

The New Legislative Principles of the Soviet Constitution

At a time when the theory of "class enemy" had failed, the search for someone to blame for the failure of the new economic measures applied by the Soviet leadership led to a process of "re-education" of the population, using methods that retained their relevance even after Stalin's death. In this context, new criminal legislation containing the political requirements of the ruling elite had become an immediate necessity. A Swiss journal conducted a broad and competent analysis of the political and legal situation in the Soviet Union at the time[50] when new legislative measures had been enacted. As a first step in the application of these new legislative measures, in December 1958, the Supreme Soviet of the USSR enacted legislation, some of which defined new Fundamental Principles regarding criminal legislation and procedures, which were to be used later as the basis of each of the Criminal Code and the Code of Criminal Procedure of the Soviet Republics.[51]

The others dealt with offenses under federal jurisdiction (offenses against the state and the military order). Subsequently, new codes were promulgated in each of the republics of the Union, with the Criminal Code of 1960 of the Soviet Federative Socialist Republic of Russia serving as a model for all others.[52]

In October 1960, the Supreme Soviet[53] of the RSFSR[54] enacted the two new codes, a criminal code and a criminal procedure code. They were to go into effect on January 1, 1961, and all the Soviet Republics followed suit, although small differences were allowed.[55]

The New Trends in Soviet Legislation Regarding Economic Crimes

The Soviet leadership feared that the degradation of the domestic economic situation that led to the emergence of the Second Economy and its years of continuity would prevent the effective implementation of a new economic policy, as had been announced in the late 1950s. Therefore, they decided to implement "group therapy" on all groups identified with those liable to impede the implementation of state economic policy decisions. This "therapy" included not only conferences and meetings where the new policy lines were explained but also threats against those who seemed to oppose government decisions.

New principles in the field of modern Criminal Law had been added to the new Codes. Thus, the number of crimes for which the death penalty could be applied was reduced and the courts into whose jurisdiction the relevant crimes fell, remained the ones to impose such sentences. This served an attempt to create the image of a Soviet justice based on principles of modern law, that were already used in Western Europe at the time. At the same time, the Moscow leadership intensified the fight against groups that appeared to pose a possible ideological and social threat to society, but especially posed an economic threat, because after the early 1950s, the Second Economy had found widespread support within the population. Individuals or groups of people considered to be enemies of socialism ("social parasites," according to revolutionary terminology), or those suspected of crimes, were liable to be subjected to very severe punishments. However, in accordance with the new principles, the application of the death penalty was restricted.

The introduction of the death penalty in the Soviet Union, as the punishment administered in the case of some of the economic crimes, was aimed at those engaged in the Second Economy.

During the course of the Soviet Union's history, the death penalty had been abolished, alternately by Lenin and Stalin, after the October Revolution (1917–1918, 1920, and 1947–1950). The death penalty was last abolished in 1947 as an expression of the Soviet people's loyalty to the communist regime and the Soviet homeland during World War II. Three years later, the death penalty was reintroduced into the Criminal Code in the context of political crimes, a category that in the Soviet Criminal Code referred to crimes of espionage, treason and sabotage. After Stalin's death in 1953, the use of the death penalty extended to other categories of crime, such as homicide. But in practice, in the period 1940–1950, and even until the end of the 1950s, the death penalty was rarely used, being applied only in very special situations. With the beginning of the 1960s, the punishments worsened, and the death penalty extended to other crimes.

The intensification of the fight against economic crimes, or parasitism, followed by vigorous campaigns for the repression of crimes that had become a source of perpetual irritation to the Soviet authorities, led to the enactment of a special criminal legislation in 1961.[56] The decrees included in this Special Legislation, already deviated from the principles that had been enshrined not long before[57] on two important points:

- First, they did not follow the principle that Soviet Criminal Laws should be stable, and measures taken against criminals should be of a general nature, rather than centered on specific problems.
- Second, this was an important feature of the special decrees. The death penalty became applicable in many cases, despite the principle set out in Article 22 of the Fundamental Principles,[58] establishing that it should be exceptional and destined to be completely abolished.[59]

Thus, some new decrees partly canceled, or diminished, the liberalization adopted with the enactment of the Fundamental Principles and the Criminal Codes between 1958 and 1960.

Some of these referred to crimes against the state, for which the penalties became much more severe, as well as for illicit foreign exchange transactions committed by a repeat offender or involving large amounts. Others reinforced the penalties for serious cases of illicit monetary transactions, and even required the death penalty in more serious cases, including a number of crimes, in particular significant thefts to the detriment of the State or society.

Consequently, with the promulgation of the October 1960 Criminal Code (also known by the name of the Criminal Constitution), the death penalty began to be applied in the case of crimes, which, before its adoption, were not considered to be subject to such draconian punishment (relative to economic crimes). During Khrushchev's time (1958–1964), despite attempts to liberalize political life in the Soviet Union, the strict legislation of the 1960s took a step back from the so-called liberal attitude that could be felt a few years earlier (1958), and thereafter the spirit of thawing was no longer allowed, nor was the adoption of measures in that direction.

Economic offenses, mostly defined as "property crimes," were among the types of crimes to which the death penalty was extended. The only known precedent of this situation, though easily comparable to punishments from Khrushchev's time, was one death sentence from Stalin's time, in 1932, for embezzling funds from state farms or cooperatives.[60]

The analysis of the Soviet legal policy of the 1960s by "The Committee" concluded that at that time, Soviet prosecutors were increasingly using the definition of "economic crime" for a wide variety of crimes, until it reached epidemic proportions. Many people were accused of this type of crime, and the percentage of those convicted was very high, as already specified. The same article comments, among other things, that the main danger of changing legal principles during the 1960s would have been the lack of coherence and precision in the use of the legal terms of the time. Those in power deliberately drafted sections of the law ambiguously, leaving room for interpretation in either direction. In a situation where both the rules and their mode of application were not sufficiently clear and precise, no fair and neutral legal procedure could be instituted from the point of view of the law enforcement authorities, which almost consistently made arbitrary decisions.[61]

From 1962 onward, the new laws regarding economic crimes began to operate regularly in almost all the republics that were part of the Soviet Union; this is what happened in the Republics of Moldova, Belarus, and Kyrgyzstan. The first example that will be analyzed in this chapter will be that of the trial involving workers at the oil mill in Balti, Moldova. Among others, Moise Ackerman, mentioned by Sorin Toma in his work, was indicted in this trial.[62]

The trial took place at the same time as the trials in Romania, analyzed in this book. I received details of the trial through an interview with Mr. Toma,[63] later from several telephone conversations with relatives in Romania, Israel, and Canada, but primarily correspondence and conversations with Mr. Pavel Ackerman, Moise Ackerman's son, who lives in Canada. Between 1962 and 1964, other criminal trials took place in Balti against large groups of employees in sugar, oil, alcohol, and fur factories. During these trials at the end of 1962, Moise Ackerman, who headed the Oil Refining Department, was also arrested, along with about 50 other people who remained in custody for about a year and a half without trial. In 1964, they were finally brought to trial before the Supreme Court of the Republic of Moldova. Most of the defendants in this trial, according to the report written by Pavel Ackerman, were Jews.[64]

The presentation of the economic trials in Evel'son's book, with numerous examples and statistical analyses, indicates a high percentage of Jews among trial defendants throughout the Soviet Union.[65] Evel'son analyzed 400 trials that took place between 1961 and 1967, in which 1,676 of the defendants were Jews. The economic crimes brought at that time to trial were divided into three categories: bribery, foreign currency trading, and large-scale theft. These types of economic crimes were among the crimes referred to by amendments to the Criminal Code in the 1960s. Of the 1,676 Jews who were convicted of one or more of the three types of crimes, the death penalty was imposed on 163 people who were executed by shooting. Another 801 people received sentences of 10 years in prison and 712 sentences of 10 to 15 years in prison.[66] Evel'son's conclusion, supported also by Gitelman, was that Soviet law used different criteria in punishing the Jewish and non-Jewish population, thus using different standards to the detriment of Jewish citizens.[67] The highest number of death sentences in the RSFSR was applied in the cities of Moscow and Leningrad.[68]

The stereotype of the Jewish speculator was not a new image for the Soviet people, and the aversion to it was well understood: the Jews were the main ethnic community accused of economic crimes, as representatives of Zionism and bourgeois nationalism.[69] Despite the formal right to freedom of choice in profession and occupation, the Jews were not integrated into the economy and were thus pushed into areas of the national economy that were considered undesirable.[70]

Evel'son's in-depth study of many of the economic trials reported by the Soviet press at the time showed that the sentences of the Jewish defendants were much heavier than those of others convicted of similar crimes. The Jews have always been portrayed as the traditional scapegoat.

With the issuance of the Fundamental Principles in 1958, the death penalty had not yet been implemented. It started to be carried out on a larger scale a little later, when these principles were incorporated into the first part of the Criminal Codes of the Soviet Republics, published only in 1960–1961. The classification of the death penalty in the Soviet Criminal Code will be considered for the comparison of the Soviet and the Romanian Criminal Codes. In fact, in Romania, the death penalty had already been introduced in 1953.

Crimes considered "economic crimes," but not political ones, in the Soviet Criminal Code, were included in chapter 6 of Berman's book.[71] In all the cases mentioned in this chapter as economic crimes, the punishments didn't exceed 10 years, which was rare, and most of the penalties for those crimes were up to 5 years and confiscation of property. Despite this special section regarding economic crimes, there were still a few that were mentioned as crimes against the State, where the death penalty was mentioned as a possibility, but all those categories were added only in amendments in1962.

The Khrushchev administration established which of these categories of crimes would be considered serious crimes punishable by death. The Soviet Criminal Code of the time applies the death penalty for three categories of crimes:

- Looting public property, but not private
- Counterfeiting
- Illicit trade in foreign currency, in which the number of transactions or the value of traded goods was high

What all these crimes had in common was the fact that they are related to property, and the severity of each one was determined by the value of the property involved.[72]

The return to repressive politics, in such a short space of time in relation to the introduction of the Fundamental Principles, was also for the purpose of detecting those who opposed Khrushchev's precepts and who had refused to adopt the norms of "collectivism" that is, subordinating individual interests to the benefit and interests of the whole society. The assumption that Soviet citizens would accept the rules of "collectivism" was one of the most irrational illusions of the communist regimes of all time and can be considered one of the obvious manifestations of the failure of civic education in any communist society.

Romanian and Soviet Criminal Codes during the 1960s

So far, I have discussed serious economic crimes that took place in the Soviet Union during Khrushchev's leadership, for which the death penalty was applied. Next, I will try to make a few specific comparisons between the Soviet Union and Romania, regarding their legal approaches in general and in terms of economic crimes in particular. Through this comparison, it will be possible to deduce some similarities and differences of approach in relation to the Jewish citizens, during the leadership of Khrushchev in the Soviet Union and of Gheorghiu-Dej in Romania.

In 2006, the president of Romania at the time, Traian Băsescu, appointed a Presidential Commission for the Study of the Communist Dictatorship in Romania under the leadership of Vladimir Tismăneanu.[73] This study ended with the publication of a large Report[74] of over 600 pages, which included extensive documentation of the totalitarian experiment of the entire Communist period between 1945 and 1989. One of the chapters of this *Report*[75] was dedicated to "repressive justice" throughout the era in question. During this period, the Criminal Codes were changed four times, namely in 1948, 1955, 1958, and 1960, the latter being the Criminal Code on the basis of which the defendants of the economic trials were convicted. The Codes contained the laws which had been enacted as the formal instruments for implementing the restrictive measures applied toward the citizens of the country.[76] The changes made over time aimed to authorize and intensify the power exercised by the Securitate. The penal codes will serve as the documentary basis for the comparison between Romania and the Soviet Union,[77] specifically with reference to economic crimes in the two countries.[78]

Criminal Codes in Communist Romania

After the communization of Romania, on February 27, 1948, the first Communist Criminal Code of 1948 was published, only four days after the arrest of Lucreţiu Pătrăşcanu, the former minister of justice. After the publication of the Criminal Code in 1948, changes and additions were made, increasing a number of penalties in criminal cases, and these were reflected in the Criminal Codes that appeared successively in 1955, 1958, and 1960.

The 1960 Criminal Code[79] was the one that served as the basis of indictment in the economic trials analyzed in this book. The Romanian Criminal Code is divided into two books, the first book, called "General Provisions," and the second book "Crimes and Felonies in Particular," including the definition of the types of crimes and the related punishments. Each book is divided into parts called "Titles," and each Title is subdivided into "Chapters." Each chapter has subdivisions called "Sections" and the Sections comprise the articles of law, in numerical order, with a continuous enumeration between the two books.

Criminal Codes in the Soviet Union

The Soviet Criminal Code used for comparison was the RSFSR Criminal Code of October 27, 1960, which was later amended on March 1, 1970.

The Code was divided into two parts, a general part, including the General Provisions as a separate chapter, and other rules and measures relating to the whole document, and the second part, called the Special Part including the charges and relevant punishments. Both parts were divided into chapters, according to the different issues they dealt with. Both the Basic Principles and the Criminal Codes for All Republics were part of the Soviet Union Criminal Code, issued between 1958 and 1960.

As already discussed in section 3.2.2.3, the deviations of the Special Legislation from the Basic Principles promulgated in 1958 were reflected in multiple declarations that reinstated the death penalty, including it among the punishments applicable to economic crime. The purpose of these sanctions was not only a personal punishment of the offender but also a means of imposing social discipline on the population of the Soviet Union.

The Principle of Criminal Attempt

Romania

The criminal codes in Romania from CP-1948 to CP-1960 established that if the law did not provide otherwise, the attempt to commit a crime would be sanctioned with a punishment whose severity is one degree less than the one for the crime itself.[80]

However, in the case of crimes considered by the communist political system to be very serious, such as political crimes, that is,, against the state, attempts to commit the crime were punished in the same way as the crime itself. This provision was included in CP-1948, the first Communist Criminal Code, and was not amended even by CP-1960. Such crimes include crimes against the internal and external security of the state, such as treason, espionage, and economic crimes, where the law provided for the death penalty, both in the case of the crime and in the case of the criminal attempt. This measure ultimately represented a strengthening of the Securitate's freedom of action in both pursuing groups of citizens considered suspects, and proceeding easily to their punishment.

The Soviet Union

The attempt to commit a crime is discussed in Art. 15 of the 1960 Soviet Criminal Code.[81] In the Criminal Codes of the Soviet Republics, the attempt is considered a deliberate act, which did not take effect due to circumstances beyond the control of the perpetrator. There may be various reasons that the crime was not committed, such as the means used by the perpetrator, or the material object of the crime, or the conditions under which it was attempted. Therefore, the punishment in the case of an attempt is lighter than in the case of the actual crime.

Although there was a tendency in Soviet Criminal Law to consider the attempt to commit a crime as if it had been committed, the Soviet Criminal Code applied a policy of reducing the sentence in the case of the attempt, in contrast to the Romanian Criminal Code, even in the case of attempt of a serious crime, like treason, espionage, and other crimes against the state or the judiciary.

This suggests that during the 1950s and 1960s, Romania escalated the punishments of perpetrators of crimes against the state (political crimes), relative to the measures taken by the Soviet Union. It will be proven later that the shadow of Stalinism continued to hover over Romania, both in its political and legal leadership,[82] lasting many years after Stalin's demise.

Crimes against the State in General and Economic Crimes in Particular

Romania

The main regulations of the repressive legislation in Romania from 1948 to1964 were included in the second book[83] of the Romanian Criminal Code, called "Crimes and Felonies in Particular" in Title I, called "Crimes and Felonies against the State." These punishments were among the most draconian measures existing in the entire Romanian Criminal Code (CP-1960) at the time when the economic trials were held. The crimes included here were classified according to the assessment of how seriously they impacted the internal or external security of the state.

In the first two decades of the history of Communist Romania, the Criminal Codes legislation went through a process of escalation of penalties. The escalation was reflected both by increasing the number of sentences and by diversifying the options for serious punishments. These measures extended the power of the Securitate Forces beyond what could be imagined to be acceptable. The Securitate was the body responsible for the surveillance and pursuit of the suspected citizens, with a view to a future arrest, and it was the same Securitate whose representatives led the investigations and manipulated the legal proceedings of any criminal trial behind the scenes. The criminal cases manipulated by the Securitate were judged by Military Courts. These measures were taken to cause panic among the civilian population, especially after the 1956 events in Hungary and Poland. Each of these popular movements shook the Romanian political system to its foundations. Prior to these movements, the Romanian authorities had issued an Order aimed at strengthening the methods of repression of the population by redefining certain offenses as being more serious than they had previously been considered, and increasing the severity of punishments through the issuance of two decrees introduced in the corresponding Criminal Codes, the first, Order no. 202/1953[84] and the second, Order no. 318/1958.[85]

Before the publication of these decrees, "economic crimes" were categorized as felonies. With the issuance of Order 202/1953, they turned into crimes against the state. Actually, economic crimes were a new category of crimes first defined in the Supplementary Section I (in Romanian, Section

I bis) of Book II, "Crimes and Felonies in Particular," Title I *Crimes and Felonies against the State*, Chapter II "Crimes and Felonies against the Internal Security of the State,"[86] which included the new economic crime of "Undermining the National Economy and Counter-Revolutionary Sabotage." This order was enacted starting with CP-1955.

On the other hand, the system of punishment for these new types of economic crimes became drastically more severe, with the addition of the death penalty. Until the issuance of Decree No. 202/1953, the maximum punishment for the most serious political crimes, such as treason (Article 184) or espionage (Article 194), was forced labor for 25 years.

The treatment of economic offenses detailed in Section I bis targeted civil servants from state institutions or enterprises. All three articles included in this section reach the most severe punishment, according to the following edict:

> If the deeds were capable of producing very serious consequences, the punishment is death and the confiscation of all property.[87]

It should be mentioned that Art. 209^4 of the same Section specifies that, referring to certain articles,[88] the criminal attempt would be treated like the crime itself. This proves that up to the 1960s, the Romanian Criminal Code consistently violated the Principle of Criminal Attempt.

Also, if in CP-1948, conspiracy against the social order was defined as a crime, punishable by imprisonment for twenty-five years, after the issuance of Decree 202/1953, this act became a political crime that in serious cases carried the death penalty. Certain punishments that were added to the Criminal Code after the appearance of Order 202/1953 became even more severe later, with the issue of Decree 318/1958. For example, the penalties for crimes of espionage or divulging state secrets (Articles 194^1 and 194^2), initially set at 25 years of forced labor, would be replaced with forced labor for life and in extreme cases could even lead to death row.

The Soviet Union

With the publication of the new Soviet Criminal Code in 1960, counter-revolutionary sabotage ceased to be punishable by death. However, the death penalty remained in force for other categories of political crimes. As discussed in the previous subchapter, the worsening of penalties in the Soviet Penal Codes followed shortly after relaxations had been introduced in Criminal Law. In reality, these harsh measures were not implemented immediately, but only in 1964, the last year in which Khrushchev served as the party's first secretary. The following are some of the Decrees that were issued and introduced in the

Criminal Codes of the Soviet Republics and which were implemented after 1960.[89]

- A second paragraph was added to the Order adopted on March 25, 1961, namely Article 25 of the Fundamental Principles of 1958, on Crimes against the State (Article 88 of the Criminal Code of the RSFSR[90]). The death penalty was imposed on the perpetrators of illegal large-scale transactions, including those involving foreign currency.[91]
  (Category 1 of the capital offenses,[92] according to Solomon[93])
- According to the Decree adopted on May 5, 1961, death by shooting was the punishment for crimes such as the theft of property on a very large scale and causing serious financial damages[94] to the state or society, as well as for counterfeiting.
  (Category 1 of the capital offenses, according to Solomon)
- According to the Decrees adopted on May 11, 1961, and May 24, 1961, the death penalty for embezzlement from public accounts was imposed.[95]
  (Category 2 of the capital offenses, according to Solomon)
- According to the decrees adopted on July 1, 1961, a long prison term was the sentence for dealing in foreign currency, and the death penalty was imposed when these acts involved very large sums of money or in the case of a repeat offender.[96]
  (Category 3 of the capital offenses, according to Solomon)
- According to the Decree adopted on February 20, 1962, the death penalty was imposed on civil servants who committed acts of corruption.[97]

In the case of the aforementioned Orders, the maximum punishment was usually imprisonment for 15 years, but in cases where the extent of economic damage was particularly high, the death penalty was imposed.

The addition to the Criminal Codes of the various categories of offenses described earlier was intended to prevent crime, social parasitism in general, and economic crime in particular.

A Comparative Analysis of Economic Crimes in Romania versus the Soviet Union

A thorough comparison of the Criminal Codes of the two countries, regarding the punishments given for economic crimes, leads to the observation that in the period considered, that of the 1960s, the Romanian Criminal Law applied harsher punishments than those applied by the Soviets. It can be seen how the toughening of punishments had evolved on different levels, such as the increased number of years of detention for the same crime and the extension of the scope of the death penalty to a greater number of cases and situations. It can also be observed, regarding the Romanian Criminal codes of 1948, 1955, 1958, that from one legislation to the next the punishments were considerably intensified. Thus, if according to CP-1948, for political crimes against the state, a sentence of three to seven years was expected,[98] according to CP-1958, this punishment was replaced by the death penalty. Between these two criminal codes, the maximum prison sentence for crimes against the state had been raised to 25 years of forced labor, while in the Criminal Code of the Soviet Union, the maximum punishment for the same type of crime was only 15 years.

Another aspect that characterized the Romanian Criminal Codes is the fact that in the case of some political crimes, the criminal attempt carried the same punishment as the crime itself. During the 1950s and 1960s, the Soviet Union was considered to be the only country where the death penalty was imposed for economic crimes.[99] This, however, was not true, since, at the same time, the death penalty had existed for some time in the Romanian Criminal Code, immediately after the promulgation of Order 202/1953. The order allowed the application of the death penalty in the case of crimes defined by the legislator as very serious, including crimes against the state.

Regarding the Soviet Union, the Committee concluded that the use of capital punishment was considered a justifiable method of punishment against those who had not mastered the "rules of behavior" imposed by communist doctrine and ideology.[100]

> The new decrees were drafted at the highest-level party and state authorities, in order to shake up public opinion who had remained indifferent to the many abuses committed against the Soviet economy.[101]

And yet, this was not the only reason for the implementation of stricter sanctions. Its other purpose was educational—to ensure that the people would respect the law and the authorities, seeing that the legislation was indeed applied in practice.

Criminal Law was considered by the communist regime, either in the Soviet Union or in Romania, as a means of achieving social and educational goals. The severe repression of the country's population by means of Criminal Law was shared by the legal systems of both countries. Engaged literature, commenting on Soviet law during Khrushchev's time, viewed socialist justice as a stage for perfection and social harmony, but its implementation in the reality of Soviet life in no way reflected this foreseen utopia.

The death penalty was reintroduced into the Soviet Penal Code only in the 1960s, when Khrushchev tried to combat the phenomena generated by the Second Economy, as explained in section 3.2.2.1. The field of capital punishment in the Soviet Union had a different profile than its application in Romania, especially in the case of economic crimes, a profile explained in the previous subchapter, in the case of crimes such as theft or widespread counterfeiting. In contrast, in the Romanian Criminal Code in force at that time, crimes such as theft or counterfeiting were not included in the category of political crimes. The promulgation of the previously mentioned Decree, no. 202/1953 underlined the importance that the Bucharest regime assigned to the crimes it considered political.

In accordance with the intentions of the legislator, those suspected of intending to harm the national economy were targeted, as explained earlier. This type of crime was introduced into the category of serious crimes against the state, as "Undermining the National Economy and Counter-revolutionary Sabotage." These articles of law, which refer to economic crimes, never fell into the category of political crimes in liberal countries, where such crimes would be considered "property crimes," even when they involved large sums of money. They were not considered crimes against the state. Of course, the theft of state property is a much more serious crime than the theft of personal property, and is punished accordingly. Returning to the Romanian Criminal codes, following the enactment of Order 202/1953, the party leadership of Romania saw in the application of the death penalty a legitimate measure against very serious crimes. After the death penalty was first included in CP-1955, it remained unchanged in the following Criminal codes, of CP-1958 and CP-1960. In the Soviet Penal Code, the equivalent punishment was not used during the same period of time. As to the application of the death penalty in the Soviet Union, a few facts should be kept in mind. The situation changed when Khrushchev initiated a return to stricter laws against those who refused to take an active part in building the communist societies. Consequently, all those who dared to violate the laws regarding state property or the manipulation of foreign currency were candidates for severe punishment.[102]

The Special Legislation in the USSR regarding economic crimes was designed to draw public attention to the corruption that had become even more widespread at that time, partly due to the Second Economy, and to stop its proliferation.

In Romania, the death penalty was rather the expression of the authorities' most effective method of control over the population, and, unlike in the Soviet Union, when an offense fell into the category of serious economic crime, it was already categorized as a clear political crime against the State.

The use of the death penalty in both countries had the effect of tightening the regime's control, discouraging "deviant" behavior, and intimidating the population.

If the Soviet Union used various media, including the local press, to publicize the course of economic proceedings, Romania wanted their conduct regarding economic crimes to be kept strictly secret, at least concerning the Economic Trials of the Foreign Trade.[103]

Another major difference between those who were accused in the Soviet Union and those convicted in the Romanian economic trials was the identity of those indicted and their social status. Although the number of Jews who had been tried in the Soviet Union was considerable, most of them were citizens without any special public status, obviously not performing administrative, political, or economic functions. Although there were some exceptions, most of them were likely to be known only in the limited circle of their family and close acquaintances in the city where they lived. Unlike these, the convicts of the economic trials in Romania were not only all of Jewish origin but had fulfilled governmental functions, being senior officials in the Romanian enterprises from the MCE. They held elite positions in Romanian foreign trade at the time and were sent abroad as official representatives of the Romanian state. The representatives of this economic elite, all Jews, were a target for Gheorghe Gheorghiu-Dej's government, a group designated for expulsion from all public positions. In the late 1950s, this target was pursued through the National Communism policy of the Romanian party.[104]

It was directed against all the national minorities existing in Romania and of course against Jews who held important positions in the country's economy. In addition, although the official definition of these crimes was that of political crimes (by their specific inclusion in the Criminal Code), their nature did not justify their classification as such.

By an Order issued on June 27, 1961, the Soviet Secret Police (KGB) was invested with even more rights of investigation into economic crimes.[105]

In the same month of the same year, on the night of June 8 to 9, 1961, the Romanian secret police, the Securitate, had burst into the apartments of Alexandru Rado and Adalbert Rosinger, the main convicts of the Românoexport trial.[106]

CONCLUSION

After the end of World War II, the representatives of the Communist Parties in Eastern Europe rose to power in their countries, under the direct influence of the Soviet Union and imposed by it. Some of the people, who held important positions in the party leadership of the new communist countries, Romania among them, were of Jewish origin. Not only did Romanian Jews have representatives in the party leadership, but some of them also participated in other decision-making factors in politics, economics, journalism, administration, ideology, even in the political police, that is, in the Securitate or Miliţia. Some of these Jews, at least, tended to believe that the practical application of an egalitarian ideology, in which ethnic origin or religion would not be an obstacle in achieving normal living conditions for all people, could be achieved by the implementation of communism in Romania. They believed that applying the socialist-communist ideas in practice would bring justice and a correct solution to the Jewish predicament in general, and that of the Jews in Europe in particular. After so many of them had been humiliated and persecuted, and millions had disappeared, being killed during the Nazi Holocaust, their support of this ideology, as a form of struggle against fascism could have been understood at the time.

But the reality did not live up to expectations, and with the consolidation of the Communist Party, a significant number of the Jews were forced to resign a few years later. Thus, they would find that the fulfillment of the past ideal had no chance of becoming a reality in the future. These changes, which took place in almost all the socialist-communist countries that were satellites of the Soviet Union, led Jews to adopt one of two attitudes: some associated themselves with the ruling political class, trying to disregard their origins, while others adopted an attitude of compromise, tacitly accepting policy without direct participation in any political life, to the extent that this was possible, and developing their own professional life in order to be integrated into the new society. The Jews of Romania also had a similar destiny.

The in-depth study of the context of the economic trials, which took place in the Soviet Union in the second decade of Eastern European communism, led to an image totally different from that of the Romanian economic trials. It can be concluded that in most countries of the Communist bloc, there have been few attempts to involve Jews with high-level positions in the national economy in economic trials. On the other hand, the economic trials that characterized the period of Khrushchev's rule were determined by specific local conditions: economic changes that led to the intensification of the Second Economy and the change of legislation, by the implementation of the Fundamental Principles and the new Criminal Codes in the Soviet republics. Through the comparison made between the justice systems in Romania and the Soviet Union, it emerged that both the law and its application in Romania were more severe than in the Soviet Union, in terms of crimes against the state in general and those of an economic nature in particular.

The norms of the Romanian Criminal Code had a direct effect on the decisions made by the Securitate, under the influence of the party bodies, as I will try to prove further. Economic trials in Romania were initiated independently and unrelated to any Soviet influence or system of justice. In addition, the economic legislation existing in Romania during Gheorghe Gheorghiu-Dej's leadership included specific laws and procedures planned in the economic context of the country. Romanian criminal legislation was a local model, which had no counterpart in any other Eastern European country of the same historical period. A more detailed analysis of this topic will be presented together with the discussion of the issue raised by foreign trade enterprises, whose officials had been convicted and incarcerated for many years, severely affecting their few remaining years after the release from difficult years of imprisonment. These details will be revealed in the following chapters.

NOTES

1. A knot from Gordios, ancient Phrygia, which no one could untie and which Alexander the Great (356 BC–323 BC) cut with a sword. It means a complicated relationship, difficult to clarify. The original concept in Greek mythology said that whoever untied the Gordian knot would conquer Asia.

2. Ron Christenson, *Political Trials, Gordian Knots in the Law* (New Brunswick, NJ: Transactions Publishers, 1994).

3. See Appendix I.

4. CP stands for Penal Code or Criminal Code, CPP for Penal Procedural Code or Code of Criminal Procedure. The acronym CP-XXXX stands for the Criminal Code of year XXXX, the acronym CPP-YYYY for the Code of Criminal Procedure of the year YYYY. This information can also be found in appendix 1. For example, the Criminal Code used for all the Foreign Trade trials was the Criminal Code of 1960, henceforth CP-1960, or the Code of Criminal Procedure of 1960, will be henceforth CPP-1960.

5. These details were gathered from correspondence between the author and Prof. Barbara Falk, faculty member in the Defense Studies Department at the European, Russian, and Euroasian Center within the Canadian Armed Forces.

6. Michal R. Belknap, ed. *American Political Trials* (London: Grenwood Press, 1994), XIV, henceforth Belknap, *Political Trials.*

7. Otto Kirchheimer, *Political Justice: The Use of Legal Procedure for Political Ends* (Greenwood Press, 1980), 4, henceforth Kirchheimer, *Political Justice.* Kirchheimer (1905–1965) was a German-born Jewish lawyer and scientist who emigrated to the United States, renowned for his contribution to social science, and constitutional and political law. His 1961 book, *Political Justice: The Use of Legal Procedure for Political Ends*, is a landmark in the field.

8. Belknap, *Political Trials*, p. XIV.

9. Eric Posner, "Political Trials în Domestic and Internaţional Law," *Duke Law Journal*, 55, no. 25 (February 2020). Eric Posner is a law professor at Chicago University (Kirk & Ellis chair).

10. Leora Bilsky, *Transformative Justice-Israeli Identity on Trial* (Ann Arbor, MI: University of Michigan Press, 2004), 2.

11. The timeline for the Cold War varies: some historians estimated it as the 1948–1979 period, others opine that it only ended after the fall of the Communist bloc, namely after 1991.

12. Barbara Falk, "Making Sense of Political Trials, Causes and Categories," *Occasional Paper*, VIII (Toronto: University of Toronto, Munk Center, 2008), 9, henceforth Falk, "Making Sense of Political Trials."

13. Falk, "Making Sense of Political Trials," 2.

14. According to this foundational document, a person is presumed innocent until proven guilty. The Universal Declaration of Human Rights was adopted on December 10, 1948 by the U.N. General Assembly. It details human rights and civic freedoms, which should be respected by all participating countries.

15. "Bring the body" (in Latin). The expression appears in the Common Law system in order to require the judge to issue an order to seize and detain a person and to determine the legality of his detention.

16. Article 87, 1952 Constitution. It refers to the usage of the habeas corpus principle which, in practice, was subordinated to the Securitate's interests.

17. Falk, "Making Sense of Political Trials," 6.

18. Otto Kirchheimer, "Politics and Justice," in *Politics, Law and Social Change,* ed. Friederic Surin & Kurt Shell (New York: Columbia University Press, 1969), 420.

19. Belu Zilber, *Actor în procesul Pătrăşcanu* (Bucureşti, Humanitas, 1997), 16, in English "*An Actor in Pătrăşcanu trial*."

20. https://www.encyclopedia.com/history/encyclopedias-almanacs-transcripts-and-maps/shakhty-trial.

21. https://encyclopedia.thefreedictionary.com/Industrial+Party+Trial.

22. Sergei Mironovici Kirov (1886–1934) Soviet civil servant during the dictatorship of Joseph Stalin.

On December 1, 1934, he was killed in Leningrad, where he held the position of the Communist Party secretary. At the 20th congress of the Communist Party of the Soviet Union, 1956, Khrushchev revealed the act of assassination as having been done at Stalin's behest.

23. Roy Medvedeev, *Let History Judge* (Oxford: Oxford University Press, 1989), 258.

24. Some other examples include "The trial of the 16" in 1937, when Kameneev and Zinoviev were the accused, "The trial of the 17," when Radek and Piatkov were the accused, "The trial of the Army Members," where Tucacev was the accused and "The trial of the 20" 1938 with Buharin, Racovski, and Vigoda as the main defendants

25. Joel Carmichael, *Stalin's Materpiece* (London, Weidenfeld & Nicholson, 1976), 163–189), henceforth Carmichael, *Stalin's Masterpiece.*

26. Laszlo Rajk (1909–1949) was an important figure of the Hungarian Communist Party, served as both minister of interior and of foreign affairs, but fell victim to Stalin's ordered show trial in Hungary. He even took part in the foundation of the State Protection Authority (ÁVH), the secret police of the People's Republic of Hungary.

27. Traicho Kostov (1897–1949) was the leading figure of the Bulgarian Communist Party until he was sentenced to death by the Bulgarian Supreme Court. Tried together with 10 other officials, in Sofia from December 7 to December 14, 1949, he was finally executed.

28. Rudolf Slansky (1901–1952) of Jewish ethnicity was one of the most representative figures of Czech communism., After World War II, he was not only

one of the organizers of the coup d'etat that established the communist regime in Czechoslovakia, but he also had a leading role in the Sovietization of the country, the abolition of private property and the repression of political opponents of the regime.

29. Carmichael, *Stalin's Masterpiece*, 163–189.

30. George H. Hodos, *Show Trials* (New York: Praeger, 1986), XIII, henceforth Hodos, *Show Trials.* He was one of the few, if not the only writer to describe in detail almost all the staged trials in Eastern Europe. He was, himself, involved in the Rajk trial and escaped with his life after serving his long sentence.

31. The conflict between Trotsky and Stalin was based on their divergent stance vis-à-vis the "Socialism in one country" theory with Trotsky supporting "The permanent revolution" theory.

32. Hodos, *Show Trials*, 1–4.

33. Karel Kaplan, *Les Processus Politiques à Prague* (Bruxelles: Ed. Complexes, 1980), 20 & *Report on the Murder of the General Secretary* (Columbus, OH: Ohio State University Press, 1990), 7.

34. Shimon Orenstein was an economic attaché with the Israeli delegation in Prague.

35. Mordechai Oren (1905–1985) was the leader of the Left-leaning Israeli party called Mapam (made out of a left coalition that included the Kibbutz movement and other Leftist Israeli parties). He was also a member of the political branch of the Kibbutz movement, Hashomer Hatzair. He was involved in the Slansky trial and nicknamed "the Prague prisoner."

36. Arthur London, *Confession* (New York, Ballantine Books, 1971).

37. Laurence Douglas, *The Memory of Judgment, Making Law and History in the Trials of the Holocaust* (New Haven, CT: Yale University Press, 2001), 14, henceforth Douglas, *Memory of Judgment.*

38. There is no connection between this term and its usage in Anglo-Saxon law. In Romanian, a legislation based on Roman Law (and French Law) is called "Drept Comun."

39. Peter Solomon was professor of Soviet Criminal Law, today professor emeritus at the Department of Political Sciences affiliated Faculty, Center for European, Russian and Eurasian Studies, University of Toronto. A group of letters from this correspondence are in the author's possession, henceforth Solomon, *Private Letters.*

40. The trial has been referred to in the literature as the Trial of the Economists. Its economic profile was not due to the nature of the accusations, but rather due to the roles played by the defendants before the trial, as economic managers in different industries, or as economists. It was prepared by the party's political secretariat on May 10, 1954, and the trial itself opened three months later, on August 7.

Jiří Pelikán, *The Czechoslovak Political Trials 1950–1954* (ed.) (Stanford: California University Press, 1971), 60.

41. Nikita Sergeyevich Khrushchev (1894–1971) was the general secretary of PCUS between 1953 and 1964 and the president of the Ministers Council of the Soviet Union between 1958 and 1964.

42. Vladimir Ilici Ulyanov (known as Lenin) (1870–1924) is the Russian revolutionary, politician, and the political theorist who led to the Revolution in Tzarist Russia and its replacement by a communist government.

43. NEP = New Economic Policy, introduced in 1921 by Lenin with the vision of establishing a sort of market-oriented economy that was nevertheless State-controlled. This policy remained until Stalin abolished it in 1930.

44. Evgenia Evel'son, *Судебные процессы по экономическим делам в СССР* (Sudebnyie protzessy po economicheskim delam v SSSR) (London, Overseas Publications, Interchange, 1986), 18–43, henceforth Evel'son, *The Economic Trials in the Soviet Union.* Evgenia Evel'son was a PhD in law, lawyer, and law professor in some Soviet universities.

45. Ibid., 18–43.

46. Sorin Toma, *Privind înapoi*,182.

47. Charles Schwartz, "Economic Crime in the USSR: "A Comparison of the Khrushchev and Brezhnev Eras," *International and Comparative Law Quarterly* 30 (1981): 283.

48. KGB (in Russian *Komitet Gosudarstvennoy Bezopasnosti*), Committee for State Security was the secret police of the Soviet Union. In 1954, the name of the old secret police, the NKVD (People's Commissariat for Internal Affairs, in Russian Naródnyy Komissariát Vnútrennikh Del) changed into KGB. The NKVD had been founded by Lenin by the Order of December 20, 1917, and continued to operate until 1954.

49. Evel'son, *The Economic Trials in the Soviet Union.*

50. Commission internationale de juristes, "Les infractions économiques en Union Soviétique," *Revue de la commission internationale de juristes*, vol. 5, no.1, summer, 1964, henceforth "Les Infractions économiques en Union Soviétique," in English "The Economic infractions in the Soviet Union." Henceforth the group of lawyers who published this article will be referred to as "The Committee."

51. Harold J. Berman, *Soviet Criminal Law and Procedure, the RSFSR Codes* (Cambridge, MA: Harvard University Press, 1972), 19, henceforth Berman, *Soviet Criminal Law.*

52. Zvi Gitelman, *A Century of Ambivalence, The Jews of Russia and the Soviet Union, 1881 to the Present* (New York: Schocken Books Inc, 1988), 259, henceforth Gitelman, The Jews of Russia.

53. The equivalent of the Parliament in the Soviet Union.

54. Russian Socialist Federative Soviet Republic.

55. Berman, *Soviet Criminal Law*, 19.

56. "Les Infractions économiques en Union Soviétique," 5–6.

57. The Fundamental Principles of 1958, then the Criminal Codes that followed around 1960.

58. This principle appears as Article 23 under the name "The Death Penalty," an Unusual Measure in the General Part of the Soviet Criminal Code published in 1960, with corrections valid until July 3, 1965, as contained in the English translation in Berman, *Soviet Criminal Law*. 131.

59. "Les Infractions économiques en Union Soviétique," 5.

60. This measure was later abolished, and the collective memory associates it with the trials that accompanied the end of forced collectivization in the Soviet Union. Evel'son, *The economic trials in Soviet Union*, 45–48.

61. "Les infractions économiques en Union Soviétique," 10.

62. Toma, *Privind înapoi*, 182.

63. On August 10, 2008, the author interviewed Mr. Sorin Toma in his apartment situated in the Israeli town of Netania. Sorin Toma was also referred to in chapter 1 of this book.

64. Pavel Ackerman's letter sent on July 16, 2008, followed several telephone conversations between us and remained in the author's possession.

65. Evel'son, *The Economic Trials in the Soviet Union*, 306–321.

66. Evel'son, *The Economic Trials in the Soviet Union*, 308.

67. Evel'son, *The Economic Trials in the Soviet Union*, 322–323, Gitelman, *A Century of Ambivalence*, 260.

68. Evel'son, *The Economic Trials in the Soviet Union*, 312, Table nr.2.

69. Chaim Potock, *The Gates of November* (London: Seckler and Warburg, 1997), 141.

70. Gerard Israel, *The Jews of Russia* (London: St Martin Press, 1975).

71. Berman, *Soviet Criminal Code*, 127.

72. George Kline, "Economic Crime and Punishment," *Survey*, 57, no. 3 (1965): 67.

73. Vladimir Tismăneanu (b.1951) is a professor of political science at the University of Maryland. He is a political scientist, sociologist, and historian whose studies specialized in the history of domestic political Romanian affairs, especially during the communist period. Tismăneanu has published a large number of books debating the issues surrounding the history of the Communist Party in Romania.

74. *The Presidential Comission* Report.

75. The chapter on Repressive Justice was written by the Romanian historian Marius Oprea (b. 1964), whose position at the time was that of Director of IICCMER (www.iiccmer.ro). Oprea wrote numerous studies and books on the methods and the institution of the Securitate. Lately he has established a new research institute for the investigation of communist crimes (www.condamnareacomunismului.ro).

76. *The Presidential Comission Report*, 189–197.

77. In this comparison, the relevant parts of the Criminal and Procedural Codes from the years mentioned earlier were used for Romania and for the Soviet Union, the book written by Harold Berman and James Spindler, an English translation of the *Soviet Criminal Code* of the 1960s.

78. Both the Romanian Criminal Code and the Code of Criminal Procedure are in the author's possession on magnetic media, copied from: Codul Penal (Bucharest, Editură Ştiinţifică, 1960) and Codul Penal Procedural (Bucharest Editură Ştiinţifică, 1960).

79. The name of the Criminal Code will be shortened to CP-1960.

80. CP-1960, Book I "General Provisions," Title VI "Misdemeanors," Chapter II "The Attempt."

81. Berman, *Soviet Criminal Code*, 129.

82. The specialized literature emphasizes that Gheorghiu-Dej never actually accepted the measures imposed by the de-Stalinization promoted in Khrushchev's secret speech; Victor Frunză, *Istoria Stalinismului*, 426 (in English, *The History of Stalinism in Romania*).

83. Both the Criminal Code and the Code of Criminal Procedure are volumes with a certain structure: their main parts are called books. Every book is made up of titles, which are made up of chapters and those are made up of sections. Each section includes a number of articles.

84. Decree/Order 202 was published in the Official Bulletin (BO) nr. 15, on May 14, 1953.

85. Decree/Order 318 was published in the Official Bulletin (BO) nr. 27 on July 27, 1958, taken from *The Presidential Comission Report*, 190.

86. Section I bis defined economic crimes for the first time in the Romanian Criminal Code. This addition was made in Romania a few years before it was added to the Soviet Criminal Codes of the 1960s. The Criminal Laws in Section I bis remained in effect in CP-1960, consequently used in the Foreign Trade trials.

87. CP-1960, Book II "Crimes and felonies in particular," Title I "Crimes and felonies against the State," Chapter II "Crimes and felonies against the Internal Security of the State," Section I bis, Art. 209^{1} paragraph II.

88. Reference is made to Art. 209^{1}, Art. 209^{2}, Art.209^{3}.

89. "Les infractions économiques en Union Soviétique," 6.

90. Berman, *Soviet Criminal Code*, p. 157.

91. Vedomosti—Ved 1961, No.13/137; Vedmosti—is the document where laws, decrees, or orders promulgated by the State were announced, similar to the Official Bulletin/the Official Monitor (BO/MO) in Romania. Hereafter, Vedmosti will be shortened by Ved.

92. Capital offenses are offenses punishable by death.

93. Solomon, *Private letters.*

94. Ved 1961, No.19/207.

95. Ved 1961, No.22/225.

96. Ved 1961, No.27/291.

97. Ved 1962, No.8/85.

98. CP–1960, Book II "Crimes and felonies in particular," Title I "Crimes and felonies against the state," Chapter II "Crimes and felonies against the internal security of the state," Section I "The attack and the conspiracy against the constitutional and social order of the Romanian People's Republic," Art. 209.

99. George Kline, "Philosophy, Ideology and Policy in the Soviet Union," *The Review of Politics*, 26 (1964): 185.

100. "Les infractions économiques en Union Soviétique," 10–11.

101. Ibid., 12

102. Harold J. Berman, *Justice in URSS* (New York: Harvard University Press, 1963), 84–85.

103. Open Society Archives, Budapest, Box 194, Item No. 1006/63, published as well by A. Andreescu, Minorități Etnoculturale, 664–665.

104. Chapter 3 will present this issue in detail.

105. "Les infractions économiques en Union Soviétique," 14.

106. Românoexport trial stands for the case study of this book, presented in chapter 6.

Chapter 3

Purging Foreign Trade of Jewish Officials

> The study of Românoexport trial criminal file P179 puts one in a similar predicament to those researchers of heresies in the Christian Church: The writings of individuals charged and condemned of heresy had been, as a rule, destroyed. Their ideas and teachings cannot be faithfully reconstructed solely from the words of their opponents—who, obviously out of polemical necessity, have altered or exaggerated theses offensive to the "true faith," which in our case is parallel to the norms fixed by the party policy.
>
> Paraphrased text after Florin Constantiniu[1]

INTRODUCTION

After World War II, Romania, as a new socialist country, encountered difficulties in resuming trade on the Western market. There were two main causes for this situation: the first one was that according to the international policy specific to the Cold War,[2] Western European countries were reluctant to develop economic and trade relations with the countries of the Eastern European Bloc; the second cause involved the competition between Romania and other socialist countries, some of which were more economically advanced and had enjoyed stable economic ties with the Western countries since the prewar period.

Given this situation, the government commercial staff of foreign trade enterprises was given a free hand in making contacts with commercial agents or companies from the West in order to renew the economic relations. And indeed, the members of this group had more than once managed to develop international trade relations, often built on the basis of personal relationships with representatives of foreign companies in the Western world. In many of these cases, either some of the foreign representatives or those coming from the Romanian side were Jews. A decade later, a large portion of those officials, who had opened the gates of Romanian trade to the Western world, lost their public and personal status, being accused of undermining the national economy and of plotting against the Romanian state. Why was the loyalty of these people questioned? How can one explain this change in the attitude of the Romanian authorities toward many of the employees of foreign trade enterprises, from that of trust and esteem to that of accusing them of being criminals and conspirators against the interests of the state? Why was the Military Court chosen to be the arena for eliminating those people, all of whom held civilian positions? Twenty-seven of the 29 defendants in the economic trials were Jews.

This chapter will discuss the following two issues:

The first is related to the way in which the Romanian commercial enterprises belonging to the MCE were founded, within the gradual development of the Romanian foreign trade, after communization. The second topic will be shedding light on a succession of political trials against senior Jewish Foreign Trade officials, who were labeled as enemies of the Regime, removed from office and eventually accused and subjected to very severe convictions.

Despite extensive and relatively long efforts, which did not lead to the discovery of the exact moment or event that triggered the pursuit of Foreign Trade officials, the staff conference of the Ministry of Commerce (Interior and Foreign), which took place at the party compound in the Tudor Vladimirescu district of Bucharest between the 14th and the 17th of October 1958, can be considered the first open expression of the authorities' intention to purge the Foreign Trade of Jews.

The meeting was held in the presence of some important officials and party members,[3] and its purpose was to have a public processing of the PMR Plenum that had taken place in June 1958.[4]

This meeting, which was attended by the official representative of the party, Florian Dănălache,[5] signified the initiation of the removal of the Jews from the Ministry of Commerce work team, but mainly from the Department of Foreign Trade.[6]

Following this meeting in October 1958, the Securitate opened surveillance files for those of the Foreign Trade officials for whom such files had not previously been opened[7] and most of those people were Jews.

THE ROMANIAN VERSION OF A SOCIALIST ECONOMY

Întotdeauna regimurile comuniste au acţionat din raţiuni politice şi mai puţin din raţiuni economice.[8]

Stelian Tănase, Elite şi Societate, p.127

Romania's Economic Position after World War II

At the end of the interwar period, Romania owned a considerable number of industrial enterprises, whose good quality products successfully competed in foreign markets. The Malaxa factories in Bucharest were famous for producing Diesel locomotives, IAR Brasov with the famous IAR[9] airplanes, ASTRA-Arad, which produced various types of railroad cars (passenger, freight, tanker), as well as textile and footwear factories.[10] The refineries in the Prahova Valley (ASTRA-Romanian, Romanian-American, Concordia, etc.) were among the most modern in the world.

During this period, Romanian industry alone covered about 80% of the needs of the domestic consumer goods market and 25% in the field of means of production. In 1935, for the first time in the history of Romania, industry surpassed agriculture in terms of export revenue. In 1938, the oil industry held first place in terms of exports, with 43.3%, while the export of cereals and their derivatives accounted for only 29.5% of the total export value. Two decades after the end of World War I, Romania became a country with an agro-industrial economy.[11]

On November 27, 1945, Gheorghe Gheorghiu-Dej was appointed President of the Superior Council of the National Economy.[12] This Council was a governmental body designed to plan, coordinate, and implement the economic and financial policy of the pro-Soviet government led by Dr. Petru Groza.[13] After communization, a socialist economy developed in Romania. The state owned most of the means of production as well as the existing natural resources, both in agriculture and in industry. This power was held by the Central Committee of the Romanian Workers' Party[14] and the MAN. The central organization of the legislative power was the Council of Ministers, whose function was the implementation of economic decisions in the centralized national economy, decisions generally made in Party Congresses. The centralized system of governing the socialist economy was characterized by the elaboration of plans, at first annual plans (1949 and 1950), and later five-year plans, the first one being the plan for 1951–1955.[15]

The five-year plans were broken down into one-year plans. The Council of Ministers formulated the general guidelines for the implementation of the plans, and then they were transferred to the relevant ministries and the units that served them.[16] The Council of Ministers was also the body responsible for coordinating, planning, and implementing work plans. Implementation plans went to institutions or other economic organizations and were further divided according to the objectives and specific nature of each. Based on these, the companies formulated their own work programs in order to achieve their assigned objectives. The planning and scheduling were carried out in collaboration with the relevant ministry, after which the work plan was sent back to the CSP for approval.[17] This was another central governmental body, whose function was to coordinate and plan the national economy. The CSP was established in July 1948 at the initiative of Gheorghe Gheorghiu-Dej. The CSP coordinated all economic institutions and its task was to report to the government on the economic situation in the country. It, therefore, had a final say in monitoring and deciding on the planned missions in different areas of the economy (including foreign trade). Another role of the CSP was to decide on issues related to the labor force available to all branches of industry, on raw materials, the volume of exports and imports and to finalize the task-fulfillment programs of subordinate enterprises. This centralized economic model was copied from the Soviet model and was applied in all areas of the economy. Forced collectivization proved to be an absolute failure, leading to an increase in the shortage of cereals and basic foodstuffs. At the same time, the obsessive development of heavy industry to the detriment of agriculture and light industry started under the leadership of Gheorghiu-Dej, and resulted in a growing shortage of consumer goods. Despite these shortcomings facing the population, the policy of industrialization pursued by the Romanian Workers' Party led by Gheorghiu-Dej continued, leading to rapid progress in industrial development in Romania. Thus, for 17 years, beginning in 1951, domestic industrial production grew at an annual rate of 13.1, the highest rate of growth known in the world at that time.[18]

Among the few Western researchers who conducted a comprehensive economic study on socialist countries, including Romania, was John Michael Montias.[19] His research confirmed the accuracy of data on the registered rate of industrial growth published by Romanian sources at the time.

By Decree no. 317 of July 28, 1949, the state monopoly on foreign trade was declared. It regulated the import, export, and movement of goods. Also, in order to regulate the country's foreign economic relations, the Trade Chamber of Commerce was established in December 1949. It centered around all the state-owned enterprises for foreign trade, an issue that will be further explained. The development of foreign trade, mainly Romania's ties with neighboring countries, was the expression of the political and economic situation of countries in the Communist bloc. After World War II, the Soviet Union and the other socialist countries became Romania's main trading partners. With the end of the war and the takeover of power by the communists, the development and recovery of foreign trade in Romania was slower than the development of other branches of the economy.[20] A main policy goal of the Romanian government, led by Gheorghiu-Dej, was to try and expand Romania's economic and trade relations with other socialist states, but the interest in developing trade relations with other countries of the world, regardless of the system, was never neglected. So, Romania also expanded its relations with the countries of the West and with third world countries on other continents. One of the difficulties encountered in Romania's attempts to achieve this goal was the country's lack of foreign exchange resources, which is why relations with Western countries required them to accept barter trade agreements, through which Romania could trade commodities without currency transactions. As a result, there was a need to expand the scope of Romania's traditional export products.[21] At the same time, there was a need to increase productivity in order to achieve a surplus in exports, and the population's requirements for the import of new consumer products increased. These two directions had the capacity to influence both the local market and Romania's relations with foreign countries by creating new future markets. Over time, the range of Romanian products for export such as various machines and finished products in different branches of industry, mainly light industry, expanded. But the chances of selling these products on Western markets were limited.[22]

CMEA and its Role in Romanian Economic Development

The CMEA[23] organization, founded in 1949 in Moscow, with the initial purpose of trying to counterbalance the Marshall Plan[24] initiative, was primarily a political and ideological entity. Although CMEA was known as an organization designed to facilitate the exchange of economic information between the participating socialist states, its existence primarily served the purpose of promoting the economic and military power of the Soviet Union, giving it a major role both in Eastern European interstate relations and in the balance of world forces. This interaction was also supported by the relations established after 1955 by the Warsaw Pact.[25] The CMEA tried to propagate the policy of centralization in the economy, in decision making and in control methods, at the level of state bodies. This policy dominated the economy of all Eastern European countries under the Kremlin's tutelage and determined that all decisions were to be dictated exclusively by the state, that is to say, by the party, giving it supreme control over the entire economy in each of the respective states. This meant the establishment and maintenance of a centralized national economy following the nationalization of the means of production, and subsequently led to the the state's permanent control over the subsidization of specific branches of the economy and over foreign trade operations.

CMEA was subordinated to a kind of centrifugal control, with the center controlling the periphery and obedience to these laws. In this way, Romania like the other socialist countries was manipulated at the Kremlin center. In fact, the connection of Romania and the other Eastern European states with the party leadership in Moscow lacked any degree of freedom and bordered on absolute subjugation. Any initiative was considered a deviation and was consequently subject to criticism.

The CMEA proved to have fulfilled its original function with some delay, and its shortcomings were immediately felt in the process of allocating and managing resources in most of the states. The economic model implemented by each of the Eastern European states was the transposition of the Soviet model at the level of that state. Among the main directions of this model were the central planning of the economy and the absolute monopoly of the state in the field of Foreign Trade. Negotiations were mostly held bilaterally, and the agreements, once concluded, were registered with the CMEA. This situation remained unchanged up to the end of 1955.[26]

Establishment of the Foreign Trade Ministry and the Foreign Trade Enterprises

Foreign trade is one of the important components of any national economy and represents a country's total trade transactions (export, import, and re-export) with the rest of the world. It includes both the flow of material goods and the associated services. Naturally, trade is characterized by the transfer of products from the sphere of production to that of consumption. In order for a foreign trade system to operate, related services are also needed, such as freight transport, telecommunications, international insurance and bank transfers in foreign currency. (Note that, in the 1950s and 1960s, the currency used most by Romania for transactions was the ruble.)[27]

The MCE was established in 1948, one year after the first Romanian transaction was signed with Moscow in 1947, by Gheorghiu-Dej, which was a trade and navigation contract with the Soviet government. Shortly thereafter, the State Enterprises for Foreign Trade were established. The activity of the future MCE was started in the small office of a house located on Orlando Street in Bucharest, and it was fixed as the meeting place of the people who were to become the main pawns of the ministry's activity. The Romanian foreign trade system had been subject from the outset to a state monopoly, established by Decree 317 of July 18, 1949. Article #1 of that Decree specifies that any activity of each enterprise, either state-owned or managed by certain private persons, had to be submitted to the MCE for approval. The Romanian Constitution of 1952 also provided for this obligation, namely that in Romania, a country of popular democracy in formation, Foreign Trade was a state monopoly.[28]

This ministry determined which of the various branches of industry would be involved in trade and which would be part of import-export programs. The type, quantity, and quality of products for export were thus established.[29] While the ministry led and coordinated important trade operations, its operational mechanisms were implemented with the help of state-owned foreign trade enterprises[30] established during the same period. The enterprises were divided according to the types of industries they represented, either for import or export, but in some cases for both. The following images show the list of the foreign trade enterprises that were established in Romania in the early 1950s and continued to exist throughout the communist era. Their names are presented in alphabetical order, and among them can be found the four companies whose officials were arrested and later convicted (figures 3.1 and 3.2).,

In addition to the enterprises, the ministry maintained a number of economic agencies in some of the foreign countries to prospect local markets, trying to detect their requirements and in some ways to penetrate them. The Romanian representatives of the economic agencies established connections with local persons or companies who showed interest in the Romanian goods. The opening of these agencies sometimes depended on branches of the local communist parties that could afford to invest some capital, such as was the case of the Italian company called URE[31] in Milan. The officials employed in these economic agencies, even if they were employees of foreign trade enterprises, were in most cases also in the service of the Securitate, thus fulfilling the function of informants regarding all the events that took place in their vicinity, both economic and socialpolitical, and even acting as industrial spies.[32] The general planning system then operating in Romania included three levels of planning: the five-year plan, the annual plan, and the special program for foreign trade. The special programs for foreign trade were to regulate trade activities, so that by supplementing the annual plans, they ultimately followed the progress of the five-year plan.[33]

Among the first officials or personalities who made an important contribution to the formation of the first Romanian foreign trade enterprises, as well as establishing relations with the Western world, were Ana Toma,[34] Silvan Vitianu,[35] Pavel Donath,[36] Andreas Fenyö,[37] Andrei Klein,[38] and the Baron von Anchau of Bucovina. These people convened to formulate a basic policy that led to the establishment of many of the future foreign trade enterprises. Each such enterprise was to represent one or more industrial sectors and develop the trade relations necessary for the import or export of an assortment of products. In this way, a single foreign trade enterprise would be in

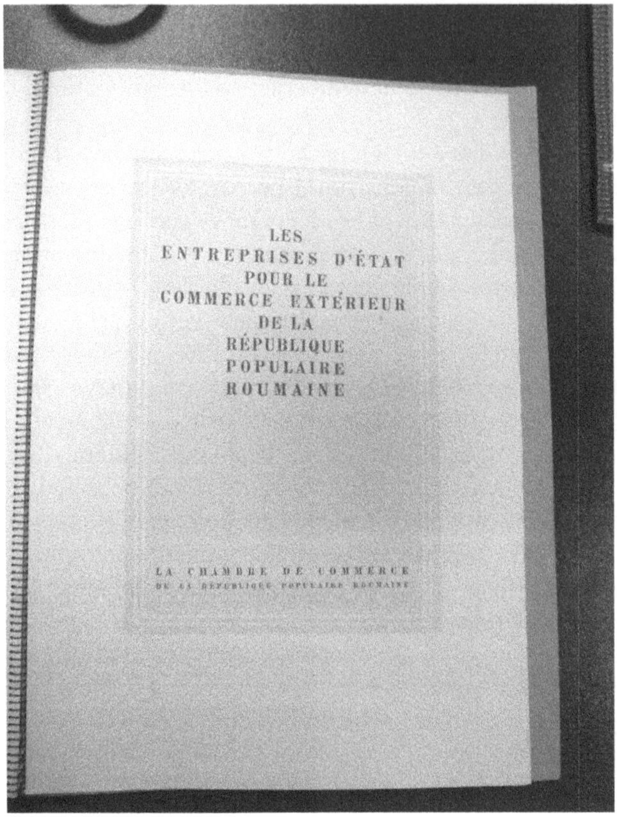

Figure 3.1 State Enterprises for the Foreign Trade. *Source: Journal of the Chamber of Commerce of Romania,* No. 1(19) A, 1956.

charge of several industrial sectors that were to produce products for export or receive raw materials for industry or imported goods for marketing and were thus connected with the relevant trade undertaking. Thus, the foreign trade enterprise became the gateway to other countries for the import and export of commodities, including both raw materials and finished products.

It follows that the import-export of products from the machinery, metal, or fine mechanics industry was associated with enterprises such as Industrialexport, Maşinimport, Metalimport, or Tehnoimport. The import and export of chemicals was the responsibility of Chimimport, the import-export of petroleum-related products was associated with Petrolexport, and the wood industry products with Exportlemn. The food industry imported products used as raw materials, but at the same time exported raw or finished plant or animal products through Prodexport and Fructexport, which was in charge of the fruit trade. Nonfood agricultural products were exported

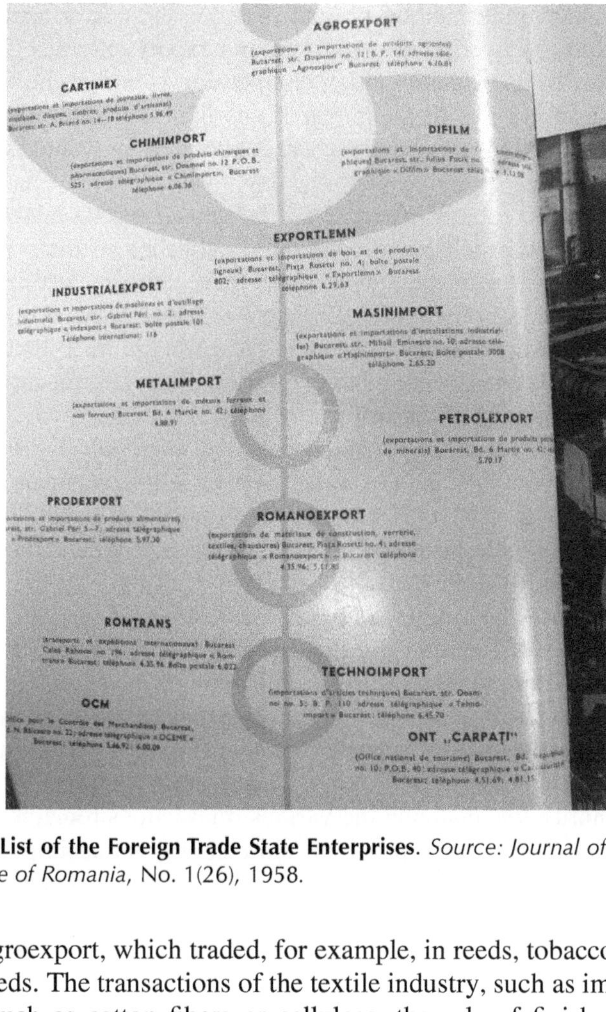

Figure 3.2 List of the Foreign Trade State Enterprises. *Source: Journal of the Chamber of Commerce of Romania,* No. 1(26), 1958.

through Agroexport, which traded, for example, in reeds, tobacco, or various types of seeds. The transactions of the textile industry, such as importing raw materials such as cotton fibers or cellulose, the sale of finished garments, or trade in leather (raw or processed), or leather goods, as well as those of the building materials industry (like glass or cement), were administered by Românoexport.

Thus, all the import-export operations of Romania related to the same type of products were executed on the foreign market by a single Romanian foreign trade enterprise.[39]

In 1949, the same year as the establishment of the CMEA, the Românoexport enterprise was founded in Bucharest. A few years later, Alimentexport was established, and its name was later changed to Prodexport, at the request of the then minister of commerce,[40] Alexandru Bârlădeanu.

The Romanian trade method presented earlier was developed in such a way as to avoid any overlap of the import and export activities of the different enterprises. In this way, although competition is one of the fundamental elements of the economic development of any liberal country, the Romanian system of organization presented earlier, deliberately prevented competition between enterprises.

All foreign trade enterprises received the annual work plans through the CSP and had to accomplish the contracts established in their annual plan. Thus, in accordance with the annual plan, each company strove to identify foreign markets for the products of the Romanian industries with which it was associated.[41] In addition to the aforementioned foreign trade enterprises and economic agencies, there were other enterprises that were meant to facilitate interaction with the rest of the world.

One of them was Romtrans, which held the monopoly for the transport of goods to and from Romania. Another enterprise that was part of the trade operation process was the Office of Goods Control.[42] The role of the OCM was to ensure quality control of export products and to establish quotas for import and export. By 1958, the rate of Romanian trade in the community of the free countries had increased by 60% as compared to 1950. From 1958 to 1962, the value of foreign trade increased by another 33%.[43] Each foreign trade enterprise had the right to trade with foreign merchants of its choice. This phenomenon was a central and an important element of the contracting system, because in this way the companies had a certain authority in concluding the transactions and signing commercial contracts. However, the supreme authority for finalizing the various transactions remained the MCE, which also drafted the trade program, ultimately granting import or export authorizations (licenses), along with some instructions or procedures to support both the auxiliary units and the enterprises themselves in completing the concluded transactions.[44] Any transaction signed by a specific enterprise ultimately required the Ministry approval, so each contract was reported. In addition, each year, the foreign trade enterprises were required to submit an annual report to the MCE on their achievements relative to the initial planning. The contribution of the Romanian Chamber of Commerce in the development of the Romanian foreign trade should also be mentioned. The Chamber of Commerce was first founded in 1919 by a group of entrepreneurs interested in Romanian trade relations with foreign countries, and immediately after World War I, they contributed to the opening of new trade markets and to the international promotion of Romania. Among the main functions of the Chamber that remained after the communization of Romania were the promotion of foreign trade and the consolidation of bilateral relations with the West.

The following is a brief presentation of the foreign trade enterprises whose officials were involved in the economic trials, which will be further analyzed.

ISCE Cartimex (CA)

Cartimex was founded in 1951 under the name of IMEX and was under the responsibility of the Ministry of Culture. Its mission was to import and export books and magazines in Romanian or in foreign languages. In 1955, the company was transferred to the MCE, and renamed Cartimex. Added to its export profile were carpets, handicrafts articles, newspapers, technical magazines in various languages, as well as the import of musical instruments and postage stamps. As in all other foreign trade enterprises, many foreign agents who had some personal ties with the CA employees showed an interest in establishing

Figure 3.3 Products Exported by CA. *Source: Journal of the Chamber of Commerce of Romania,* No. 1(34), 1960.

commercial relations with CA. The number of CA employees was around 228, of whom 50% were employed in "operative" positions, that is, they were in the front lines of those who traveled abroad, thus coming into contact with foreigners and establishing future trade relations (figure 3.3).

ISCE Prodexport[45]

PE, founded in 1949, was the descendant of Alimentexport. Its main activities included the import of citrus products, as well as raw materials for the food industry. It was also an exporter of meat and internal organs of cattle, pigs or poultry, feathers, oil, and sugar. A division of it, Fructexport, handled the export of fresh or partially processed fruit and wine (figure 3.4).

Figure 3.4 Cheese and Wines Exported by PE. *Source: Journal of the Chamber of Commerce of Romania*, No. 1(26), 1958.

ISCE Agroexport[46]

AE was a foreign trade enterprise established to coordinate the export of various Romanian agricultural products, including reeds, cereals, seeds, and various types of tobacco, peas, beans, and fodder (figure 3.5).

ISCE Românoexport[47]

The RE enterprise was the first foreign trade enterprise established in 1948 as an import-export enterprise. The company was an exporter of construction materials such as cement, glass, and wood; textiles; various clothing and knitwear products; and footwear fabrics. RE imported raw materials for textile production, raw cotton yarn or various categories of processed yarns for the footwear industry, and sometimes imported leather or finished products for

Figure 3.5 Seeds and Forage Plants Exported by AE. *Source: Journal of the Chamber of Commerce of Romania,* No. 1(26), 1958.

Figure 3.6 Portland Cement Exported by RE. *Source: Journal of the Chamber of Commerce of Romania,* No. 1(26), 1958.

the domestic market. In April 1950, another company with an exclusively textile industry profile, Textilimport, separated from RE. A year later, in 1951, it was reintegrated into RE (figures 3.6 and 3.7).

At the top of the pyramid of the hierarchical organization of most foreign trade enterprises was the director of the enterprise, called general manager or coordinating director. He was followed by the deputy director, also called technical director. Following were the advisers, according to the different branches of specialization, and next, the heads of the different services that corresponded to the economic operations carried out by the enterprise. There were several services, even when it came to a single product, such as "meat." Various services dealt either with different types of the marketed product or with parts of the same product, which were sometimes marketed separately.

Some of the future convicts of the economic proceedings, employed in the aforementioned enterprises, published specialized articles in the Official

Figure 3.7 Textiles and Clothing Exported by RE. *Source: Journal of the Chamber of Commerce of Romania*, No. 1(26), 1958.

Journal of the Chamber of Commerce of Romania, whose purpose, as the purpose of the magazine itself, was to document the activities of these enterprises in all their fields of business.[48]

THE FOREIGN TRADE ECONOMIC TRIALS

The Specificity of the Trials

The specificity of the Foreign Trade trials can be characterized by two aspects:

- The first refers to their uniqueness as compared with other trials held in Eastern Europe during the same period of time.
- The second refers to the so-called political predicament of the Securitate after the end of the revolution in Hungary.

The Uniqueness of the Foreign Trade Trials

Against the background of the realities presented previously, between 1960 and 1964, six trials of some senior officials from foreign trade enterprises took place in Romania. These trials were destined to remain unknown and unexplored, more than 25 years after the fall of the Iron Curtain. According to the previous analysis,[49] in none of the political regions of the Eastern Bloc states did economic proceedings of such magnitude take place. As shown, Eastern Europe trials that took place at the time were not based on economic issues, with the exception of the isolated cases of the Czechoslovak economists' trial[50] or the intended indictment in Poland, of a person called Josef Kutin, who could somehow be related to economy.[51] In addition, the detailed study of Soviet Union economic trials, during Khrushchev's rule, showed that they targeted a population totally different from the one to which the Romanian convicts belonged.[52]

The Romanian economic trials had something in common with the show trials of the Great Purge in Moscow, in the mid-1930s, though they were secret, as opposed to those that took place in the Soviet Union. The defendants in the Romanian trials, which took place between 1960 and 1964, as well as those in the Moscow trials of 1936–1938, were members of the new sociopolitical order in the state, none of whom could have been suspected of belonging to the Old Regime or identified with "the class enemy," who were supposed to have been eliminated after the communists took power and forced the abdication of King Michael I in 1947. Otherwise, they would not have held the important positions they did in the new economy of socialist Romania. The elimination of class enemies in the Soviet Union had also taken place many years before the Great Purge.

Another similarity between the two groups of "criminals" in Bucharest and in Moscow was that, almost without exception, they were Jews. And yet, the Jews suspected of undermining and plotting against the state order in Romania were members of the elite in the governmental economic system, which, in part, they had founded[53] and had represented only a few years earlier. In the Soviet Union, in contrast, the accusations in the Great Purge trials had an almost exclusively political background. Most of the heroes of the Great Purge in the Soviet Union were Jews with key roles in the political leadership of the party. It should be remembered that in socialist Romania, all foreign trade enterprises were state-owned, and therefore, the delegations sent abroad were official representatives of the Romanian government.

In addition to the similarities presented earlier between the Great Purge trials in the Soviet Union and the foreign trade trials in Bucharest, there were a number of differences.

While in Romania they took place without any involvement of the media, the trials of the 1930s were fully publicized. The trials in Romania took place in total secrecy,[54] without spectators other than the defendants, members of the judiciary, investigators, and members of the institutions involved, and of course family members.

Another characteristic that differentiated the two groups of trials was the group to which the defendants belonged: those of Romanian economic trials were well-trained professionals in the field of economy and trade with applied knowledge in these fields from before the communization of Romania. In their positions, with the takeover of power by the communists, they became state officials and were sent abroad for expanding Romania's trade relations with the West or with third world countries.[55]

However, the defendants in the Soviet Union economic trials, during Khrushchev's time, had generally belonged to the middle class. They had been small traders, small business owners, who had tried to improve their economic status, either through methods provided by the Second Economy,[56] or through the use of foreign currency, both procedures being considered illegal. For the most part, they had not held political or economic positions, as had the Romanian defendants.

Another difference between the two types of economic trials can be found in the conduct of the court proceedings. While in Romania, the record by the court clerk was a brief summary, and therefore incomplete, in the Moscow trials, as well as in other Eastern European trials, a fairly accurate documentation and an almost complete transcript of the protocol of court discussions were made.[57] In this way, the dialogue of the parties, appearing before the court, could be completely reconstructed. However, in Romania, neither the speeches of the prosecutor, of the lawyers, nor even of the president of the Military Court, the one who read the sentence of the trial, were completely transcribed.[58] It should also be noted, for example, that during the reading of the sentence in the RE,[59] trial, statements with some anti-Semitic connotations made by the president of the tribunal, a senior military officer, were not included in the protocol.

The Securitate's Endeavor to Regain Its Position before the Party and State Bodies

The economic trials were also a means for the Securitate to rebuild a stronger, more authoritarian image in the eyes of its main manipulator, the party. After Khrushchev's "secret speech,"[60] the population was apparently granted a short period of reprieve. But during the "terror" days of the Hungarian revolution in late October 1956, Romanian political leaders were faced with a scenario in which the workers' dictatorship could collapse within 24 hours, as had happened in the neighboring country, and they feared that such a thing could easily take place in their own country. Following this dramatic event, the Securitate was determined to try to regain its former reputation in the eyes of the party. During the years 1958–1960, it took action to remedy its tarnished prestige and recover its position in relation to the party and state bodies, rebuilding its image as the "armed arm" of the party leadership, and applying measures of intimidation and subjugation of the population.[61]

The facilitation of these measures, as well as the legitimization of the Securitate's attitude, took place in the context of the hardening of the national policy initiated by the Gheorghiu-Dej government.[62] Some of the objectives of this policy were

- the gradual reduction of any political and economic dependence of Romania on the Soviet Union until its total elimination; and
- the termination of Romania's economic dependence on professionals from the old guard, a majority of whom were Jews.

Thus, the push to remove Jews from positions of influence was accelerated, extending to various branches of the economy—obviously Foreign Trade, but also industry, the army, and medical and cultural institutions.

For the first time, Romanian foreign trade, as mentioned earlier, could count on ethnic Romanian graduates of the Academy of Commerce[63] for its future development. The academy's Faculty of Foreign Trade was then in the first years of its existence. Some of the Jewish officials were still being sent for some important missions abroad, due to their knowledge and relationships, sometimes despite the rather persistent opposition of the Securitate. These officials were not all representatives of Romania's party members, although a large part of them had been affiliated with the PCR, or known as sympathizers during the interwar period. Over time, with the strengthening of the socialist state and its policy, former Jewish foreign trade workers were increasingly suspected of disloyalty to communist ideals and the Romanian state, with some of them applying to emigrate to the state of Israel.

After a decade of socialist Romania's existence, the ideal emerged of a "new man," committed to fulfilling the objectives of the state. The new party leadership showed confidence in this type of "new man," coming from a "healthy" social background, ready to take the place of the old generation. In addition, this created the new economic elite meant to march on the socioeconomic scene of the country at the end of the sixth decade of the twentieth century.[64]

JEWS, AS THE SOLE VICTIMS OF THE FOREIGN TRADE TRIALS

The people against whom the Foreign Trade lawsuits were filed represented a group of senior officials with elite positions in the Romanian economy. They were trade specialists, mainly in various branches of light industry, and were hired after 1947 to represent the new socialist state and its economic institutions, in order to renew trade relations with states of the free world at the beginning of the Cold War. These people had the qualities required to establish multilateral ties outside the socialist camp, toward building an economic and trade base for Romania and strengthening its international relations. The majority of people employed in the Foreign Trade were Jews.

The main reasons for this were related to the individual profiles of these officials, many of which included prewar experience in various branches of the economy, or involvement in various private foreign trade companies that had ceased to exist after nationalization or had continued operations throughout the transition phase of Romania, as companies still holding capital at that time.

Also, some of the Jewish officials had remained in touch with commercial agencies, present before the war in Romania, that were run by former citizens who had left the country, or by locals who had been their employers. Knowledge of foreign languages (some of these officials, if not most of them, were born in Transylvania, so they knew Hungarian and German and many of them even French or English) as well as the higher education that some of them had acquired, but especially their interdisciplinary professional experience, and their connections or personal relationships with various foreign traders were a real advantage in the eyes of the authorities. They brought the nascent Romanian state significant advantages.

On the one hand, Foreign Trade officials were the much-needed bridge between the Romanian state and the capitalists beyond the Iron Curtain, but on the other hand the suspicion and distrust of the party authorities hovered over them. Nevertheless, they created the only links through which there could be opportunities for trade relations that would be a source of foreign currency, so important and necessary for Romania. For members of the Securitate, every Jew who negotiated—according to ministerial directives—various transactions with Western businessmen, "the capitalists," was a potential spy or an emerging underminer who favored some capitalist partners in exchange for present or future material advantages. The capitalist goodwill, demonstrated through foreign exchange, would be approached in such a way so as to render it suspicious and conducive to investigation, providing targets for Securitate's bayonets, starting with the arrest of Cartimex's Jewish director Octav Botnar in 1960. It should be noted again, that only two people involved in all these trials were non-Jews.

Jewish officials employed in Foreign Trade, a privileged group with special rights (permission to handle currency and maintain direct links with foreign nationals), had been the central preoccupation of the Securitate for many years, but after the Plenum of June 1958 and the MCE Working Meeting of

October 14–17, 1958, the drive to reveal them as enemies of the state was intensified.

Evidence of this could be seen in the speech of Alexandru Drăghici, the minister of interior at that time of the 1960s.[65]

Between 1950 and 1958, when Alexandru Bârlădeanu and Marcel Popescu were the Foreign Trade ministers, the Securitate bodies failed to transform this sector into a free zone for witch-hunting. This was done later when people with important and relevant positions were replaced by successors who could no longer oppose the arrest and prosecution of senior Foreign Trade officials.

EVOLUTION OF THE PCR'S ATTITUDE TOWARD JEWISH OFFICIALS IN FOREIGN TRADE

The following sections present a series of events in the political life of the PCR[66] in Romania between 1952 and 1961. The mentoring party and the Securitate worked hand in hand to isolate a group of senior Foreign Trade officials in order to "cleanse" the Ministry of Commerce of its Jewish staff as much as possible. Under the party's protective umbrella, the Securitate meddled in the affairs of institutions and businesses in an effort to identify and eliminate some of the Jews who had reached key positions in Foreign Trade. In my original research, there were detailed references and examples to what I considered to be the sequence of events, which led to the obvious intention of eliminating the Jews from the Foreign Trade. The following description is only a compendium of my research in this field.

About the Activity of MCE Officials

Within the National Archives of Romania, at the fonds entitled CCPCR, Economic Section (SE),[67] a few documents dating from 1952 to 1953 were found, concerning the MCE employees, their previous affiliation, as well as the follow-up correspondence written by Rusu Clement,[68] head of the SPFC, and addressed to Ady Ladislau,[69] head of the SRE. Both sections were like the party indirectly supervising the activities of the foreign trade enterprises.

The three documents, written by Rusu Clement, head of SPFC, are listed here:

1. A paper written by Rusu Clement for the SC of the CCPCR On April 22, 1952
2. An information report regarding the nature of the work of the MCE staff, written on July 11, 1952

3. A minutes document of the transfer of materials from the SPFC to the SRE dating from January 16, 1953

These documents show the critical standpoint of the Cadre responsible for the MCE, vis-à-vis its employees. Perusing these documents more closely, one can observe a succession in time, which spans a number of years, and points to CCPCR observers' "critical" attitude toward both MCE functionaries, and with a detailed presentation concerning each company.

The Paper[70]

In this paper, Rusu Clement emphasizes the fact that the workers in the Foreign Trade are mostly former officials of the former Ministry of National Economy, Industry and Trade[71] and of some import-export enterprises that belonged to capitalist companies from the pre-communist period, companies in which they were employed as civil servants or were even co-owners.[72] In his opinion, they all show weak ideological training, a shortcoming that jeopardizes the activity of the entire ministry, since in his opinion, they are capable of becoming the perpetrators of acts of negligence and even acts of sabotage or treason.[73] At the same time, members of the current leadership of the ministry tend to disregard the achievements of young workers, new graduates of the School of Foreign Trade, keeping them in lower positions, as the ministry considers their academic background to be insufficiently specialized as yet.[74]

Clement emphasizes the following two points:

- The choice of MCE officials is made according to their professional level, instead of being made according to their political credentials (this is indicated as a disadvantage, an error committed by the ministry).[75]
- The background and initial political training of officials were not sufficiently taken into account at the time of their employment, as their social background was not verified. By this, reference is actually made to the "special attention" paid by the party leadership to the selection of employees with a "healthy origin,"[76] so that they comprise a majority of the workers of the ministry.

The serious denunciation of the "insufficient ideological training of workers in Foreign Trade enterprises," reported in Rusu Clement's 1952 report, can be viewed as the start of a procedure of pursuit and mostly, as the disclosure of the intention to "re-educate" those who would be victims of the economic trials 10 years later. The remarks of the SPFC director signal the identification of a "suspicious area" that was already in the sights of the

Securitate, who followed nearly all the activity of the party cadres in different fields with a frightening "vigilance," but especially of those working in Foreign Trade.

Clement's attitude was not an individual one, but in the perspective of the political world of the time and its system of references, one can understand the reluctance of the head of the SPFC to trust those who were categorized as not being of "healthy origin."[77]

Moreover, these people, whose origins were thought to overshadow their professional activity in the ministry, were identified with a group of so-called enemies of the state and the party. It can be surmised they had reasons to be suspected, as their almost daily activity was carried out on the interface between East and West, when the party had already completed its checks on the authenticity of party members, but not to the extent of washing away the sins of those of Jewish ethnicity.

As a conclusion to all his remarks, Clement suggests taking some steps in the future:

- Improve the social and national composition of the ministry's work force, by promoting elements with a healthy origin, for the good functioning of the ministry in the future.
- Purge the ministry of hostile elements as a measure for the prevention of possible future sabotage and espionage operations.
- Appoint a large commission from the party apparatus of the CCPCR and the party organization of the city of Bucharest for the execution of the proposed verifications.

The Information Report[78]

A few months after the submission of the report, on July 11, 1952, Rusu Clement drafted another larger document in which he criticized the Cadre work regarding the MCE staff even more harshly.[79] What was understood as Cadre[80] work was a periodic investigation of employees and the clarification of several tasks and purposes. This kind of activity was organized and run in most cases by members of the Securitate. Personal cases were publicly discussed, as well as the individual files of some of the employees. Participants were urged to write down recommendations or information about other people, in order to facilitate the professional or political advancement of workers, the demotion of others, or the detection of persons harmful to the collective, who are liable to organize acts of sabotage against the enterprise, the state or the regime. Another purpose of those meetings was to locate potential informants for the Securitate.

It should be mentioned that these documents were issued in the middle of 1952, when several party representatives were accused of right-wing deviationism.[81]

At that time, Gheorghe (Gogu) Rădulescu[82] was the deputy minister of the MCE, while Alexandru Bârlădeanu was the minister. Gogu Rădulescu himself was among those who were accused of right-wing deviationism and therefore discharged.

The same recommendations earlier in the text were mentioned as possible measures to be taken in the future within the MCE, but in addition, the author was of the opinion that those with important positions in the ministry, such as senior directors, should be replaced.

The Proceedings

This is the third document[83] referring to the MCE activity that was found. It is a protocol for the transfer of materials between the SPFC and the SRE. The protocol includes a letter written on January 16, 1953, about the transfer of 35 files between the two sections. It is mentioned that the files bearing the numbers 15–28 refer to the activity of the import-export enterprises from MCE. Mentioned in the protocol, for example, are "Problems of the Foreign Trade Enterprises," as well as "Work plans and reports relevant at that time." A list of all enterprises existing on that date within the MCE is registered, including those that would later be involved in the economic trials (CA, PE, AE, RE).

Unfortunately, the files mentioned in the protocol were not found in the Romanian National Archives and it is very likely that they could have provided particularly important information about the activity of the related enterprises.

As indicated earlier, the evaluation index of the officials of the foreign trade enterprises was not based on their professional value, but on their political training. It is certainly one of the reasons that put the loyalty of those officials in question in the following years. Starting in the early 1960s, this led to a type of pursuit, virtual at first, real afterward, which included Jews in foreign trade. The reports submitted to the SPFC undoubtedly served as a kind of preamble to the subsequent process of denigration, arrest, and prosecution, when the economic trials began. The way in which the investigations of the defendants in all the trials were conducted also proves that those who served as investigators had a thorough training. Even without finding specific references and records in the Romanian archives to indicate the veracity of this assumption, the pursuit of future defendants, carried out for many years by the Securitate, sometimes through Special Bureaus[84] as well as the thorough preparation of future investigations, cannot be challenged.

Tortured and subjected to Securitate brutality, the defendants remained at the center of an extended operation to find evidence of their wrongdoing and questionable decisions, which would later be labeled “crimes of undermining the national economy” in the context of the indictment.

The special bureau, with a representation in each of the foreign trade enterprises, knew how to pursue any activity that could be of interest to the Securitate in its quest to carry out its intentions. The activity of the Securitate representatives, be they agents, informants, or collaborators, was permanently under the guidance and orders of the party leadership.

CCPCR Plenary Session of June 9–13, 1958

On June 9–13, 1958, the CCPCR Plenum took place, with the reconsolidation of the PCR and the establishment of the mandate of Gheorghiu-Dej as its main purpose. At the same time, the session managed to make it clear that no critical point of view and no questioning of the position or policy pursued by the party’s Political Bureau, under the leadership of Gheorghiu-Dej, would ever be allowed. This meeting was of essential importance in the strategy elaborated by Gheorghiu-Dej, in order to consolidate the communist regime in Romania, both by strengthening his own position as absolute leader and at the same time, that of the political police, that is, the Securitate. After the dangers “from inside” had been gradually but surely eliminated,[85] this occasion had offered the opportunity to remove members of the Central Committee who questioned the so-called policy of de-Stalinization led by Dej from key positions. These steps had to be taken in order to ensure the undeniable continuity of the party leadership in Bucharest, but also to assure the Kremlin of the political stability of the Bucharest regime and the indisputable authority of its leader, as a proof that the departure of the Soviet armies from Romanian territory would not pose any danger for the future.[86]

But the Plenum session of June 1958 had other intentions: Gheorghiu-Dej announced that in a short time he would proceed to eliminate some comrades from the party, some of them old illegals, who had dared to raise their voices against the leader with absolute powers, manifesting a critical point of view toward his policy. The purges included countless party members, both from the party apparatus and from public institutions, such as ministries, hospitals, publishing houses, and research centers, as well as the removal from public office of “Jewish elements” so that the general process included a subprocess for the exclusive removal of a large number of Jews from some institutions in the country.[87] The years 1957–1959 were the time in which tens of thousands of former members were expelled from the party, many of them intellectuals, and among those targeted were a large number of Jews. Thus, the Jews, considered in part as “producers of ideology,” in that they worked in the fields of press, culture, media, and publishing, were eliminated, not only from the sectors of economy and sociopolitical life but also from the cultural world and the press. During this period, the practice of the famous circulars sent to almost all the offices of ministries, publishing houses, or enterprises was also known, and it specified the immediate need to remove a certain percentage of Jews from office. This measure was invoked as a "party directive" so it had to be implemented immediately. The circulars were accompanied by texts referring to the need to "improve the social and national structure" in all sectors.

This key phrase can be seen as an updated equivalent of the well-known phrase "Numerus Clausus,"[88] transposed from the times of fascist dictatorships to the communist period.[89] The resurgence of Stalinist ideological dogmatism together with the illogical administrative measures were applied despite the alleged "thaw,"[90] which in the opinion of the communist leader had a detrimental effect on Romanian society.[91] The Romanian repressive apparatus, represented by the Securitate, would expand its composition and sphere of influence, tighten its means of repression, and intensify its intimidation of the population.

During the same period of 1957–1958, there was an apparent change in the policy of the Romanian government regarding the reopening of the gates of Jewish emigration to Israel, after a break of about five to six years.[92] In 1958, Moses Rosen met Ion Gheorghe Maurer, president of the Great National Assembly of Romania, of which Rosen was also a member, and asked permission to tell him the following story:

> After Friday's service at the synagogue, the rabbi loudly invited everyone who likes fish to come and visit him at home. Many parishioners, fish lovers, arrived at the rabbi's house in the evening. He sat at the table and ate the fish with obvious pleasure. He invited the guests to sit down, they sat down and waited to be served fish, but it was late in coming. The rabbi continued his meal without seeming disturbed by the eyes of the visitors. When they expressed their astonishment, he looked at them very sharply and said:
>
> Did I say I would give someone a fish? Of course not. What I said was that I would like to know how many of you are fish lovers.[93]

After recounting the tale, Dr. M. Rosen asked Maurer: "Is there any chance that the Romanian government has invited so many Jews to the police headquarters just to see which of them are 'fish lovers'"?

The implications of the Party Plenum of June 1958 targeted not only Jews but also groups of non-Jewish intellectuals, people who through their sociocultural activities could have been identified as hostile to the system. The later economic trials of the Jewish Foreign Trade officials were the result of the conjunction between Gheorghiu-Dej's interest of applying his national policy and the consolidation of the coercive, oppressive, terror-based system under the responsibility of the Securitate, the "sine qua non" condition for imposing this policy.

General Assembly of the Employees in MCE

The first institutions from which Jews were massively purged were the Ministry of Foreign Affairs, the Ministry of the Armed Forces, and the Ministry of the Interior. Jews in these sectors were transferred to other positions, some of them within the Ministry of Internal Trade, to various workshops or to less influential institutions, such as in various cooperatives.[94] This transfer of people from one job to another was one way of applying the measures taken by the June 1958 Plenary, meant to replace Jews holding key positions in various ministries, with persons of Romanian ethnicity. In 1958, it was the turn of the MCE to meet the required clearance rate. The official disclosure of the intentions and the laying of the groundwork for the impending decisions was at the General Assembly of Employees of the Ministry of Commerce-Department of Foreign Trade between the15th and the 17th of October 1958.[95] The foreign trade sector was considered by the members of the Securitate as a suitable ground for staging large-scale processes. The official purpose of the working meeting was the elaboration of the resolution of the Plenary of June 1958. The meeting was itself a particularly stormy[96] "theatrical plenary,"[97] and created an atmosphere of criticism and condemnation directed against a large number of officials in the ministry and in foreign trade enterprises. One of the purposes of the meeting was the replacement of some of those officials with members of the new generation.[98]

The party leadership of the city of Bucharest was represented at this meeting by Florian Dănălache,[99] the secretary of the Party Committee of the city of Bucharest, by the MCE leadership, represented by Marcel Popescu,[100] the minister active at the time, and also by some of the deputy ministers, like Gheorghe (Gogu) Rădulescu, Mihail Petri, and Vladimir Steriopol.

During the meeting, the positions of the chief of the Cadre, and of the Securitate representatives, some of which had been covert, were disclosed. Their speeches revealed the renewal of specific methods of action of a threatening and terrorist character, which had characterized party meetings of those times. The role of "first violin" played by Jewish officials in the Ministry in the "show" given by the "imaginary orchestra" in front of the Party Leadership of Bucharest, with Florian Dănălache as its main conductor, cannot be neglected. Scapegoats were to be singled out, for various irregularities within the ministry. In particular, they could not be other than the Jewish officials of the foreign trade enterprises, or sometimes of the ministry itself.

It is under these circumstances that the balanced approach of the minister of Foreign Trade in charge at that moment, Marcel Popescu, should be noted. He was dismissed shortly after this meeting.[101] Dănălache and the other representatives of the ministry urged the officials present to confess to their shortcomings, both in terms of mistakes made at work, but also in terms of disregarding party discipline, in all aspects. Many office workers took the floor, highlighting the mistakes they had made, in the presence of the "great inquisitor." They proceeded to criticize their own actions, pledging future identification with the strict procedures that Dănălache presented as steps that should be strictly observed for the future smooth running of Romanian trade.

> It can be noticed, that there are comrades with a very low ideological and political level and still they play a leading role in the Directorates of the Ministry. These bourgeois tendencies are also influenced by the contact they maintain with capitalist firms.[102]

Shortly after this speech, it became even clearer that most of the former employees of the ministry, Jews employed in the MCE enterprises, were about to be fired and replaced by people considered more "suitable" by the party leadership. The attempt to connect the professional training to the ideological level of the employees reminds us of the report written almost a decade earlier by Rusu Clement,[103] warning the Foreign Relations Committee, existent at that time, about the low ideological level of the ministry's employees.

Although the meeting was apparently aimed at auditing the ministry's work and aligning it with the June 1958 Plenary Decisions, in reality it was intended to expand the ministry's ranks by promoting young, motivated people with a "healthy origin" for supporting and serving the party, on the basis of an ideological educational training meant to give rise to a new generation. On the other hand, there was another purpose, namely to incriminate most of the Jewish officials employed at that time in Foreign Trade.[104]

Important members of the party, including Dănălache, came together to form a group of "people's judges and assessors" to assume the status of "people's tribunal," which would eventually declare the widespread guilt of many among the employees of the ministry, creating an atmosphere of criticism and accusation reminiscent of the show trials of Stalin's time. In this context, the MCE deputy minister Nicolae Anghel gave a speech, presenting a concept regarding the working alternative that was supposed to dominate in the future.

Minister Anghel's intention was to replace "people with outdated perceptions," those who had acted as experts in foreign trade, with "people associated with our regime and our party." As follows:

> I would like to end with this phrase: to open wide the windows of our Ministry, to let in fresh fresh air, as we were instructed through the documents of our party, the documents of the CCPCR Plenary of June 9-13, 1958.[105]

This meeting was really a preamble to the actions, which were taken by the party in the following two years, ending with the Foreign Trade economic trials. The words spoken by Dănălache[106] can be seen as a warning that, for those who had eyes to see and ears to hear, signaled the beginning of a series of measures that would massively change the human makeup of the MCE. This was achieved by professionally blocking all those who could be identified by the Securitate as "bourgeois," Zionist, anti-party, or those who had been linked in the past to the activities of the legionary movements.[107] Shortly afterward, a large group of Jews who had applied for emigration to Israel, together with their families, were removed from the party.[108] At a subsequent meeting on November 13, 1958, the staff of the Ministry's Party Committee was changed, and in a report published on the occasion, following measures to be applied were outlined:[109]

- The national and social composition of the ministry must be changed.
- Those persons with an inappropriate attitude or behavior must be eliminated from the ministry.[110]
- Positions must be taken against directors who have behaved inappropriately, with an attitude of liberalism, hypocrisy, and opportunism, manifested for personal gain, or against those who misuse principles and show an attitude of reconciliation.[111]
- Finally, a senior staff policy must be advanced, to promote young and qualified people in key positions in the MCE, in order to be able to replace all those belonging to the older generation.

One of the most prominent principles reflected in the party documents specific to the MCE expressed the need to combine professional work with party work, as a condition for successfully carrying out the tasks assigned to the ministry and subordinate enterprises. One of the examples that reflects this concept that characterized the party leadership at that time, but today can be seen as absurd in its own way, is the speech of Ana Toma,[112] who served as deputy minister of Foreign Trade:

> Today I admit that I was wrong, because instead of waiting I should have asked for the help of the Party Committee, because together we could have solved the problems that existed then, in the Ministry of Foreign Trade. I had to admit, the party support in improving the professional results of the Ministry must be emphasized. We had the duty to put the instructions that came along the lines of

the party and the state into practice in the work carried out, because in this way we could involve party members in our work, and in this way, we could have improved our professional achievements.[113]

This strange connection between professionalism and what was considered the quality of being a party member, revealed by Ana Toma, in the aforementioned lines, highlights the obligation that the employees of the MCE had to consult their party comrades, bearers of supreme authority, in making professional decisions.

PCR Plenary Session of November 1961

Partidul nostru nu trebuie să reabiliteze pe nimeni post mortem.[114]

(From the speeches of the Plenary Plenum[115])

In October 1961, the 22nd Congress of the Communist Party of the Soviet Union opened in Moscow. On the agenda, the resumption of Stalinist politics after it had been condemned five years earlier by the famous "secret speech" of February 1956. On the eve of the opening, the Romanian delegation used the occasion to lay a wreath in the Red Square at the graves of both V. I. Lenin and his successor, I. V. Stalin. N. Khrushchev's speech to the congressional delegates was scathingly critical of Stalin's policies. As a result of this unforeseen situation, the Romanian delegation felt compelled to lay a wreath at the recently inaugurated Karl Marx monument.[116] The leadership of the Romanian delegation was concerned about the way it was targeted in the speech. In fact, the party leadership in Bucharest had not moved away from the practice of Stalinist personality cult, primarily aimed at the one who was in charge of the Romanian delegation to the Congress, Gheorghiu-Dej. The anecdote about the Romanian delegation laying wreaths at both monuments was another practical demonstration of the double standard that characterized Gheorghiu-Dej throughout his political career. During Khrushchev's speech on the Stalinist policy of terror, some of the delegates to the Congress ostentatiously turned their heads in the direction of the Romanian delegation.

Shortly after the return of the Romanian delegation to Bucharest, the Plenum of the PCR was opened. Romanian leaders staged a kind of "game" with which they presented themselves during the plenary meetings to prove how aware they were of the campaign carried out in Moscow against the personality cult and its consequences. Through these maneuvers they tried to create the impression that they should be appreciated as those who put the precepts of the opposition to personality cults into practice "avant la lettre."[117] Gheorghiu-Dej made every effort to make the Soviets forget his faux pas in

Moscow in the Red Square and for this he would have to show that the PCR's program was precisely following the lines set by the 22nd Congress.

The intention of the Plenum was to revise and even rewrite the modern history of the Romanian Workers' Party, so that if Gheorghiu-Dej's policy was targeted, and indirectly even criticized in Moscow, the "game" of Romanian politicians through this Plenum was intended to purify the image of the leader.[118]

During this Plenary meeting, there was a dialogue between the party secretary, Gheorghiu-Dej, and his minister of interior, Alexandru Drăghici,[119] who was also the head of the Securitate. The dialogue took place on a free stage, in front of the participants of the Plenum, and its purpose was to cancel any attempt to attribute to Gheorghiu-Dej some of the horrors attributed to Stalin. But, in reality, the dialogue turned out to be a farce, in which Drăghici addressed the leader of the party with flattering words, in order to give the impression of Dej's perfection of action. Gradually, in the dialogue between the two, both encouragement and expressions of mutual support intensified, so a variety of episodes in the history of the PCR were highlighted, although the party leadership and the Securitate would have preferred to hide some of them or at least keep them in the shade. Various characters stood before the audience, many of whom were among the victims of the Romanian partisan terror, exposed in the utter ugliness of the facts and the total collaboration of those present in the hall. All of them, from the "patron" Dej to his "servant" Drăghici, but also the others, who through their applause gave their support to the acts of hypocrisy and demagoguery, were attempting to counteract the impression created in Moscow, namely, that in Romania, Stalinism never ceased. Through the farce[120] of the staged dialogue between the two main protagonists, Gheorghiu-Dej and Alexandru Drăghici, the latter tried to wrap the "wolf" in a verbal "sheepskin" defending him against the allegations "candidly" in front of the spectators.

CONCLUSION

This chapter describes both the environment and the political and economic atmosphere in which the accusations against some senior Jewish officials were conjured up after a period of activity of about a decade in Romanian foreign trade. The period starting from the beginning of the 1960s in Romania saw the economic restructuring of the state, started after the communists took power. This was achieved gradually by shifting from a market economy to a centralized one and by adopting, for the most part, the Soviet economic model.

In the framework of researching the existing documents referring to Romanian political life, it was not possible to pinpoint the exact beginning of the events that led to the future condemnation of the Jewish officials in Foreign Trade. According to the written and oral testimonies referred to in the previous chapters, as well as the interpretation of the related events, it can still be concluded that the starting point of the elimination of Jews from Foreign Trade was the Working Meeting of the MCE, in October 1958.

In accordance with the attitude expressed in this meeting, the completion of a process that took nearly a decade could have been foreseen. The stages of this process were rigorously prepared in advance by the Securitate representatives by designating the group of senior Jewish officials who would later serve as easy targets to pursue. Only one month after the working meeting of the MCE employees, during the Plenum in Bucharest between November 30 and December 5, 1961, no reference was made to those who had already begun their journey to the hell of communist prisons.[121]

Striving to the point of absurdity to establish some "facts" and fabricated events that lacked any connection with reality, the November 1961 Plenum, which was apparently meant to enshrine Stalinism, approved the Romanian party's own fiefdom, the continuation of repressive actions precisely reminiscent of those of Stalin's time.[122]

NOTES

1. Alina Pavelescu, Dan Catănuş, *Amurgul Ilegaliştilor, Plenara CC al PMR, iunie 1958* (in English *Twilight of the Illegalists, CCofPMR Plenary, June 1958*) (Bucureşti: Vremea, 2000), 243. The quoted fragment is a paraphrase of the afterword of this volume, written by Florin Constantiniu, henceforth Pavelescu, Catănuş, *Amurgul* (in Romanian).

2. The Cold War period can be considered to be the period of time between 1945, the end of World War II, and the dissolution of the Soviet Union, 1991. It is also understood as a policy struggle between the Western capitalistic countries and the new communist countries, somehow, almost all being under Soviet Union's influence.

3. The protocol of this meeting can be found at DMBAN, PMR Fond / File 18/1958 (DMBAN, Bucharest Municipality Directorate of the National Archives). Lately, this Directorate has acquired the new name of a service and that is why its present name used today, is SMBAN, instead. At the time this document was analyzed, the name of the archive was DMBAN.

4. DMBAN, PMR Fond-Bucharest City Committee, Tudor Vladimirescu district / File 18/1958, pp.75–79.

5. Florian Dănălache (1915–1984), the party secretary of the town of Bucharest, member of the Executive Committee of the CC PCR between 1947 and 1967.

6. The Ministry of Commerce was partly divided into two departments of Interior and Foreign trade, but at times two ministries existed, Ministry of Internal Trade and MCE.

7. The Securitate file types held at ACNSAS will be explained in appendix II.

8. "Communist regimes have always acted for political resons and less of economic ones," Stelian Tănase, *Revoluţia ca eşec: Elite si Societate* (Bucureşti: Humanitas, 1993), 127, in English: *Revolution as failure: Elites and society*.

9. IAR, Industria Aeronautică Română (The Aeronautics Romanian Industry, airplane factory).

10. Buhuşi, cloth factory; Guban Timişoara, shoe factory.

11. Ioan Scurtu, "Economia după 20 de ani. De la Teorie la Realitate," Accessed on Internet on June 11, 2020. http://www.ioanscurtu.ro/?s=Economia+dup%C4%83+20+de+ani.+De+la+Teorie+la+Realitate.

12. In Romanian, Consiliul Superior al Economiei Naționale.

13. Petru Groza (1884–1958), a Romanian politician, held the position of prime minister in the first communist Romanian government.

14. The Romanian Workers' Party held this name between 1954 and 1964, then eventually changed its name to the Communist Party.

15. *Colecția de Legi, Decrete, Hotărâri și Deciziuni*, Vol 28 (Bucureşti: Editura de Stat, 1950), 45–47.

16. Jay A. Burgess, "Direct Foreign Investment in Eastern Europe: Problems and Prospects of Romania's Joint Venture Legislation," *Law and Policy in International Business*, 6, no. 4 (1974): 1063, henceforth Burgess, "Direct Foreign Investment in EE."

17. In Romanian, Comitetul de Stat al Planificarii, henceforth CSP.

18. Titu Cristureanu, *Romania Foreign Trade* (Bucureşti: Meridiane Publishing House, 1969), 14, henceforth Cristureanu, *Foreign Trade*.

19. John Michael Montias, *Economic Development in Communist Romania* (Cambridge, MA: MIT Press, 1967).

20. In the legal context of the 1952 Constitution, Article 17 (c) stated that Romania's economy is a centralized one, whose purpose is to expand its ties with as many states as possible.

21. Oil, wood, and grain.

22. Letter from the Israeli representative at the Israeli Embassy in Bucharest to the Economic Section for Eastern Europe of the Israeli Ministry of Foreign Affairs, National Archive of Israel, Het-Zadei Fonds 1956/10 (Romania's Foreign Trade with Developing Countries, 1961).

23. In Romanian, CAER.

24. The Marshall Plan was a US-initiated plan, for helping to rebuild the European economy after World War II. Its implementation started in 1948.

25. The Warsaw Pact was founded on May 14, 1956, as a political and military reaction of the Eastern European countries to the creation of NATO, namely Western Germany being accepted as part of this Treaty.

26. Oana M. Văsioiu, *Evoluții ale comerțului exterior românesc în perioada 1950–2000*. România de la CAER, summary. Accessed on Internet on June 4, 2010.

http://bibliotecatest.ase.ro/resurse/resurse_electronice/teza_capitole.php?tid=977&qs=sort%3Dtitlu%26dir%3Dup%26pagina%3D11.

27. Comertul Exterior Accessed on July 3, 2016. http://www.scribd.com/doc/55874512/Comertul-Exterior.

28. Found in the Constitution of 1952, Art. # 14, Accessed on November 2, 2020. http://ro.wikisource.org/wiki/Constitu%C5%A3ia_Rom%C3%A2niei_(1952)#CAPITOLUL_1_-_ Oranduirea sociala (Social Order) accessed on November 2, 2020.

29. Decisions made through Plenaries of the PCR Central Committee.

30. Evidența și Analiza Activității Economice a Întreprinderilor de Comerț Exterior (București: Editura Didactică și Pedagogică, 1965), 9–14, henceforth *Manual de Comerț* (this book was used in the service of the Romanian People's Republic regime).

31. URE was an Italian company located in Milano, Unione Representanze Estere.

32. Titu Simon, *Pacepa : Quo vadis ? Din culisele Serviciilor Secrete Românești* (București: Editura Ștefan, 2009), 149–177.

33. Burgess, "Direct Foreign Investment in EE," 1064.

34. Ana Toma (1912–1991) was a PCR activist, secretary of Ana Pauker during her term as minister of foreign affairs of Romania (1952–1947) who later held the position of deputy minister of foreign trade. She served as a witness in the Pătrășcanu trial, against one of the other defendants, Remus Koffler.

35. Silvan Vitianu was born on July 23, 1906. He took over the position of economic adviser at the Romanian Embassy in Bern, he was the director of the Relations Department II (see the Foreign Trade ministry structure, in Appendix IV), and between 1950 and 1952, he held the position of export director. Until 1954, he occasionally worked in the Cadre Department of the MCE.

36. Pavel Donath (1911–1981) was one of Romania's official representatives in Moscow, at the CMEA organization, and later the PE general manager. Donath was one of the main defendants and convicts in the PE trial, which began in 1961.

37. Andreas Fenyö was a merchant and businessman from Cluj. He was employed at Dermata factory in Cluj. He was later employed in Bucharest at a raw leather processing enterprise. Being a person with initiative, he contributed to increasing the productivity both at Dermata and at the leather goods factory.

38. Andrei (Bandi) Klein was part of the management of the Dermata leather factory, where he worked as a director of the company, being also married to the owner's daughter. In 1949, he started his employment at Românoexport, and in 1952 was expelled from the party.

39. *Manual de Comerț*, 11. ISCE, meaning State Enterprise for Foreign Trade (in Romanian, Întreprindere de Stat de Comerț Exterior), was used as a prefix in all the names of the Foreign Trade state enterprises.

40. The Ministry of Commerce comprised two different ministries, the Foreign Trade Ministry and the Ministry of Internal Trade, and acted at times as a common forum uniting the two, at times, the two were separate ministries.

41. As explained before.

42. In Romanian, Oficiul de Control al Marfurilor, henceforth OCM.

43. The Romanian Statistic Journal, in Romanian, Revista de Satistică, Bucureşti, Octombrie 1963, 54–56.

44. Burgess," Direct Foreign Investment in EE," 1064–1065.

45. Henceforth Prodexport will be abbreviated as PE.

46. Henceforth Agroexport will be abbreviated as AE.

47. Henceforth Românoexport will be abbreviated as RE.

48. Pavel Donath, PE Manager, "Les produits alimentaires roumains s'affirment de plus en plus sur le marché international," *Journal of the Chamber of Commerce of Romania*, no. III (36) (1960), Gheorghe Manheim, RE Counselor, "L'Industrie roumaine de la laine et le commerce des matières premières pour l'industrie de la laine," *Journal of the Chamber of Commerce of Romania*, no. II (23) (1957), Alexandru Costin, RE Manager, "Confections et tissus roumains, entretien avec M.A. Costin, directeur de l'entreprise Romanoexport," *Journal of the Chamber of Commerce of Romania*, no. I (34) (1960).

49. See chapter 2.

50. Ibid.

51. Michael Checinski, *Poland, Communism, Nationalism, Anti-Semitism* (New York: Karz-Cohl, 1982), 221.

Kutin was a French Resistance fighter, against whom an attempt was made to stage a trial around 1967, but in the end the intention did not turn into reality.

52. See chapter 2.

53. The people involved in the trials were among the founders of the Romanian foreign trade in its first years of existence. In order to strengthen its economic structure, the state needed, among other things, a Foreign Trade authority, in charge of satisfying the basic requirements of raw materials not found in the country.

In the field of trade and especially of foreign trade, there were few non-Jewish Romanian specialists as mostly Jews had dealt with trade in previous years.

This information is based on my correspondence (July 2016) with Mr. Geza Kornish (1917–2019), a resident of Bad Homburg, Germany, who himself had been employed at ISCE Fructexport.

54. Botnar's testimony in the CA trial, ACNSAS, P7893/Vol. /p.103.

55. At that time, relations between Romania and the United States were in their infancy.

56. See chapter 2.

57. Meir Cutic, *The Prague Trial* (New York: Herzel Press, 1987), or Daniel Magen's seminary paper about Bukharin Trial, written at the Faculty of Law, Tel Aviv University, under the direction of Professor Liora Bielski.

58. The information regarding the documenting of the criminal trials in the communist period was made available to me by Ms. Oana Axinia Soare, lawyer at IICCMER, during personal discussions and through our correspondence, which is in the author's possession, on April 11, 2012. These facts can also be consulted in CPP-1960, Book III "The Judgment,, Title I "General Provisions," Chapter 5 "On the finding of debates,, Articles 312, 314. IICMER is the acronym of Institutul de Investigare a Crimelor Comunismului şi a Memoriei în Exil (www.iiccmer.ro).

59. The RE trial sentence was pronounced by the Court on July 4, 1964.

60. See chapter 1.

61. This situation can be assumed by reading Alexandru Drăghici's speech during the CCPCR Plenum, which took place between November 30 and December 5, 1961, Arhivele Naţionale, Fond Cancelarie (English, Chancellery Fund), File 55/1961, pp. 226–258, as well as the Protocol of the Working Session with the workers from the Ministry of Commerce, DBAN, File 18 / pp. 79–201.

62. The elements of this policy as well as other of its relevant aspects were discussed in chapter 1.

63. Academy of Economic Sciences, ASE (http://www.ase.ro) (in Romanian, Academia de Ştiinţe Economice), is the current name of what was previously known as the Academy of Commerce, in Romanian, Academia Comerciala. This institution, with a long tradition of economic studies, was inaugurated in 1913, but the Faculty of Foreign Trade began to operate only in 1951, so the first graduates appeared on the market only starting in 1954–1955.

64. StelianTanase, *Elite si Societate, Guvernarea Gheorghiu-Dej, 1948–1965* (Bucureşti: Humanitas, 1998), 192–193, *in English, Elites and Society, The Gheorghiu-Dej Government.*

65. Alexandru Draghici's speech delivered at the Plenum of CCPCR held between November 30 and December 5 1961, National Archives, fond CCPCR, Chancellery Department, File 55/1961, 226–268.

66. As already mentioned in "Introduction" and chapter 1, we use the term of PCR for the Romanian Communist Party (in Romanian, Partidul Comunist Român, PCR), though its name at the time of the economic trials was Romanian Workers Party (in Romanian PMR). The reference as PCR was preferred because in the National Archives of Romania, the documentation referring to the party is held under the name of PCR. For instance, part of the references following are to the Fonds "CCPCR" (meaning PCR Central Committee, in Romanian, Comitetul Central al Partidului Comunist Român, or CCalPCR, in short, used in the book of CCPCR).

67. Partly, the activity of CCPCR was divided among various sections (bureaus), each of them being responsible for a different subject; among these were External Relations Sections (in Romanian Secţia Relaţii externe, henceforth SRE), Economic Section (in Romanian Secţia Economică, henceforth SE), Chancellery (in Romanian, Secţia Cancelarie, henceforth SC), Plan, Finance and Trade Section (in Romanian, Secţia Plan Finanţe şi Comerţ, henceforth SPFC), and ASO. The various categories are divided in different archival fonds (in Romanian Fonduri for plural, Fond for singular).

68. Rusu Clement, member of the CC of the PCR between 1960 and 1974, deputy and then director of the SPFC section between 1952 and 1955, website http://www.cnsas.ro/documente/2004%20-%20Membrii%20CC.pdf, accessed on the Internet on June 28, 2008.

69. Ady Ladislau was for several years the head of the SRE department, and after the elimination of the "right-wing group," he was appointed to a senior position in the Ministry of Internal Affairs and the Securitate. He served as deputy minister of interior beginning in 1952. He was director general of penitentiaries. In 1959, he

was dismissed and later brought to trial, on the grounds that he had collaborated with prewar Romanian Siguranta, which is the name under which the Romanian secret service operated until November 13, 1940, or later, with the Special Intelligence Service (SSI), a service that was active until September 15, 1944.

70. The paper, issued on April 22, 1952, ANR, Fond CCPCR, Economic Section, File 18/1952, pp.1–5.

71. The Ministry of National Economy was founded in 1938 and was divided into the Ministry of Industry and Trade and the Ministry of Mines and Petroleum in 1945 (Order 188/24 March 1945). On April 29, 1949, the Ministry of Economy (Order 9 of the Presidency of the Grand National Assembly) was founded and continued its activity under the name of the Ministry of National Economy, Industry and Trade.

72. ANR, Fond CCPCR, Economic Section, File, 18/1952, p. 2.

73. Ibid, p. 2

74. Ibid, pp. 4–5.

75. It is worth mentioning the lack of logic of this statement by Clement, emphasizing that in socialist trade, professionalism is measured not by the professional level of the employee, but by his political level.

76. Healthy origin, in Romanian "Origine sănătoasă," was an expression referring to people coming from working class or peasant origin.

77. Accessed June 28, 2020. http://www.jurnalul.ro/stire-istoria-comunismului/prinsi-in-vartejul-vremurilor-102997.html

78. ANR, Fond CCPCR, Economic Section, File 18/1952, pp. 22–28.

79. Ibid., 28.

80. Cadre was frequently used for Personnel, mainly Party members' personnel. Cadre work meant the processing of political documents and instructions in popular meetings.

81. The right-wing deviation was a political accusation against several highly positioned PCR party members, such as Ana Pauker, Vasile Luca, and Teohari Georgescu in 1952, as a result of which they were excluded from the party.

82. Gheorghe (Gogu) Radulescu (1914–1991) deputy of the Foreign Trade Ministry (1949–1952), minister of Internal Trade (1956–1959), then of the Foreign Trade, vice president of the Council of Ministers (1963–1979), vice president of Council of State (1979–1989). He also held the position of CCPCR member (1960–1989). Once excluded, Vasile Luca and Teohari Georgescu were arrested and condemned, while Ana Pauker was put under house arrest.

83. ANR, Fond CCPCR, Economic Section, File 12/1952.

84. "Special Bureau" (in Romanian, Biroul Special) was the name of a section existing in almost in all State enterprises, composed of representatives of the Securitate being present on the spot.

85. From the elimination in 1946 of Stefan Foriş to that of Lucreţiu Pătrăşcanu in 1954, through the treatment applied to the "right-wing deviators group," in 1952.

86. Pavelescu, Catănuş, *Amurgul*, 6.

87. Toma, *Privind înapoi*, 121–122.

88. Rabbi Dr. Moses Rosen, *Dangers, Tests and Miracles* (London: Weidenfeld & Nicolson: 1993), 183, henceforth Moses Rosen, *Dangers, Tests and Miracles.*

89. Bity Caragiale (1920–) a journalist at the youth newspaper "Scânteia Tineretului" and later at "Realitatea Evreiască." Employed in this newspaper from the late 1950, she confirmed the existence of these circulars during the personal discussions we had together. Ms. Caragiale left Romania in 1990, emigrating to Israel, from where she assiduously continued her publishing activity at Romanian-language newspapers in Israel.

90. Toma, *Privind înapoi*, 204.

91. Vladimir Tismăneanu, "Gheorghiu-Dej and the Romanian Workers' Party: From De-Sovietization to the Emergence of National Communism" (*Woodrow Wilson International Center for Scholars*, May 2002). Accessed November 4, 2020. https://www.wilsoncenter.org/sites/default/files/media/documents/publication/ACFAF5.pdf.

92. Moses Rosen (1912–1994) was the Chief Rabbi of the Mosaic Cult in Romania between 1948 and 1994 and president of the Federation of Jewish Communities in Romania (1964–1994). He became a deputy in the MAN in 1957 and a honorary member of the Romanian Academy from1992.

93. Rosen, *Dangers, Tests and Miracles*, 187.

94. Rosinger, *Cartea neagră*, 2.

95. DMBAN, Direcția Municipiului București a Arhivelor Naționale, Fondul PMR,Comitetul orășenesc București, raion Tudor Vladimirescu, Dosarul 18/1958, pp.79–201.

96. About the stormy atmosphere of the session, reported also Moni Marcel, employee of the Ministry of Internal Trade, participant in the Meeting, who was eliminated from the Ministry on the occasion of this meeting, DMBAN, File 19/1958, p. 108.

97. Narrated in the Memoirs of Rosinger Adalbert, written between 1979 and 1980.

98. DMBAN, Dosarul 18/1958, p. 1

99. Florian Dănălache (1915–1984) former member of the PCR Executive Committee between 1967 and 1974, first secretary of the Party Committee of the city of Bucharest.

100. Marcel Popescu held the position of minister of Foreign Trade, between 1957 and 1959.

101. Popescu's dismissal was not for professional reasons, but due to the dissolution of his family relationship with Gheorghiu-Dej's daughter, Lica Gheorghiu.

102. DMBAN, File 18/1958, p. 143.

103. Referred earlier.

104. The intentions that could be observed during this session were found in two primary sources, the first Rosinger Adalbert' partially written manuscript, Rosinger, *Cartea Neagra*. The second source is an oral statement made by the Jewish official Moni Marcel, present at this meeting, who was himself dismissed from the Ministry of Internal Trade, because shortly before, he had submitted documents requiring for emigration to Israel. This source was confirmed by the wife of another RE defendant, already mentioned, Silvia Chinzbrunner (1914–2014), with whom the author spoke in Frankfurt, Germany, at her home.

105. DMBAN, Direcţia Municipiului Bucureşti a Arhivelor Naţionale, Dosarul 18/1958, p. 175.

106. Ibid., 186.

107. Ibid., 188.

108. DMBAN Dosarul 19/1958, p. 108.

109. DMBAN, Dosarul 19/1958, p. 126.

110. Ibid., 125.

111. Ibid.,127; reconciliation was considered an attitude inconsistent with communist morality.

112. Ana Toma (1912–1991) was a communist activist and served as deputy minister of the MCE from 1952–1966.

113. DMBAN, Dosar, 19/1958, p. 53.

114. In English "Our party shouldn't rehabilitate anyone, post mortem."

115. ANR, Fond CCalPCR, Chancellery Section, File 55/1961, pp. 226–258.

116. G.M. Razi, "Rumania: Don't Rock the Boat," *Problems of Communism*, 11, no.3 (May–June 1962): 18–21.

G.M. Razi was a member of the District of Columbia Bar and published numerous articles on international law and Eastern European affairs in both French and American journals.

117. Vladimir Tismăneanu, "'Gheorghiu-Dej and the Romanian Workers Party': From De-Sovietization to the Emergence of National Communism," published by Woodrow Wilson International Center for Scholars, May 2002 Accessed November 4, 2020. https://www.wilsoncenter.org/publication/gheorghiu-dej-and-the-romanian-workers-party-de-sovietization-to-the-emergence-national.

118. Ion Mihai Pacepa, *Cartea Neagră a Securitatii* (Bucureşti: Omega SRL, 1999), Vol. II, 99, henceforth Pacepa, *Cartea Neagră a Securitatii.*

119. As head of the Securitate, Draghici was directly responsible for the personal safety of the Party Secretary Gheorghe Gheorghiu-Dej.

120. ANR, Fond CCalPCR, Chancellery Section, File 55/1961, pp. 226–258. Sectia Cancelarie, File 55/1961, pp. 226–258. Apart from this file, which shows the events of the Plenary of November-December 1961, it was repeated in the historiographical literature on other occasions.

121. Vladimir Tismăneanu, "The Ambiguity of Romanian National Communism," *Telos*, 60 (Summer 1984): 69.

122. Frunză, *Istoria Stalinismului*, 433.

Chapter 4

The Criminal Procedure Followed in the Economic Trials

Official truth is not actual truth.

Lord Acton[1]

INTRODUCTION

After many years in the service of the Romanian Foreign Trade Ministry, a group of high-level functionaries were entrapped by the Securitate and accused of undermining the national economy and plotting against the social order of the Romanian state. These events took place in a historic period of time characterized by general suspicion, fear, and tension toward the Eastern European communist countries, already vilified by the narrative politics of the Cold War.

The great majority of the charges brought against these functionaries were connected to economic contracts with Western European, Asian and African countries, nations outside the Eastern Bloc. The prosecution tried to show that these contracts were damaging to the Romanian economy in that they sold local products at lower prices and bought imports at higher prices. The investigation considerations that aimed to do so were, at best, haphazard and did not take into account the specific circumstances in which these contracts took place, the factors that determined their terms, and the fact that most Romanian companies at the time, although capable of delivering contracts, were not receiving sufficient offers. These price differences mentioned by the prosecution were presumptuous, and no evidence was ever provided to attest to their existence. The Criminal Procedure refers to the entire process, including the arrest, the investigation by the Securitate investigators, the appearance in the court, the judgment, and the conviction. As far as the officials in Foreign Trade were concerned, all the legal procedures took place in a Military Court.

I would like to emphasize that this chapter represents a personally conceived description of the Criminal Procedure in the economic trials. My description is based on archival documents, all of which have been analyzed in this book. Yet, my analysis is certainly not a paradigm of the various political trials that took place in Gheorghiu-Dej's Romania. Although those political trials were analyzed in various papers[2] that have appeared in recent years, their documentation does not refer to the same legal procedure that in the Foreign Trade trials led to the specific accusations of undermining the national economy. The uniqueness of these trials lies in the fact that the Foreign Trade officials' purge from office, arrest, and arraignment to a Military Court cannot be linked to any attempt to eliminate political rivals who could have competed for Gheorghiu-Dej's position.

PRELIMINARY STAGES OF THE ECONOMIC TRIALS

In reality, the criminal proceedings that defined the economic trials were initiated by the Securitate, years before the actual trials took place, under the direct control of the Communist Party, which it conscientiously served. The surveillance steps involved are presented here, including the scenarios entrapping the defendants in situations that would later warrant their arrest and trials.

Criminal Surveillance of the Foreign Trade Functionaries

In order to gather as much information as possible, the Securitate started a complex surveillance campaign that intruded into the personal lives of those who were to later become "guilty." If we were to wonder if these actions were based on the Romanian authorities' express intention to build a case against those accused, the answer is affirmative, as the surveillance had been in place long before the trials started.

The idea of eliminating Jewish functionaries from the Foreign Trade Ministry had already been introduced—and quite clearly—during the Working Meeting of the Workers from the Ministry of Commerce[3] of the same ministry, attended by Florian Dănălache,[4] the party secretary of Bucharest city, at that time. During this meeting, some of these Jewish functionaries were labeled problematic, lacking both moral and professional conduct vis-à-vis the companies where they worked.[5] A decision was made at this time to replace some of them[6] with Romanian functionaries or educated peasants and blue-collar workers, graduates of the Academy of Commerce in Bucharest.[7]

Due to the nature of their work, Foreign Trade Ministry officials used foreign currency in their interactions with their foreign counterparts, either for the exchange of goods or for facilitating economic transactions. Years before their arrests, some of them were ensnared in a "spider web" created by the Securitate precisely for this purpose. Consequently, some of the future defendants became, by choice or coercion, its collaborators and informants. Once the surveillance procedures were initiated for those labeled problematic, the Securitate opened files on them. In the first stage were "verification" files and then, as the process developed, a second type of files was developed, "under surveillance" files.[8] The great majority of these files were opened in 1958 and 1959, with some predating these years.[9] Entrapped by the Securitate's machinations, and fearing for their future, some of the defendants gave in and became either informants or collaborators of the Securitate. Yet, even though they collaborated with the authorities and informed on targeted people and events, when the economic trials started, some of them were arrested and were subjected to the same treatment as other defendants. The methods used by Securitate to coerce them into submission were among the most brutal methods used by the Eastern European totalitarian regimes, even without reaching the brutality of those used against political detainees in the 1950s.

FROM THE OPENING OF THE CRIMINAL PROCEDURE TO THE APPEARANCE BEFORE THE COURT

Preliminary Stages

For starting each of the Foreign Trade trials, a warrant was issued.[10] The Criminal Procedure refers to the entire process: the arrest, the investigation by the Securitate investigators, the appearance in court, the judgment, and the conviction. The Criminal Surveillance Bodies at that time were the Police and the Securitate, each in charge of different criminal procedures and each known by a different Romanian name.[11] The first warrant, initiating the Criminal Procedure, refers to only one person, but, as the investigation continued, more names were added to the defendant list. Some of the articles of the law under which the defendants would ultimately be convicted already appeared in this first warrant.

The Arrest

Initially, upon their arrest, the defendants in the economic trials were presented with an "arrest warrant," issued by the Securitate, which did not require the signature of a prosecutor. This type of documents was issued just one or two days prior to the actual arrest. Soon after, a second type of order, a "remand warrant" was issued. This document justified the extended holding of the prisoner for varying periods of time, sometimes many years. Two other orders were issued at the time of the arrest: a "search warrant," and a "seizure warrant," the latter allowing the seizing of personal property (not only of the person being arrested but of his family living in the same place).

The search warrant allowed the Securitate agents to purposefully look for "incriminating"[12] evidence among the belongings of the defendant. Regardless of the inculpating potential of the objects found, they were recorded in writing and seized. Sometimes, the seizure of goods took place later, after the initial search warrant was conducted, in the presence of another family member or a neighbor. Romania was in principle a popular democracy and an adherent to the Universal Declaration of Human Rights,[13] which presumed an individual innocent until proven guilty. Its 1952 Constitution, the one valid at that time, and particularly its article 87,[14] stated: "The citizens of the Romanian People's Republic are guaranteed their personal inviolability. According to the existing law, nobody could be arrested unless thus decided through a court order or judge order." The constitution delineated guiding principles, which were then detailed by the Code of Criminal Procedure, as in the present case.

More precisely, according to the CPP-1960 in effect at the time, arrest warrants could be issued by the criminal surveillance bodies or the prosecutor in charge of the case. The criminal surveillance bodies could be either investigators associated with the General Prosecution office or the Securitate investigators.[15] In the case of the Foreign Trade trials, the Securitate was the criminal surveillance body, through its criminal investigators. The main reason given was, that Foreign Trade defendants' accusation, undermining the national economy,[16] fell into the category of crimes against the Internal Security. In this way, the Securitate investigators could issue an arrest warrant[17] whereby defendants, those charged with crimes, requiring criminal investigations (as was the case in Foreign Trade), could be detained first for 24 hours and the detention could be extended up to 2 months. This course of action was also legitimized by the Code of Criminal Procedure. The military prosecutor issued extensions of the initial remand warrant, which were addressed to the Securitate Criminal Investigation Division. Their purpose was to maintain the legality of the arrest. The procedures used during the Foreign Trade trials were based on the Criminal Code and the Code of Criminal Procedure, both of which had been updated in 1960.[18]

It can be assumed that the major decisions regarding the conviction of the Jewish functionaries originated within the higher ranks of the PCR. The execution of these decisions was carried out by the Securitate and the legal procedures by the Military Court, despite of the fact that none of defendants had military ranks. Under these conditions, once the arrest warrants were issued, the defendants were as good as sentenced.[19]

In theory, however, it seemed that the criminal procedures were carried out according to the law in effect and the principles dictated by the Universal Declaration of Human Rights. Among its principles, stands Habeas Corpus,[20] which states that before a person could be arrested, he had to be brought in front of a judge and presented with the facts warranting his arrest. If no such facts existed and he was found innocent, he was supposed to be exempted from arrest and released.[21] According to this principle, a judge had the power to issue an arrest order but not the power to decide the innocence or lack thereof of the defendant. Yet, this law principle was not observed during the Foreign Trade trials, as the arrest orders were issues not by a judge but by the investigators of the Securitate and, the extension of the arrest was later approved by a prosecutor associated with the same institution. At no stage of this process was a judge involved. The Habeas Corpus principle was bypassed under the cover of article 87 of CP-1960 that granted the investigation units the right to issue arrest warrants. One of the reasons that such an action was possible had to do with the fact that, according to the communist constitution in effect at the time, the separation of state powers was not implemented.[22]

The Investigation

> None of the means and the procedures used by the investigatory services required a task as laborious and complex as the investigation of a prisoner.
>
> Alexandru Drăghici, 1955[23]

Investigation was the main procedure used by the Securitate to compile the files that were necessary for the defendants' arraignments. According to Alexandru Drăghici, the Ministry of Internal Affairs in Romania to whom the Securitate belonged and reported to, had, as one of its main responsibilities, "the investigation of the defendants."[24] The preparation of the investigation file by the criminal investigator was one of the most important steps. Through the way it was organized and presented, it had the power to shape or decide the future sentencing of the defendants. The sentence itself was closely related to the way the investigation file was compiled, to the extent that not only its length but also the defendant's quality of life after release were determined by the way the file was composed and presented.

When it came to the methods used by the Securitate during Gheorghiu-Dej's leadership,[25] distinct periods exist. The difference between them lay in the harshness of the methods used against the defendants during the investigation and later on against the prisoners. Khrushchev's famous speech in February 1956 resulted in a temporary softening of the methods used by the Securitate to investigate and interrogate political prisoners. This attitude, however, was done away with during the last years of Gheorghiu-Dej's leadership and replaced with drastic methods of terrorizing and frightening the general population and the political prisoners in particular.[26]

The repressive methods exercised upon them were an efficient means to force admission of guilt and, from the very beginning of the criminal procedures, ensure the defendant's belief in the inevitability of the outcome. Not surprisingly, these activities were meant to generate material that placed the defendant undeniably in the category of an enemy of the status quo and the state. More precisely, the defendant was removed from the personal sphere, that is, his personal home, into the public space where the arrest and investigation where to be conducted. This removal of the person from a space perceived as supporting and protective into one where anything could happen was justified through the use of an "arrest warrant." The prisoner's encounter with the investigator was no more or less than an encounter with his own personal fears and a constant attack on his personal psychological structure. From the moment he was arrested and started the ride to jail (in the cases presented here, the Securitate basements in the Malmaison building), the defendant was led to believe that he would arrive in a place where his personal safety and his future were uncertain. This constant subordination of the defendant to the Securitate investigator resulted in a constant and debilitating state of terror and fear. Intentionally, this state of mind started with their arrest when their eyes were covered with black tin eyeglasses and, as they were forced into the Securitate vans, were told, "from this moment on, shut up, and answer only when asked."[27]

Although this abuse was pervasive and obvious, the Securitate forces attempted to show that they respected the existing laws and procedures of the criminal code. Yet, then and now, it is common knowledge that the Securitate investigators had free reign when it came to arriving at "the truth," or the version of it that served the interests of the PCR and was formulated prior to initiating criminal procedures. As such, this truth did not correspond to the truth of the defendant and did not reflect the actual services he had performed for the state. According to the Securitate, what constituted "truth" was a fabricated system of models and profiles that allowed only one course of action and outcome for the defendants in custody. The rooms that housed the investigations were, for the most part, underground, so that the cries of pain and despair of those being investigated and the beatings and the torture they were subjected to doing interrogations could not be heard from outside.

The methods used at Malmaison were intentionally geared toward creating a state of fear and terror, a warped sense of reality in the defendants who, more often than not, succumbed to the state of mind associated with uncertainty and powerlessness. It is relevant to note that almost all of the daily reports written by the main investigator and signed by the defendants themselves, with very minor exceptions, used formal, polite language, devoid of vulgar expressions, or threats and curses. Yet, these reports did not reflect reality. Curses, invectives, threats, and beatings were a daily occurrence in the interrogations conducted by the Securitate officers.[28] According to primary sources belonging to the economic trials investigations, this approach was generalized and present in all such encounters. These constants also illustrate the labor-intensive documentation that accompanied the interrogations, documentation that included reports written by the investigators, signed, in the majority of the cases, by the defendants themselves, or, in a few cases, supplemented by typewritten documents produced by functionaries assigned to this task. Here, we could ask to what extent, if any, these documents reflected the actual conversation between the investigator and the investigated. As they were produced and compiled by those in power with a vested interest in the sentencing of the defendants, these documents could not reflect the reality of the events in question.

As such, we acknowledge the partiality of these primary sources and advise the reader to maintain a critical distance from the events they detailed as having happened a certain way in the basement cells of the Malmaison building. It is not possible to know, from these biased primary sources, the extent of the psychological manipulations or the exact language used by the investigators. This is particularly true, when their primary goals were to bend the defendants' will and behavior to exact certain responses and reactions. The investigations vacillated between psychological and physical torture and the methods included physical isolation, physical humiliation through savage beatings, including strikes with fists and boots, and strikes with sticks in the sensitive groin area, verbal humiliation, and threats. These forms of torture impacted not only the defendants sequestered in their cells but their immediate families (wives, children, parents) as well.[29]

While it is true that the Securitate torture methods were even harsher during the 1950s (including forcing the defendants to eat their own excrements or to be naked during the interrogations), and that they had been toned down prior to the economic trials, there was no actual "improvement" in the interrogation procedures in the following decades. No such changes could be observed and deduced from the existing records of these interrogations. In themselves, the records compiled by the Securitate functionaries, although very detailed, well indexed and catalogued, function only as impersonal accounts of the events.

The investigation of the defendants in the economic trials started immediately after their arrest by the Securitate agents from the Criminal Investigation Division[30] of the Ministry of Internal Affairs.[31] The length of these investigations depended on the time needed by the Securitate agents to gather sufficient information and extract collaboration agreements from those investigated, most often through violent means. In themselves, the investigations followed the format of questions and answers recorded and archived as transcripts or, in some cases, the format of declarative confessions, signed by the defendants. The latter were either answers to posed questions or extensive explanations the defendant felt necessary to say, either independently or under coercion.

It may be assumed that under these conditions, the validity of these records is murky at best and might not reflect the truth about the confessing defendant or about what he said concerning others, who were subjected to the same treatment. In fact, these confessions were extracted with the intention to procure incriminating information against the other defendants, being subject to interrogations that took place in parallel and were sometimes conducted under the promise that the one doing so could benefit from better living conditions or a reduced sentence. More often than not, the entire interrogation was carried out by the same Securitate agent to ensure consistency of method and record.[32] When the interrogator was replaced, the intent was to prevent a personal relationship from developing between him and the defendant, to corrode his sense of empathy and any trust developing in the defendant that he could improve his situation and condition.

In addition to the daily interrogations, information on each defendant was gathered from their cellmates, who were asked questions about their behavior and their own thoughts about the interrogations themselves.

The following passages will detail the various warrants issued by the Securitate investigators and the reports solicited by the interrogators, as well as the methods used to secure them.

Warrants Issued during the Investigation

- Warrant for the execution of financial assessment

This warrant was issued in order to assess the losses and damages incurred by the supposed undermining activities of the defendants and was a sine qua non document for the investigation. The committees in charge of conducting these investigations were allegedly industry "experts"[33] who, very likely, had collaborated with the Securitate in the compiling of files for the RE trials and others. Under the alias Horia Mihai, one of these experts appears in countless records as a main player in the investigations. He was a Securitate collaborator with the real name Constantin Dobrescu. He was a jurist by profession and worked as legal counsel at RE. He later acted as a financial expert in several of the financial audit committees.[34] The warrant for a financial assessment was ordered as soon as the investigation proper was initiated and provided material evidence to be used for sentencing during the economic trials. In the case of the RE trials, the financial assessments were ordered even before the defendants were rounded up and investigated. Unfortunately, no personal information on these financial experts could be found in the archives of the CNSAS and, it is safe to say that a direct relation with the Securitate could not be established. While, based on the existing documents, it could be established that none of them had held any qualifying position in commerce or, by extension, in the Foreign Trade Ministry.

The presence and actions of people like Constantin Dobrescu, a Securitate collaborator, and the lack of evidence regarding the exact relationship between the financial experts and the Securitate highlights the possibility that many of them (or perhaps all of them) were collaborating with it. According to their known positions at the time, none of these so-called financial experts were proficient in the economic sectors and, very likely, their audit findings were dictated by the agents of the Securitate. These findings are available for consultation in voluminous files included with the criminal file of the defendants.[35] They contain specific economic contracts, established between 1950 and 1960, which were later used to incriminate the defendants during the actual trials. Here, it is important to note that part of the contracts was considered successful and beneficial to the Romanian economy and those who established them had actually been recognized and honored with medals and honorary titles for their efforts and services to the country.

Yet, despite these past honors, the financial audits of the RE functionaries found them guilty of suspect activities that undermined the national economy and were later used as primary evidence during the trials. The damages mentioned in these reports and in the documents supporting the prosecution's claim were presumptive damages. The actual damages were, as the Securitate investigation managed to point out, the result of selling Romanian products at low prices and buying imports at high prices. The damages alleged by the financial audits were the result of the difference between actual prices and prices that it was claimed could have been obtained. These alleged damages were then used as evidence that a criminal act was committed against the Domestic security of the Romanian state.[36] As such, the "crime" committed was perceived as political and the defendants treated as political prisoners during the investigation and the trials.

- Warrant for the inclusion of material evidence and official documents in the defendants' surveillance files

This type of warrant was issued, for example, during the ISCE Agroexport trial in order to add its results to the financial audits that were part of the criminal file.[37]

- Warrant to conclude the criminal investigation

Toward the end of the investigation, this type of warrant was issued and presented to the defendants to mark its conclusion. The defendants were expected to sign this document and most of them complied. Still, there were some cases where defendants refused to sign, while recording their reasons at the bottom of the page.[38]

- Indictment Warrant

As part of the investigation process and immediately after the defendants' arrest, the Securitate investigator issued an Indictment Warrant. Quite frequently during the investigation several such warrants were issued in order to secure the Indictment document, which was issued by the criminal investigator according to the Code of Criminal Procedure[39] in effect, on an individual basis, which required the specific defendant's signature upon receiving it. The latter could actually comment on its content. At the conclusion of the investigation, the court received a document called Indictment Conclusions,[40] a document that referred to the entire group of defendants. Its drafting was the responsibility of the investigating unit.[41] These concluding documents were passed to the court when the investigating unit decided that the gathered evidence was sufficient and, together with the testimonies of the defendants, justified the beginning of criminal proceedings. They were submitted to the court, but not before the defendant could (a) read his entire file and find the nature and gravity of the accusations against him and (b) decide if he had questions about the conclusions of the criminal investigation and if he wanted to submit additional statements to his file.[42]

Between Investigator and Defendant—Diversification of Investigation Methods

Of special importance in the investigation process was the relationship between the person being investigated and the Securitate agent.[43] Some of the facts described further were disclosures made by Foreign Trade convicts, or by members of their families, others were in the primary sources accessed at CNSAS. Among the documents that detail this relationship are the investigation files themselves, various documents and statements, and the emergent literature[44] that appeared in recent years presenting the legal psychology used during the criminal investigations. According to the latter, regardless of the investigation being conducted by the same agent or by a series of them, the defendant was considered guilty and his infractions well-known.

> From a psychological point of view, the surveillance and the court proceedings were the total sum of the relationships between the investigated, the Securitate investigator, and everyone else involved in this process.[45]

As such, psychological manipulations during the economic trials' investigations were common practice and aimed to make the defendants admit the claims detailed in the investigation file. Naturally, when the same investigator conducted the entire interrogation process, he and the defendant developed knowledge of each other, which he could then use in his favor. Namely, the investigator became aware of the defendant's way of thinking, his weaknesses and panic points, and his social behavior and milieu. In time, he was able to read his facial emotions, the motivations behind his words and actions, even the inherent fear brought about by the investigation itself and the uncertainty of the defendant vis-à-vis his own future. This acquired knowledge represented one of the advantages of having one investigator for the entire duration of the process, which could last from a few weeks, to several months.

Yet, this knowledge was mutual and, in time, could weaken the resolve and efficiency of the Securitate agent in his function as an interrogator. While the developing trust could be conductive to confessions that could not be extracted otherwise, it could also result in the investigator developing sympathy toward the defendant and deflect the goals of his actions. To avoid such developments, every investigator was subjected to rigorous training (including personality tests) prior to his assignment to the function, to prove that he could perform the activities associated with it to the satisfaction of his superiors.[46] The meetings between the investigator and the defendant under his charge could happen daily, but not always consecutively and could be scheduled weeks or months apart. They could last from a few hours to longer sessions of 8–10 hours or even more, 15 or 20, with or without a break. During these sessions, the defendant was kept standing or sitting and, not infrequently, he was refused water. The main reason of these extended sessions and the conditions in which they were carried was to exhaust the defendant, both physically and mentally, so he would become malleable and amenable to the investigation goals.[47] To amplify their effect, the defendants were asked a barrage of questions with occasional, but not guaranteed, breaks between them. In certain situations, additional participants were present in the investigation room, among them, the chief of the investigation unit.[48]

The investigation itself followed one of the two distinct methods:

- A dialogue, with the interrogator asking questions and the defendant answering them; the resulting conversation was registered in a standard form called Transcript of Interrogation (PVI).[49]
- A declarative procedure, when the interrogated person had to write information required by the investigator. Part of some defendants' investigation abounded in this type of declarations, instead of the usual filling out of the PVI form.

Both types of investigations collected information under pressure and often with physical violence. The intended purpose was to incriminate either the writer himself or the other defendants. Consequently, the information contained therein could neither be verified nor authenticated. In these circumspect conditions, it was impossible to separate truth from lies. There are cases in which, removed from these conditions, the defendants retracted their own statements a few days after giving them.[50]

Some of these interrogation sessions were carried by the same investigator for reasons detailed earlier. The final investigation report, the PVI, was signed by hand, on each page, by the defendant and on the last page by his investigator. There were some cases when the defendant refused to sign the PVI, and, in these cases, the note "I refuse to sign" was written at the bottom. The format of this report was relatively constant throughout the investigation. At times, it was backed up in typewritten format. Only a small percentage of the criminal files contained double versions of PVIs. Instead of the hand-signed name, on the last page of each typed document, there was the investigator's signature together with the acronym, SS, meaning in Romanian, "illegible signature."[51] Some of the documents have questions in the margins, written by the investigator's superior, most likely added immediately after the investigation.

At the end of the investigation, the defendant received the entire file for revision. Yet, although he had access to both his own and the other defendants' files (including the results of the financial audit), he had very little time to revise, clarify, or make changes on it.

Confrontations between Defendants and Prosecution's Witnesses

During the investigations, it was common to stage cross-examinations between defendants in the same trial, or between them and witnesses for the prosecution.

Cellmates Working as Spies for the Investigators[52]

One of the most common information-gathering techniques used by the investigators was spying performed by the cellmates on each other. In most cases, those doing the spying were, or had been, defendants in other political trials. They were strategically placed in cells where the defendants, just interrogated and thus unsettled and unnerved by the process, were more likely to slip or to break and divulge secrets. In such moments, the former acted as impromptu confessors and trustworthy friends who, as soon as possible, delivered the information collected to the investigators for immediate recording. In itself, the information was detailed, complex, and aimed to capture important details about the defendant in the case. Its delivery depended on the collector's personality, education level, comprehension, and capacity for empathy. Those informing on their cellmates were moved around, as needed, to spy on defendants in the same or separate trials.

In exchange for their collaboration with the investigators, these informants could receive shorter sentences, better conditions, and benefit from attenuating circumstances. In turn, they reported casual and targeted conversations, their cellmates' frustrations, their physical behaviors, emotional and psychological states of being, even their preferred postures. As these reports were delayed by the circumstances in which they were collected, it is possible that they were "padded" and some of the scenarios they described reimagined. After they were delivered, they awaited the inspection and approval of higher-ranking investigators and, when possible, were used to conduct subsequent interrogation sessions.

In essence, these sessions were geared not only towards information collection but also towards building a body of evidence that benefited and cemented the prosecution's case. They ensured that the defendants were found guilty of crimes against the state and its social order and that they were found guilty of undermining the national economy.[53]

Defendant and Prosecution Witness Depositions

As already mentioned, all the witnesses deposed in these economic trials belonged to the prosecution.[54] The defendants tried to present their own witnesses, but their requests were always denied. Both their verbal and written requests to introduce witnesses who could attest to their innocence or confirm their side of the story were summarily dismissed by the investigation agents. This decision was, of course, against the procedures allowed by the criminal code, which stated:

> The defendant had the right to representation both during investigation and during the trial proceedings, most precisely, after the first interrogation and could, after consulting his lawyer, decide whether or not to take security measures.[55]

The defendants' lawyers were keenly aware of this transgression and how minute their chances for a fair trial were when appearing in front of the

Military Court. In fact, in these specific trials, the lawyers were a simple formality. The prosecution's witnesses were selected to introduce and reinforce evidence against the defendants and were, in the great majority of cases, their work colleagues from the same ministry or related industries. Some of them were in the process of serving their own sentence in communist penitentiaries.

The Ending of the Investigation

The investigations leading to the economic trials lasted, at times, several years. Their length was dependent on the complexity of the accusations, the number of defendants involved and the ability of the Securitate investigation units to obtain irrefutable evidence. Even though the defendants were presented with their criminal files and could review them, their request for any revisions was, in the great majority of cases, summarily denied. Yet, a few defendants were granted their request to recall the prosecution witnesses take the stand during the trial in order to clarify certain information. Once the criminal investigation was completed, a medical committee issued a certificate of mental and physical health clearing the defendant for court. As the defendants were accused of economic crimes against the state, these and the rest of the documents were then sent to a regional Military Court in Bucharest. The ensuing trials took place behind closed doors and in secret, and after the formal conclusion of the investigations, they could be postponed for several months. Not infrequently, during these trials, the bar was announced at the last minute so that a designated lawyer had very little time to prepare the customer's defense.[56] While the defendants, with their families' help, had the option of securing their own counsel, the time they had together was very short. Additionally, their lawyers were limited in what they could say to defend their clients and, in fact, were mostly a formal presence in court.

THE COURT SESSION

The Military Court as the Trials' Location

As already mentioned, the defendants in the MCE trials were primarily accused of undermining the national economy[57] and plotting against the social order of the state.[58] For these reasons, they were judged by a Military Court, which was the Supreme Court in cases of political nature. Even though defendants without military ranks should not have been appearing in front of such a court, this type of practice was common in Eastern European communist states.[59] In Romania, there was a law school whose students were recruited from among the ranks of blue-collar workers, public transportation functionaries or agricultural workers. They were between 38 and 42 years of age, and, as long as they had at least four years of high school, they were considered qualified to attend this institution. After only two years of study, they received their diplomas and then worked as lawyers and prosecutors. In 1949, the Romanian justice system saw the addition of people's assessors to its courts. Their role was to represent and defend the interests of the Communist Party, participate in criminal investigations and in sentencing, especially when the trials were of a political nature. The statute of peoples' assessors was inspired by the Soviet justice system.[60] During this time, the Romanian Military Courts were coordinated in accordance with law 33/1948, which also informed the new Code of Military Justice.[61] The latter was introduced in order to "support the new social order and improve the efficiency of the military legal system."[62] Other institutions (e.g., the Ministry of the Interior, responsible for the state's security, its judicial and prosecution institutions, people's assessors, and the changes to criminal codes) were founded in order to prevent any resistance from the general population against the agenda and the actions of the communist state.

The Defendants' Testimonies in Court

The Romanian legal system is based on continental law,[63] which in turn is based on Roman law. The conducting of court proceedings is based on the inquisitorial method.[64] According to this method, the judge participates in the investigation, controlling it and participating in the dialogue with the defendants or witnesses, thus contributing to the discovery of relevant evidence for the decisions that will be made at the end of the trial. Thus, some evidence may be omitted by the representatives of the two parties in court, the defense and the prosecution. In this context, information that might have been relevant is missing from the data included in the documentations of the trials, as, unfortunately, the only written evidence was recorded by the clerk. Had the recording procedures used during such trials included all the materials presented, the accuracy of the information contained therein could be verified

In the case of the economic trials, held in absolute secrecy, except for the defendants, very few persons appeared as audience in the court: members of their families, agents of the Securitate, legal authorities, and some representatives of their old workplaces. Their testimonies and the statements of the defense lawyers and prosecution were transcribed in shorthand in a document called the *Conclusions*. There were two additional documents, the *Minutes* and the *Sentence.* While in court, each defendant had the right to use his testimony to bring evidence in favor of his own defense. The defendants who had served in higher positions were granted extended time as their accusations were more complex and the expected sentence lengthier and harsher.

The Witnesses for the Prosecution

The witnesses brought forth by the prosecution appeared in court after having been deposed by Securitate agents during the investigation proper. Prior to their first deposition, they were given information relating to the reasons for their presence in court and details about the defendants.

The Defense during the Economic Trials

As already mentioned, the defendants' lawyers were, in part, hired by their families. Mostly, however, the defendants were appointed a lawyer by the court and had very limited, if any, time to meet with him and build their case. Sometimes, the lawyers met with their clients only after the court proceedings had started.

The Conclusion of the Criminal Trial and the Issuing of the Sentence

Once the court proceedings concluded, a trio of documents was recorded and the last one, the Sentence, was read in front of the entire court. Next, the three documents are presented in detail. All three started by mentioning the names of the court representatives and, if they had any, their military ranks.[65]

The Conclusions[66] described the trial itself, the summaries of the sessions, witnesses' testimonies, and the statements of the defense and the prosecution. According to these conclusions, each trial started with the reading of the Indictment Conclusions drafted by the Securitate during its Investigation and presented to the Military Court. In the absence of complete recordings of the court proceedings, it is difficult to assert the exact nature of the exchanges carried out in court between the prosecution and the defense.

The Minutes[67] was a kind of short protocol, containing the sentence summary and the names of the accused. It detailed the complete sentence and, after it was recorded in the court's register, was read out loud to the entire audience.

The Sentence[68] was then read by the president of the court, or his substitute. Sometimes, the document was as long as 500 pages and contained a brief introduction of the defendants' names, a summary of their accusations, and the punishments demanded by the prosecution.

During the rest of the court proceedings, the documents collected by the prosecution were presented: the Securitate investigations, various versions of the financial audits, and the prosecution witnesses' testimonies. A close examination of these documents shows that the court adopted the arguments of the prosecution in their great majority. This attitude and practice actually permeated all the economic trials against the Foreign Trade officials.

THE APPEAL

After the sentence was pronounced, the defendants had the right to file an appeal. The period allowed for this procedure varied from case to case and the appeal could take place as late as half a year after the sentence was read.[69] Both the defendants and their lawyers could present documents in their defense. In the economic trials, changes produced by this new evidence were minimal and granted only to a small number of defendants. Only in a few cases, were the appeals successful in diminishing the sentences of the accused.

THE CARRYING OUT OF THE SENTENCE

Life in the Romanian Sing-Sing[70]

In Romanian jails,[71] the prisoners were separated according to their gender and placed in different locations. Some locations, however, like Jilava,[72] had prisoners of both genders, temporarily housed there before departing for more permanent locations. During the investigations, the political detainees in the economic trials were housed in the underground cells of the Malmaison building, which belonged to the Securitate.

> Originally belonging to a guard regiment, later assigned to the S.S.I., which became the Securitate in 1948, the innocuous building housed thousands of detainees, who heard the animation of the street without passers-by suspecting their existence beyond the lead facade. A few dozen yards away, in a building in the green courtyard, the trials of a military court were taking place.[73]

After their sentencing, the Foreign Trade prisoners were transferred to Jilava,[74] until their appeal. Following the appeal, the defendants were sent to three Transylvanian prisons. Most of the men were transferred to Aiud, while the women convicted in the same trials were transferred to women's prisons, either in Oradea or in Miercurea Ciuc.

Regardless of the location, life in these institutions was harsh and filled with cruel and unusual punishments. For example, the Malmaison cell had two cement beds topped with straw mattresses and a bucket to be used for the biological needs of the inmates. During the day, the inmates could not lie down and were allowed only to sit on their beds with their legs hanging down.

If caught in breach of this rule, they were beaten or subjected to other kinds of punishment. The cell door was made of metal with only one small opening through which the meals were delivered daily. This opening only served as an observation point for the wards in charge of surveilling the prisoners. As already mentioned, the latter were spied upon by their own cellmates who reported on their behavior, actions, and words to the Securitate agents.[75]

At the Jilava prison, the so-called "rooms" were divided in four and housed metal bunk beds which were oriented perpendicularly to the windows facing one of the three jails' interior courts. They were covered by straw mattresses and, sometimes, a wool blanket covered in a white bedsheet. Some of the cells had a wooden bench, or a few wood planks in the center, which could serve as a sitting or eating place. The windows were barred by closely grouped metal rods, making escape impossible. Even sunlight could barely reach into the cells. Although the cells had wooden stoves, they were placed closed to the windows. The prisoners had a very small allowance of wood that barely warmed the room, and even then, only for a limited amount of time. To keep themselves as warm as possible during the cold nights, most of them lit their stoves in the evenings.[76] The daily food rations consisted of 100 grams of bread (1/4 of a pound), 300 grams of cooked corn (about ¾ of a pound), and a meal, which the prisoners called "turtoi."[77]

At another prison, in Aiud,[78] the dimensions of the holding rooms were of monastic size, yet housed four prisoners.[79] Here, the political prisoners were held separately. During the day, the prisoners spent their time braiding metal rods into supports for the metal beds or making straw baskets. Gardening, a less physical chore, was also part of daily work obligations. Prior to the arrival of the political prisoners, the prison had undergone some renovations: the wooden floor had been replaced with a cement one, the walls had been repainted, and the wall separations had been redistributed. Some of the old woodwork shops had been repurposed into living and bathroom quarters. Some of the buildings themselves had been repurposed to serve as workspaces. The work schedule itself was a seven-day schedule, meaning that the prisons worked every day on various projects. A few select prisoners had some light privileges, which included the ability to spend time outside in conversation with other prisoners or to play ball, both activities taking place under the scrutiny of the prison's guards. The hangar adjacent to the prison served as a workplace and personal hygiene space. There, the prisoners could clean and shave themselves during set hours. In return for their work, the prisoners were allowed to receive one 10-kilogram care package (about 20 pounds) a month, and a visit with one of their family members. This visit, however, took place under the watchful eye of prison guards.

The political prisoners associated with the Foreign Trade spent lengthy sentences at Aiud and saw these living conditions deteriorating rapidly. After

1965, the frequency of care packages received and visits changed from once a month to once every three months. If the prisoner was ill or could not perform his daily work obligations, these privileges were revoked, which resulted in bouts of despair and increased loneliness. Those who fell ill did not receive medical attention and care. Both the dehumanizing conditions of their imprisonment and the rare generosity and charity of their mates remained engraved in the memories of the detainees. Not infrequently, these difficult conditions sparked incidents of hate, antisemitism, anger, and envy as outbursts and responses to the dehumanizing conditions of the prison. These conditions that had developed at Aiud were harsher even than those used in Transnistria.[80] When a gesture of sympathy or caring occurred, it had the power to carry the recipients through dark moments and ensure their survival though otherwise very dire circumstances.

Perhaps the best description of these particular conditions is stated in the following lines:

> There were radical differences between the prison conditions during the previous dictatorial bourgeois system, in place before 1945, and the communist regime that replaced it. Namely, the former living conditions of the prisoners could be described as convenient, as compared to the ones of the communist prisons.[81]

CONCLUSION

In the case of the economic trials detailed in this book, the laws of the Romanian Criminal Code were used and manipulated to serve the interests of the prosecution. In service of the PCR, the Securitate dictated the course of the interrogations. In turn, the investigations and the prosecution, in service to the Securitate, dictated and decided the outcome of the proceedings. De facto, the PCR was in charge of the entire legal proceedings, carried out in its name by the Securitate. At the latter's request, exchange rates for the foreign currency used in the MCE's transactions were manipulated in such a way as to incriminate the defendants. Some of the reports it relied on for its accusations were written after such transactions took place, without observing proper procedure.[82] The following chapters will describe the ways in which the six Romanian Foreign Trade trials unfolded between the years 1960 and 1964.

NOTES

1. John Dalberg (1834–1902), also known as Lord Acton, was a British noble, historian, and politician proponent of political freedom within the state.

2. Andrei Muraru, Sorin Cucerai, Dumitru Lăcătuşu, Clara Mares, Constantin Petre, Cristina Roman, and Marius Stan, *Dictionarul penitenciarelor din România comunistă (1945–1967)* (Institutul de Investigare a Crimelor Comunismului în România, Iaşi: Polirom, 2008), Mircea Stănescu, *The Reeducation Trials in Communist Romania (1952–1960)* (New York: Columbia University Press, East European Monographs, 2011), Lavinia Betea, *Lucreţiu Pătrăşcanu, Moartea unui lider comunist* (Bucureşti: Curtea Veche, 2006).

3. This particular meeting was detailed in chapter 3.

4. Dănălache was the party secretary for the city of Bucharest during the 1950s.

5. In 1958, many Jews contacted the Romanian authorities to express their interest in emigrating to Israel. Before 1958, such opportunities were very rare for the Jewish population. Soon after emigration papers were filed, most of them were fired from their respective places of employment. The Foreign Trade Ministry was one such place.

6. As previously mentioned, 27 of the 29 defendants in these economic trials were Jewish, versed in commerce and speakers of several foreign languages. Most of them were from Transylvania.

7. The ASE, previously the Academy of Commerce (In Romanian "Academia Comercială"), was founded in 1913. The Foreign Trade Department, established in 1951, produced its first graduates in 1954–1955.

8. These types of Securitate files, today at ACNSAS, are described in appendix III.

9. Some of these files were actually open prior to the 1958 work meeting, but could not be located for consultation.

10. CPP-1960, Book II, "Criminal Surveillance and Arraignment," Title I, "Criminal Surveillance," Chapter IV, "Documents for Criminal Surveillance," Section I, "Initiating the Trial Procedures, Art. 195."

11. These names were either the Criminal Inquiry or the Criminal Investigation. The former was in charge of the Police, the latter in charge of the Securitate. The cases, where the second type of investigation was mandatory, were those referring to State Security crimes, like the ones attributed to the Foreign Trade defendants. Cases like that were covered by CPP-160, Book II "Criminal Surveillance and Arraignment," Title I, "Criminal Surveillance," Chapter III, "Criminal Surveillance Bodies," section 186(3).

12. Such objects could include personal letters, foreign books and newspapers, small gifts like cigarette packs, and other consumer goods not found on the scarce local market.

13. The General Assembly of the United Nations adopted the Universal Declaration of Human Rights on December 10, 1947 (Decision 217 A (III). Romania adopted it on December 14, 1955.

14. The 1952 Romanian Constitution. Accessed November 7, 2020. http://claudiuefta.wordpress.com/2010/10/12/constitutia-romaniei-1952,

15. CPP-1960, Book II, "Criminal Surveillance and Arraignment," Title I "Criminal Surveillance," Chapter III "Criminal Surveillance Bodies," Art. 186, 186b.

16. CP-1960, Book II "Crimes and Felonies in particular," Titlul I "Crimes and Felonies against the State," Capitolul II "Crimes and Felonies against Domestic security," Section I bis. Art. 209[1], "undermining of the national economy and counter-revolutionary sabotage.

17. CPP-1960, Book II "Criminal Surveillance and Arraignment," Title I "Criminal Surveillance," Chapter III, "Documents for Criminal Surveillance," Section IV "Warrants and preventive arrest," Art. 253.

18. The previous versions of the Romanian CP and CPP were dated 1948, 1955, and 1958.

19. As already mentioned, the law articles used in the defendants' arrest would also count in their final sentencing.

20. See chapter 2.

21. While this principle is applicable to the Common Law, it has its equivalent in the Continental Law, on which Romanian Law is based.

22. The Separation of Powers is a model for the governance of a democratic state and refers to the separation of its legislative, executive, and judiciary branches.

23. ACNSAS, Fond Documentar, D100, p.100, henceforth ACNSAS, DXXX/Vol yy/pp. z1-z2.

24. ACNSAS, D100/pp.51–52.

25. From 1948 to 1965.

26. Chapter 1, a chapter dedicated to Romania, as a communist country, details among others, the way Gheorghiu-Dej, acting as the leader of the PCR, largely bypassed the application of those measures mentioned in Khrushchev's speech during the XXth Congress of the PCUS.

27. Rosinger, *Cartea neagră,* 7.

28. The memoirs written by those who survived the Securitate's investigations and detention contain many references to these events, detailed from the perspective of those tortured and interrogated. Yet, for obvious reasons, their accounts do not benefit from primary sources (hand or typewritten) that could corroborate their accounts. Among these memoirs, there is Adalbert Rosinger's manuscript and, in interview format, the testimony of Tertulian Langa (1922–2013), a Catholic Transylvanian priest who was sentenced to 20 years, of which he served 14 in several jails, Aiud included. He was interviewed by Lucia Hossu Longhin and presented the ways the Malmaison interrogations were conducted in chilling detail. Accessed May 18, 2015. http://old.clujeanul.ro/general/afisare_articol.php?id_obiect=148&cat=50. Virgil Ierunca, *Fenomenul Piteşti* (Bucureşti: Humanitas, 2007), in English *The Piteşti Phenomenon.*

29. "Anchetele Securităţii strategie şi tactică în demascarea duşmanilor poporului." Accessed November 7, 2021, http://www.scritube.com/stiinta/stiinte-politice/Anchetele-Securitatii-strategi123112149.php, 1–12, henceforth *Anchetele Securităţii.* After the 1989 revolution, countless books delved extensively into the repressive measures of the communist regime and its campaigns of misinformation and abuse, including their application in the case of the economic trials. Among them are: Adrian Cioroianu, *Pe Umerii lui Marx, O introducere în istoria comunismului românesc* (Bucureşti: Curtea Veche, 2005), Romulus Rusan, *Cronologia şi geografia represiunii comuniste în România* (Bucureşti: Fundaţia Academia Civică, 2007), Marius

Oprea, *Banalitatea Răului, O Istorie a Securităţii în documente* (Iasi: Polirom, 2002), Dennis Deletant, *România sub Regimul Comunist* (Bucureşti: Fundaţia Academia Civică, 2010).

30. In Romanian, Secţia de Anchete Penale.

31. During the 1960s, the Criminal Investigation Division of the Ministry of Internal Affairs and, as such, its agents held military ranks.

32. This information comes from Ms. Gina Radu, an investigator with the Bucharest Police (known as Militia during the communist regime) and a 2013–2014 researcher with "The Institute for the Investigation of Communist Crimes and the Memory of the Romanian Exile" (www.iiccmer.ro). The notes and letters relevant to this professional meeting are in the author's possession.

33. These so-called specialists had never held official positions in the MCE (ACNSAS, P179/V32/p.1). Their personal files could not be found at CNSAS Archive.

34. It is very likely that those named financial experts in these committees had their own files at Securitate. CNSAS identified Horia Mihai as Constantin Dobrescu, who acted as the financial expert in some of the financial audits, ACNSAS, I257122.

35. For the RE trials, the financial assessments can be found at ACNSAS, P179/ Vol 32 and Vol 28.

36. CP-1960, Book II "Crimes and Felonies in particular," Title I, "Crimes and Felonies against the State," Chapter II "Crimes and Felonies against the Domestic Security," Art. 209, Section I bis, "The Undermining of the National Economy and the and counter-revolutionary sabotage."

37. ACNSAS, P8004/Vol 3/p.1.

38. ACNSAS, P179/Vol 4/p.274.

39. CPP-1960, Book II "Criminal Surveillance and Arraignment," Title I "Criminal Surveillance," Chapter IV "Preparing the criminal surveillance documents," Section II" Accusation," Art.248superscript[1]–248superscript[12].

40. In Romanian Law, the document concluding the investigation and initiating the criminal trial is called "Rechizitoriu" (Indictment Conclusions).

41. CPP-1960, Book II "Criminal Surveillance and Arraignment," Title II "Arraignment," Chapter I "Arraignment by a Prosecutor, Art. 269.

42. CPP-1960, Book II "Criminal Surveillance and Arraignment," Title I "Criminal Surveillance," Chapter IV "Preparation of the criminal surveillance documents," Section VI "The Presentation of the Criminal Surveillance Documents," Art. 264(1)–264(6).

43. Some of these processes were shared with the author by the defendants themselves or by their family members. Additional details were found in their files and the primary documents included there.

44. Tudorel Butoi, *Psihologie Judiciară* (Bucureşti : TREI, 2012), henceforth Butoi, *Psihologie*.

45. Ibid., 192.

46. Butoi *Psihologie*, 192.

47. *Anchetele Securitatii*, 12.

48. Nicolae Dumitrescu, who was in charge of the Criminal Department of the Ministry of Internal Affairs during the 1960s, held a military rank superior to the investigators involved in the economic trials.

49. In Romanian, "Proces Verbal de Interogatoriu," henceforth PVI.

50. ACNSAS, P179/Vol 2/pp.258–259. In these pages, Adalbert Rosinger revisits the statement he made on March 30, 1962. Additional information could be found at ACNSAS, I257122/Vol 1/p.136. Another document is a letter written by Geza Kornis (1917–2019) on October 27, 2007. The letter details a conversation Kornis had with Rado Alexandru, one of the accused in RE trial, upon his release from prison. Rado confessed that some of his statements during the interrogations were coerced.

51. In Romanian, "semnatura indescifrabila."

52. The Securitate called those spying on their cellmates "cell agents."

53. *Anchetele Securitatii*, 17.

54. Those who were close to the defendants and were summoned by the prosecution as witnesses could not refuse to do so. The author received this information during an August 24, 2010, conversation in Dusseldorf with the late Gheorghe (Gyuri) Leuchter. He was one of the last remaining witnesses of the investigations.

55. CPP-1960, Book I "General Procedures," Title V "The Parties, the Prosecutors, and the Defenders," Chapter V "The Prosecutors and the Defenders," Art. 76, para. 1.

56. A letter issued by the Ministry of Justice to the bar association asked the organization to appoint several lawyers in the RE defendants. The letter was dated May 12, 1964, and the trial was scheduled for June 9 of the same year, so the defense had less than one month to prepare for court, ACNSAS, P179/Vol.34/p.5.

57. Article 209^1 is part of Section I bis and refers to the undermining of the national economy.

58. Articles 209(1) and 209(2) mentioned various infractions of plotting against the social order of the state.

59. CPP-1960, Book I "General Procedures," Title II "Competence," Chapter I "Specialized Competence," Section IV "The Competence of the Military Courts."

60. Information relating to the Military Courts can be found in one of Ms. Gina Radu's letters, with whom the author corresponded between 2012 and 2013. Ms Radu worked both for the Bucharest police and IICCMER (www.iiccmer.ro).

61. Law no. 33 was issued on February 26, 1948, to alter some of the regulations pertaining to the Code of Military Justice.

62. DGSP order nr. 100, issued on April 3, 1950 (General Directorate for the People's Security, "Directia Generala a Securitatii Poporului." Its meaning was explained in chapter 1.

63. The Continental Law is actually called in English Civil Law and stands against the Common Law system used mostly in Anglo-Saxon countries. However, the main definitory features of this system is the fact it takes its origin from the Roman system of Law and continues with the Napoleonic/French one, being also implemented in Romanian Law.

64. The inquisitorial system is a legal system in which the court, or judicial clerks, play an active part in determining the events and facts deemed relevant in the case presented before the court. The opposite method is the adversarial system in which

the judge has a passive role, while the prosecutor/State in Criminal Law and defendant make their claims in front of a jury whose members are people without a legal education. See also appendix I.

65. The names and ranks of the members of the Military Court for the RE trial, in appendix VI. Even though the documents started with the phrase "The members of the Military Court of the Bucharest Region met in a public session to discuss issues pertaining to," none of the court sessions were really public and took place behind closed doors. Andreescu, *Minorităţi etnoculturale*, 605 (item # 20).

66. In Romanian, "Incheierea."

67. In Romanian, "Minuta."

68. In Romanian, "Sentinta."

69. In case RE, after the sentence was pronounced on July 4, 1964, the appeal decision was granted much later, in January 1965.

70. A famous, maximum security American prison, in Ossining, 50 kilometers north of New York City. Adalbert Rosinger compared the Romanian prison to its American counterpart in his memoirs, chapter XXVIII.

71. The details that follow refer to the events that took place during the 1960s at Aiud and during the late part of the 1950s at Jilava. These prisons treated their prisoners less harshly than the communist prisons at the beginning of its "reign."

72. Jilava prison was built in a village near Bucharest on the site of a fortress built by King Carol to defend the capital city. During the communist regime, the prison served as a stopover point in the selection and detention of prisoners before they were distributed to other prisons in Romania.

73. Romulus Rusan, "The Topology of Terror," in *Centrul Internaţional de Studii asupra Comunismului out of Memorialul Victimelor Comunismului şi al Rezistenţei* (Bucureşti: Fundaţia Academia Civică, 2011), https://www.memorial-sighe.ro/bucuresti-topografia-terorii-2/, Accessed July 12, 2021.

74. Valentin Saxone, *Speranţe în întuneric* (Bucureşti: Viitorul Romanesc, 2004), 159–160, henceforth Saxone, *Speranţe în întuneric*.

75. Saxone, Speranţe în întuneric, 223.

76. Ibid., 159–160.

77. Ibid., 185–189. The term comes from the word "turtă," which refers to a variety of sweet bread. It is an ironic name as the variation given to the prisoners was made on corn flour and water and had minimal nutritional value.

78. The Aiud prison was founded in the eighteenth century and remains functional to present day. During the communist regime (1945–1989), it was known as the "intellectuals' prison." Accessed November 7, 2020. http://asapteadimensiune.ro/analiza-dictaturii-comuniste-xlix.html

79. The dimensions of the cells varied by locations. According to George Carazza, who was imprisoned at Aiud in the 1950s, the dimensions of his cell were a mere 4 × 2 meters (about 12 × 6 feet). Sometimes the cells were a bit larger and there was a correlation between their size and the number of prisoners therein. Aiud cetatea mortii (in English, Aiud the City of Death). Accessed November 7, 2020. http://www.fericiticeiprigoniti.net/aiud/724-zarca-mariei-tereza.

80. During the twentieth century, Transnistria was a much-contended territory. After it was appropriated by Nazi Germany during the World War II, it became home to a series of work camps for the Jews from Bukovina, Bessarabia, and the Romanian portion of Moldova who were displaced by the Ion Antonescu regime. The deportations of the Jewish populations to Transnistria took place on September 15, 1941, and, with some breaks, continued until the fall of 1942. Most of the work camps held communist sympathizers and Jews. As opposed to the work camps ruled by the Nazis, when the Romanian controlled them, there were no mass murders and the detainees were not to be killed there. Yet, those arriving from Romania lacked proper lodging, food, medical supplies, and adequate hygienic conditions.

81. Rosinger, *Cartea neagră,* chapter, XXVII, 23.

82. ACNSAS, I257122/pp136–152.

Chapter 5

The First Economic Trials

The first Foreign Trade economic trials took place during the years 1960–1964. The accused were officials holding positions of responsibility in 4 of the more than 20 import-export enterprises, existing at that time, as part of the MCE. These trials have never been investigated so far, and no case study of any of the trials has been published to date, more than a quarter of a century after the fall of the Iron Curtain.

The accusations against the foreign trade defendants were economic in nature. However, the Romanian Criminal Code law articles in force, CP-1960, on the basis of which they were convicted, referred to crimes against the internal or sometimes external security of the state, that means charges of political crimes.[1]

Allegations of this type of crime[2] were among the harshest forms of repression introduced by Romania's communist regime in order to enhance its political power. The Criminal Code of 1960, in force during the Foreign Trade trials, represented a continuation[3] of the previous criminal codes, with the harshness of some clauses even more extreme.

The fact that these trials were staged trials, and also their political-economic characteristics, as proven by the sentences passed on their defendants, makes them uniquely specific to the sociopolitical context of Eastern European countries, a few years before Gheorghiu-Dej rule over Romanian came to its end following his death in (1965). The inclusion of Foreign Trade economic trials in the political trials category followed the Securitate's intention of proving how closely linked the economic and the political contexts were in the Romanian society, an intention that fully satisfied the party's policy guidelines. Ties between the Securitate and the Romanian Workers' Party were mainly established as hierarchical ones, but as it will be seen further, the members of the Securitate extended their influence over some of the political party leaders. Gheorghe Gheorghiu-Dej, the party secretary, together with his "right hand," Alexandru Drăghici, the head of the Securitate, were at the top of the government's hierarchy in terms of their control over the country's citizens. The close collaboration between the party and the Securitate was legitimized by the Romanian Criminal Law through its criminal legislation.

The first five out of the six economic trials that took place during the years 1960–1964 will be further analyzed, whereas the sixth trial will be analyzed separately in the next chapter, as the case study of this book.

The trials will be presented in chronological order of their development and partially following the structure of the criminal procedure, described in chapter 4. The trials will be referred to by the shortened name of each enterprise: Cartimex (CA), Prodexport (3 trials, PE1–PE3), Agroexport (AE), and the last one, Românoexport (RE) trial.

As a complete analysis of each one of the trials, except the RE case study, was beyond the scope of this book, the pattern described in detail in chapter 4 will be used as the theoretical mold to be filled in with as many elements as possible, characterizing the trials, derived from the extensive documentation. Every trial described further in this chapter will be analyzed using that mold, whose outline contains the procedures used by the Securitate in surveillance, arrest, and arraignment, in order to achieve its final goal, the conviction of the defendants.

The witch-hunt of Foreign Trade employees began in 1958,[4] but the action initiated then was completed only in 1960, with the arrest of Octav Botnar, manager of CA. Four years later, in 1964, the sixth and last trial of this series, the RE trial, would begin. The investigation in the first trial, the CA one, lasted one year, while the investigation in the RE trial lasted three years, which proves there were significant differences between processes, such as the different number of contracts involved, the way the investigations were conducted, the Securitate's ability to obtain evidence in each case or the way the Military Court handled the sentences of the defendants. Despite the existing differences, all the trials had as a common denominator the fact that they were judged at the Bucharest Regional Military Court, and that the defendants' convictions were based mainly on the same articles of law, namely undermining the national economy and plotting against the social order of the country.

CARTIMEX—CA TRIAL

CA[5] was the first foreign trade company whose general manager, Octav Botnar, of Jewish ethnicity, was involved in an economic trial. During the period of time referred to in the CA trial, CA specialized in the export of decorative items and handicrafts together with the export of newspapers, magazines, and books. Another main activity of CA was the export of carpets from Romania to Western European countries.

CA transferred the requests of foreign buyers to Romanian companies producing carpets for export and then performed their quality control by using verification methods in accordance with the standards of foreign partners. If the goods did not meet the requirements, the product was returned to the manufacturer. The quality control was rigorous in accordance with the demands of the world market. More than once this rigor caused the revolt of Romanian producers, who claimed that the percentage of disqualified and returned carpets established by CA was too high. If the product passed the quality control imposed by CA, it was sent abroad, to the carpet agent who was to present it to the buyer. Octav Botnar and Ioan Pantazescu were among the officials of the company who dealt with the export of oriental carpets.

At that time, Romania was not among the countries exporting oriental carpets to the West. Romania, which had begun production of Persian carpets only in 1954–1955, did not dare to enter the existing competition on the European market, beside the Soviet Union or Iran. At first, the carpets were of inferior quality in terms of dyeing, weaving method, and lack of homogeneity. The length of the wool threads was uneven, and so the uneven ends of the threads were visible at the edge of the carpet. These production defects began to diminish until they disappeared, following the export contract with the company Atico, owned by the Iranian carpet trader Ayatollah Atigeschi, from Hamburg. The basis for the CA officials' convictions was the sale of Romanian carpets to the Iranian trader Atigeschi.

Preliminary Stages

The warrant for initiating the CA criminal trial[6] included, in addition to Octav Botnar, five other suspects. Two of them went through an investigation, but were released following its conclusions. The three remaining defendants of the trial were:

- Octav Botnar was general manager at CA.
- Ioan Pantazescu, an expert in the science of commodities, was arrested for his involvement in some of CA's commercial contracts, as well as for having close ties to Botnar.
- Eugen Virgil Perianu was an officer with the rank of captain[7] at the Ministry of Internal Affairs. Perianu was not a CA employee. His arrest was due only to his family relationship to Botnar, as his brother-in-law.

The Surveillance

The Securitate started the surveillance of Octav Botnar on March 21, 1959. Seven months later, it opened a surveillance file.[8] There has been no information available concerning the other defendants, Pantazescu and Perianu, despite repeated requests I have addressed to CNSAS.

From the Initiation of the Criminal Procedure to the Appearance before the Court

The Arrest

The three defendants of the CA trial were arrested on the same day, April 26, 1960, based on an arrest warrant issued by the Securitate.[9]

The Investigation

Octav Botnar's investigation started as soon as he was arrested and continued until September 3, 1960, when Captain Stefan Nedelcu, a Securitate investigator, handed him the Indictment Warrant.[10]

After reading this document, Botnar addressed the Investigation Body and requested that additional documents be made available to him to aid him in proving his innocence by describing his contribution to the development of CA. The whole investigation was led by Captain Stefan Nedelcu. In his opposition to the accusations, Botnar stated that over the years a person inside the company was used as a Securitate informant, providing data about his work, partly true and partly falsified. This activity was used to incriminate him, whereas, in the absence of those pieces of information, the investigation would have lacked accusatory data. During the investigation, some other evidence was brought against Botnar, associating him with the Ioanid[11] brothers' activity.

Although the actions of the Ioanid group are beyond the scope of this work, it is very possible that the anti-Jewish atmosphere may have become even more pervasive, as a result of the events related to this group consisting exclusively of Jews. In fact, Pantazescu's connection with some members of the Ioanid group was one of the reasons for his arrest.

Perianu's investigation also started on April 26, 1960, soon after his arrest, and continued until August 20, 1960, when Captain Stefan Nedelcu handed him the Indictment Warrant.[12]

Pantazescu's investigation started on April 26, 1960, as soon as he was arrested and continued until January 10, 1961, when Captain Gheorghe Puscoi, another Securitate investigator, handed him the Indictment Warrant.[13]

It should be noted that although Pantazescu's initial accusation was the disclosure of state secrets (Art. 506 of the CP-1960), later, following his investigation, the Indictment Conclusions also charged him with plotting against the social order of the state (Art. 209 (2a) of CP-1960).

Following the investigation, which included arranged confrontations of the defendants with each other and with some of the prosecution's witnesses, the Securitate established the conclusive materials for the prosecution. These were presented to each of the defendants toward the end of the investigation, together with the delivery of the final form of Indictment Conclusions. Upon receipt of the indictment findings and the investigative materials, the defendants were given the opportunity to express their views in writing.

As a general feature of all the trial investigations, both in the CA trial and in the following ones as well, it will be observed that the Securitate investigators consistently used all possible means to intimidate and frighten each individual, vehemently questioning the plausibility of their statements. This behavior was repeated whenever the answers of the accused did not correspond to the "facts" claimed by the investigators to represent the actual course of events. For example, when the anti-revolutionary activity attributed to Botnar was cited, his categorical and prompt refusal to accept the accusations led the investigator to chastise him, telling him: "you are dishonest." From there, he was only a step away from frightening Botnar by accusing him of outright lying.

This attitude was consistently adopted in all the investigations and the phrase "you are dishonest," was the transcript written in lieu of the much harsher words that were addressed to the victim—violent, aggressive, and threatening words. It was a euphemism used by the transcribers of the PVI[14] themselves (usually the investigators) in order to hide verbal violence directed at the defendants. These threats often extended to the families. The violent language was accompanied by blows. The defendants were beaten with a rubber cane and other instruments and kicked by the boot-clad investigators, who targeted sensitive parts of their bodies. Thus, the defendants were intimidated, sometimes easily, and the investigators were able to get the responses they wanted.[15]

Witnesses

A feature that characterized all the foreign trade trials was the fact that there were only witnesses for to the prosecution. Witnesses for the defense were not accepted, and even requests by defendants or by their lawyers to summon witnesses who, through their testimonies, might have reduced the gravity of the accusations were rejected. Despite this, and in the total absence of defense witnesses, a nearly unique event took place during the CA trial, and recurred only once more, in one of the later convictions.[16] Some witnesses, even unwillingly, supported Octav Botnar's claim of innocence, as well as his personal merit in concluding the first contract for the export of carpets in Romania. This led to the dropping of one of the original charges, which the Securitate was finally forced to remove from Botnar's indictment.

Formulation of the Indictment Conclusions

The Indictment Conclusions in the CA trial were issued by Captain Stefan Nedelcu, on January 25, 1961.[17]

- Octav Botnar was charged with the crime of plotting against the constitutional social order of the RPR (Art. 209 (2a) of the CP-1960), while the initial accusations were those of espionage by the disclosure of classified documents or state secrets (Art. 194^2 of CP-1960) and undermining the national economy (Article 209^1 of CP-1960). The change in the charges against Botnar between the issue of the Indictment Conclusions and the final formulation of his accusation was an extraordinary occurrence in the economic trials of the Foreign Trade.
- Eugen Virgil Perianu was charged with the crime of disclosing secrets (Art. 506 of the CP-1960).
- Ioan Pantazescu was charged with the crime of conspiracy against the constitutional and social order of the RPR (Art. 209 (2a) of the CP-1960).

The other two initial defendants, Alexandru Isoveanu and Dumitru Arsene, were acquitted following the investigation but were demoted from their positions.

Before the Military Court

The Sentence

On May 23, 1961, five months after the presentation of the Indictment Conclusions, the criminal trial began at the Military Court of the Bucharest Region. On May 25, 1961, Sentence no.129/161 was handed down by the same Military Court. The prosecutor agreed with the Indictment Conclusions as presented by the Securitate investigator, as well as with his legal classification of the defendants' crimes. This full agreement and direct and indisputable support of the decisions of the investigative body, represented by the Securitate, was characteristic not only of CA but of the whole series of Foreign Trade trials.

- Octav Botnar was charged with the felony of plotting against the state social order and sentenced to seven years of correctional imprisonment, the total confiscation of his property and the suspension of his civil rights for four years.[18]
- Eugen Virgil Perianu was sentenced to three years of correctional prison.
- Ioan Pantazescu was sentenced to five years of correctional imprisonment, the total confiscation of his property and the suspension of his civil rights for three years.

The Appeal

On June 28, 1961, Decision no. 8/1961 of the Supreme Court of the Romanian People's Republic was handed down, regarding the appeal in the CA trial. The decision was to leave the sentence unchanged both in the prison term and civic degradation. Botnar was released from prison after about four years on July 29, 1964.

About the Background and the Allegations of the Cartimex Trial

In the Warrant for Initiating the Criminal Procedure against Octav Botnar and others, there was a note regarding the contracts concluded by Botnar, for the sale of Romanian goods to capitalist companies in Western Europe.

According to this, Botnar caused damage to the national economy by disregarding the legal norms for concluding contracts, among which are the following:

- Failure to take into account the terms and prices achieved by other socialist states in contracting the sales of similar products (e.g., a comparison between Romanian prices for the sale of carpets on the Western market, in relation to the prices requested by other states)
- The way in which certain markets were chosen for sales contracts or the preferential choice of some companies over others (as derived from the testimonies of some prosecution witnesses)

At that time, it was known that Romania had failed to conclude any long-term contract for the sale of carpets on advantageous terms with any Western European company.

In 1957–1958, after a long period of failures in the export of Romanian carpets, CA, after a thorough prospecting of foreign markets, managed to initiate an export operation in the West, through the Iranian agent, Ayatolah Atigeschi, owner of the Atico Carpet Company in Hamburg, West Germany.

Atigeschi undertook the selling of Romanian carpets to agents and carpet sellers in the West and signed a contract with Botnar.

The suspicions cited by the Securitate against Botnar during his arrest and investigation were rejected by him on the basis of the failure of any other Romanian efforts before 1958 to export carpets to Western markets, and based on the fact that Atigeschi was the first and only foreign trader who agreed to undertake the sale of the carpets in the West, as a long-term arrangement. He was seriously committed to serving an important purpose for the Romanian foreign trade. In addition, Atigeschi showed his good intentions by promising to send specialists to Romania to help improve the Romanian carpets' quality.

Regarding the price set in the contract, it is true that both the prosecution and some witnesses showed that the sale prices were lower than the prices of other Eastern European countries, but the Atico-CA contract lasted for a long time and sales were in much higher quantities than those of Romania's neighboring countries. Thus, a consequence of the success of signing this contract (and not of its failure, as the accusation tried to prove) was the continuity of the export of carpets through the same company from Hamburg.

In addition, the contract signed by Botnar was not made and signed by him, as an individual, but rather it was seen, discussed, and approved by the relevant directorate of the MCE.[19] The corresponding directorate of the MCE had also approved the future export contracts for Atigeschi, which included an exclusivity clause regarding carpet sales, a contractual advantage common to many foreign agents who undertook to sell Romanian products on Western markets.[20]

CA Trail Conclusions

The contract between CA and Atico was, just a few years after its signing, the basis for the conviction in the CA trial, and the main defendant was the manager of the enterprise, who denied the first charges made against him during his arrest and investigation. The investigation tried to invoke the conditions of the contract concluded with Atico as an expression of his lack of good faith toward the company and the country, to which was added the accusation of lack of responsibility in his activity, which together would have undermined the economic interests of the Romanian state.

The knowledge and information possessed by Octav Botnar characterized the attitudes and discussions he held at work. They came from the contacts he used to maintain with foreigners, and from written media or the radio stations he listened to. At that time, such information was not made available to the general public in Romania. Knowledge of foreign languages and possession of a wider general culture gave Botnar a broader vision whose origins date back to his stay in France as a fighter of the Resistance during World War II in the Maquis.[21]

During his career, Botnar often had discussions with colleagues in the company about issues related to the essence of their joint work. Some of Botnar's statements were considered insults to Communist Romania. Therefore, together with Pantazescu, Botnar was accused of participating in the organization of a plot to undermine the social order in Romania. This accusation was based on two things—first, slander of the homeland and the existing sociopolitical order, and second, his connection with the Ioanid gang, the group with which the two defendants had maintained social relations around that time. His statements were seen as a critical approach to the regime, and therefore a threat to it.

As we have shown earlier, there were two cases in which the accusations made by the Securitate in the Indictment Conclusions were later dropped in the sentence issued by the Military Court. One was Octav Botnar's case, explained earlier, and the second was Samy Edelstein's case, which will be detailed in the analysis of the AE trial.

The reasons for canceling some charges in the CA process were determined by the limited scope of exports made by CA abroad and the relatively short period in which Botnar served as manager of the company, and last, but probably not least, as we have mentioned earlier, there were indirect testimonies in favor of the activity carried out by Botnar. It is noteworthy that there were some witnesses in the first Foreign Trade trial who could not be completely manipulated by the Securitate. They managed to sketch a positive image of Botnar's work, pointing out that after the company's multiple failures, he was the one who almost single-handedly contributed to improving the quality of carpets for export, thus opening the way for Romania to export oriental carpets to Western countries.

Although some of the initial charges against Botnar were removed from the final sentence, Botnar was not acquitted but was charged with conspiracy against the social order of the state. The allegation of plotting against the social order, as a leitmotif against senior Foreign Trade officials, has not only characterized the defendants in the CA trial but reappeared in each of the six trials discussed. In the case of Foreign Trade officials, the purpose of the Securitate was to refute their good faith and at the same time their devotion, especially as Jews, to the state. I must point out that the "labeling" of Jewish Foreign Trade officials, which had its roots in the Working Meeting of the MCE Workers in October 1958, was also mentioned by Botnar when he appeared in court.[22]

The Securitate's argument was that these high-ranking officials, in the context of their functions, would have turned into criminals who intended to act against their own country. This argument, regardless of whether it refers to the sale of carpets (CA), agricultural products (AE), oil, sugar and meat products (PE), or building materials and textiles (RE), is a recurring theme in the development of all six lawsuits.

PRODEXPORT TRIALS

Between 1961and 1963, three trials took place in which Jewish officials of the PE enterprise were involved. In the first PE trial,[23] PE-1, among its 14 defendants, the Jewish citizens charged were of two categories:

- seven Jewish officials who held senior positions in PE
- seven other Jewish citizens who did not hold positions in the enterprise, but maintained family ties, or other friendly relations with its officials

The defendants in the later trials, PE-2 and PE-3, were two women, both senior officials of the enterprise, while in the PE-2 trial, the general manager of the company, Pavel Donath, who had already been convicted in the PE-1 trial, was also involved, alongside the woman defendant. While in the first lawsuit, most of the incriminating contracts were those in which meat products were sold to Western companies, the last two lawsuits focused on sales and purchases of other products marketed by PE, such as oil, sugar, feathers, and eggs.

The First Prodexport Trial (PE-1)

PE[24] was one of the foreign trade enterprises within the MCE dealing in food products. Romania's exports to the Western market in terms of meat (pork, beef, poultry) and fresh or processed internal organs had begun to develop in the early 1950s. The incriminating contracts in the PE-1 trial were mostly contracts with agents working for either Italian or French companies, employing either the barter or the clearing system of compensation for meat export transactions.[25]

From the testimonies of both the defendants and the prosecution witnesses, it arises that meat export was hampered by Romania's economic situation at that time and the consequent lack of proper means of refrigeration and of optimal transport conditions. To this was added the reluctance of foreign governments to grant local companies licenses to import meat products from Romania.

During the PE-1 trial, a large number of people in senior positions in the enterprise were arrested, one after the other, as well as some who were not PE employees, but only related to them through personal connections. However, knowledge of this trial did not go far and was confined to only those employed in the field of foreign trade and their families. The Jewish defendants, whether they were senior officials of the enterprise, as were those accused in the PE-1 trial, those accused in the PE-2 and PE-3 trials a year later, or the defendants in the subsequent trials (AE and RE), were all subjected to nearly impossible situations.

Many of the contracts or agreements they had made with the sales or buying agents of foreign companies included commissions paid to these agents and decisions that had been established, more than once, through talks based on personal relationships. These people held various trade relations with some of the agents they had known from the past, especially during the interwar period. They might have worked together and consequently established mutual trust. The encouragement and maintenance of such economic links often required offering the foreign agents exclusivity in certain markets and increasing their commissions for achieving the execution and promotion of the trade between the Romanian state and that country they represented. These were established conventions in international trade, and it was natural to abide by them, especially in the early times when Communist Romania's foreign trade with the West was just beginning. These methods soon became a handicap for the company's employees. After a decade of playing a key role in the bilateral relations established with Western European countries, they had been accused, among other things, of following these common practices of international commerce.

In the early 1960s, it came about that Jewish Foreign Trade officials were sidelined. How did this change of position take place?[26] At that time, young Romanian people graduated from the Bucharest Academy of Economic Sciences in the Foreign Trade Department, and of course many of them entered positions in Foreign Trade enterprises, and even some senior positions. The Romanian administration, under the influence of the party's plenary sessions, especially the one held in October 1958 with the staff of the MCE, also made its mark on the decision to remove as many Jews as possible, in order to create vacancies for future graduates. Accused of lack of patriotism (some of them had expressed their intention to emigrate to Israel) and of pursuing personal interests to the detriment of the Romanian state, Jewish Foreign Trade officials, within a few years, became the target of Stalinist-like trials, at a time when such trials had already descended from the stage of history. In this way, all the Romanian Foreign Trade economic trials can be considered an anachronistic remnant of the trials that characterized the Stalinist period.

Preliminary Stages

The Warrant for Initiating the PE-1 trial[27] was issued by Lieutenant Iosif Bistran, a Securitate criminal investigator,[28] on March 15, 1960, in the Criminal Investigation Section of the Ministry of Internal Affairs. The arrest warrant was issued against Viorica Vrânceanu, one of the main PE-1 defendants and later against other officials of PE. Vrânceanu's arrest warrant was based on Art. 194^2 and 194^3 with 194^4, articles of Criminal Law, referring to betrayal of the homeland.

The Surveillance

As indicated earlier, surveillance files[29] were opened for all officials who had been employed in foreign trade enterprises, but especially for those slated for indictment. It was not possible to obtain the personal information files of all the defendants in the PE-1 trial from CNSAS, which does not mean, of course, that they did not exist. The opening of surveillance files for the main defendants in PE-1 is supposed to be dated as usual, in the years 1958–1959, but during the extensive investigation at CNSAS, most of them were impossible to locate. I only found some information concerning Milea Wulich,[30] but her surveillance file was different. A file in her name was opened through the Foreign Intelligence Service[31] and transferred to microfiche. The pre-surveillance files were switched to a surveillance file as soon as the person became a potential candidate for indictment.[32]

The main defendant of the PE-1 trial was Pavel Donath. There was only a single surveillance file[33] found in CNSAS, that had been opened for him, but it was dated after 1968, the year of his release from prison and his employment at the Federation of Jewish Communities under the leadership of Rabbi Moses Rozen, the chief rabbi of Romania at the time. It is impossible to believe that there was no previous surveillance file in Donath's case, given his involvement as a leading figure and defendant, in both the PE-1 and the PE-2 trials.

Viorica Vrânceanu's surveillance was done indirectly, through the opening of a surveillance file for Regis Chomienne.[34] This happened in November 1959 when Chomienne was the sales agent of the French Collectorgane Company. Chomienne was an intermediary in one of the main PE activities, the commercial sales of meat to various companies in France and later in Italy.

The surveillance file[35] for Micu Suzin and Alfred Schwartz was conceived as a joint one.

No other surveillance files for the main defendants were found.

From the Opening of the Criminal Procedure to the Appearance before the Court

The Arrest

Cited on the Indictment Warrant of Viorica Vrânceanu, the first PE-1 trial defendant to be arrested, as the reason for both hers and the others' indictment, was an article of CP-1960, that would later become part of the final charge, the undermining of the national economy, Art. 209^1 (CP-1960). The arrests of the 14 people accused in the PE-1 trial were carried out gradually between March 1960 and June 1961.[36]

The following list represents the names of the people involved in the PE-1 trial. There were fourteen persons, seven of them employed by the company, the others connected to them through family or social relations. Here are the main people and the positions they held:

- *Pavel Donath*, Prodexport manager.
- *Milea Wulich*, economist, previously the director of export within the MCE. At the time of her arrest, she was working in a Bucharest department store, where she had been transferred after her dismissal from foreign trade in 1958.
- *Micu Mordechai Suzin*, economist, and consultant at PE.
- *Alfred Schwartz*, lawyer, chief of the meat export department at PE until 1957.
- *Viorica Vrânceanu*, chemical and textile engineer, head of the meat export department at the PE Enterprise from 1957, after Schwartz's departure.
- *Radu Simion*, former consultant at PE, retired at the time of his arrest.
- *Csendes Andrei*, PE commercial manager, who passed away during the investigation.

The other PE-1 trial defendants did not work for PE and ultimately received sentences of five to eight years for their personal connections to the accused. Their charges were mainly related to foreign currency exchange matters. Here are their names and connections:

Andrei Ascher, chemical engineer, related to Alfred Schwartz, Silvia Simon, Viorica Vrânceanu's sister, Veronica Suzin, Micu Suzin' wife, Jacques Marcus, Milea Wulich's husband, Baruch Morgenstern, Ernestina Rusu, and Misu Cristescu, all related to Alfred Schwartz.

The Investigation

The duration of the PE-1 trial investigation was relatively short, considering the large number of defendants and the amount of time other investigations required. The investigation began with Vrânceanu's arrest on March 16, 1960, 11 months before the arrest of the PE manager, Pavel Donath, on February 25, 1961, and ended on July 27, 1961, 1 year and 4 months later.[37]

The investigations in the PE trials, especially that of the PE-1 trial, showed almost no strong objections made by any of its defendants in order to deny the charges made against them.

The draconian system of investigation and the pressures PE officials were subjected to drove them to nearly complete confessions and made them agree, with very little opposition, with the accusations leveled against them.

The real conditions to which the prisoners in the Securitate's cellars were subjected, in order to force them to acknowledge the accusations as fact and incriminate themselves were published more than once in the Romanian specialized literature of recent years.[38] In support of the aforementioned assumption, I'll refer to some incidents that characterized part of the investigations. For instance, among the unusual events found in the PE-1 files were Donath's later attempts to prove his innocence.[39] During the investigation (1961), Donath was forced to accept the statement made against him (under pressure from the Securitate, as would be seen seven years later) by one of the witnesses, named Gheorghe Ardeleanu. Ardeleanu claimed that Donath was a Siguranţă[40] collaborator in the interwar period, while living in the city of Arad.[41] During the investigation, Donath agreed to sign a declaration accepting this accusation, which led to one more charge being added to his conviction. Seven years later, during his detention in Aiud, a short time before his release, Donath sent a memorandum to the Romanian Supreme Court in order to partly prove his innocence.[42] In order to advance his request, Donath revealed facts that were part of his 1961 investigation at Malmaison. They are quoted here:

> Ardeleanu was brought to Bucharest—I presume under arrest—there was a confrontation with me in the office in the presence of Colonel Dumitrescu,[43] Captain Bistran and one more person. What Ardeleanu said at the beginning of the confrontation was totally unfamiliar to me because it wasn't true. Then I signed.[44]
>
> None of Ardeleanu Gheorghe's statements are true, everything is fabricated, and adhering to his first declaration during my investigation and even intensifying his initial statements during the confrontation, was justified from his point of view considering his false claims of being employed by the police.

In the aforementioned testimony made by Donath in 1968, the year in which he submitted his request for the reversal of his conviction, he claims that the statements he made during the investigation were false, and that he had been forced to confirm Ardeleanu's false testimony. The example of such a testimony, later denied, demonstrates Donath's state of mind under the well-known conditions of the investigation, and why he failed to support his claim of innocence. From the description of this event, it can be deduced that Donath was not the only defendant obliged to sign a false confession under the conditions of the investigation, and yet it is not easy to find primary documents to prove this. We have no way of proving how many and what other statements were signed by the defendants in the economic proceedings under the harsh conditions of the investigations, whether they were coerced, dictated by the investigator, or the defendants, compromised by the circumstances, agreed to sign any document. Donath's memorandum included the next paragraph as well:

> I have never been an informant of the Siguranţă, and do not judge me for the fact that I accepted this charge before the court, which convicted me, - the fact that statements from the Investigation were signed does not mean that they correspond to the truth, but that they are due to the conditions in which the Investigation was carried out. They are well known to the Investigation Body.[45]

Although found at a later time among the pages of the P7955 file, the information regarding this incident does not explain why Donath did not request the annulment of the other charges of which he was convicted when he filed the application. The event took place seven years after the final decision of the Appeal, following the PE trial sentencing and almost a year before Donath's release. (It is very likely that at the time of the application, Donath was not aware of the date of his upcoming release.)[46] His request was first rejected by the Bucharest Regional Military Court on February 28, 1969. Later, after his release in January 1969, Donath addressed the Supreme Court again, this time requesting a reconsideration of the decision, or an appeal. This time, the Supreme Court accepted this new request for an appeal that was issued by Decision no. 79 on May 10, 1969.[47]

Another outstanding case of PE-1's defendants' investigation was that of Milea Wulich. Wulich's testimonies hinted at a special phenomenon that accompanied not only her testimony but others as well. It happened that after a period of time in which they claimed their innocence (in Wulich's case for a period of six months), most of the defendants changed their position quite suddenly, accepting almost all the charges from that moment on.

Wulich acknowledged that as a child she had lived in Bessarabia under difficult conditions of deprivation and humiliation and often suffered from anti-Semitic attacks, a situation that contributed to her later adoption of Zionism, which was certainly unacceptable to the communist regime.

The stories told by Wulich were documented in countless pages signed by Anca Ionescu, her cellmate from Malmaison. Asked by the Securitate investigators, the prisoner Anca Ionescu offered them various intimate and personal episodes that Wulich spoke about in her moments of distress, upon returning from investigation, or during the days spent in the joint detention cell in Malmaison.[48]

Another person whose inquiry raises many questions and concerns was Alfred Schwartz. Schwartz was arrested on June 10, 1960, and a few days later his investigation began. During the first three months of the investigation (until November 1, 1960), he denied all of the charges, boldly, even refusing to accept the testimonies of other defendants supporting the accusations brought against him by the investigators. He even opposed the testimony of his wife, Any Schwartz, and that of his brother-in-law Deutch. Confronting him with documents of the company he worked for did not lead to any change of attitude on his part. Schwartz did not give in to either the verbal or the physical threats to which he was subjected. He did not admit to any of the crimes the Securitate accused him of.

However, after a period of three months, the situation was reversed. From that moment on, Schwartz thoroughly cooperated with the investigators and he confessed to all the allegations. May it be concluded that the physical and psychological pressures he was subjected to, skillfully executed by investigators who specialized in annihilating the strength of resistance of those under investigation, were among the causes of Alfred Schwartz's change of attitude? There is no written evidence, but the testimonies of some people, as well as literature describing the methods used during the Securitate investigations of that period, can suggest an affirmative answer.

Apparently, Schwartz was the most enigmatic figure among the defendants in the PE-1 trial. All the others agreed, sooner or later, to confess to nearly all the accusations, after a period of time in which they were under the Securitate investigators' pressure.

Schwartz's situation was completely unusual, if not unfathomable, in the austere landscape of the PE-1 trial investigations in 1961. This was learned from information received later, after his son, Liviu Schwartz, was located in Brazil.[49] The information found in the investigation file shows that Schwartz's wife, Any Schwartz, was arrested and remained under arrest between July 1, 1960, and October 17, 1960. It should be noted that the date of Schwartz's sudden change of heart was close to November 1, 1960.

During the investigation, Any Schwartz disclosed particularly important information related to the events in which she and her husband, Alfred Schwartz, participated. For example, she reported about clothing packages and sums of money received by the Schwartz family from the Italian agent with whom he had concluded numerous meat export contracts for PE. Some of these contracts were among those under investigation by the financial assessment executed during the investigation. Any Schwartz was released from Securitate custody in a manner that is difficult to explain considering the time the events took place (the 1960s). Soon after, she received a permit to leave the country along with her son Liviu, who was then 15 years old (born in 1945), with their destination being Brazil.[50] Any Schwartz, whose maiden name had been Goldenberg, was born in 1926, was a seamstress by profession, and left Romania two weeks after her release from custody on November 5, 1960, with her son.

What really prompted Alfred Schwartz to change his attitude during the investigation? Was this a means of freeing his family (son and wife) from Romania, with the approval of the Securitate, on the condition that he cooperated and confessed to what the Securitate had alleged during the investigation? The acquisition of a permit for the family of a detainee to emigrate was almost impossible in the political context in which the trials took place. Was this the reason why Schwartz, in a moment of despair mixed with the hope that he would be able to save his family, agreed to sign whatever was put in front of him by the Securitate investigators? Schwartz's change of attitude occurred only after the Securitate granted his family permission to leave Romania.

Either the version to which Schwartz testified in the PE-1 trial was true, or it was obtained after defendant Schwartz could no longer stand the physical conditions to which he was subjected in the custody cell, or perhaps what determined his willingness to accept the testimony was the hope that he could save his family. Any of these versions remains only an assumption that cannot be fully confirmed. However, the events described in the case of Alfred Schwartz and his family remain unique in the context of the trials analyzed here. Such unexpected coincidences, if they can be called that, raise one of the main questions referring to PE-1 trial: Were those accused in the PE-1 trial really guilty?

Witnesses and Testimonies

The only witnesses to participate in the trial were the prosecution witnesses, while the investigative bodies rejected any attempt by the defendants or by their lawyers to bring any favorable evidence to their defense. Thus, any existing legal option for defense was totally canceled, both in the investigation and later in court. The witnesses were sometimes other defendants, or people who had already been convicted and were serving their sentences in prison. Out of weakness or inability to withstand the Securitate's interrogation, or hoping that they would be able to receive better treatment in the future, some witnesses agreed to sign false statements written by the Securitate, denouncing others. Cellmates were often used as witnesses by Securitate investigators during the economic trials. They often tried to persuade the defendants to admit to being guilty, and in this way to collaborate with investigators. Going through the cellmates' reports, whether they were true or made up, one can see how significant their observations were at times for the progress of the investigation, including investigators' notes and recommendations written next to the comments. From this, we understand that through those people, present in the cell, the defendants were under almost constant pursuit during their long stay in Malmaison for the compilation of their investigation file and later the Indictmente Conclusions. It is not possible to verify the testimonies given during the trial or the statements made by witnesses, either free or already convicted.

Formulation of the Indictment Conclusions

The Indictment Conclusions against PE-1 defendants were issued on June 30, 1961, by Iosef Bistran.[51] The defense in the PE-1 trial, like in others as well, was simplistic and superficial. One week before the official opening of the trial,[52] on August 1, 1961, the Tribunal applied to the Bar Association to appoint a defense lawyer for each defendant, if they had not already been specifically appointed in private. The meetings between the lawyer and the defendant lasted not more than one hour.[53]

There is no evidence of longer meetings and according to the criminal records of other trials, this information is true.

Also, the lawyers' pleas are not documented, save for the summary of their presentations written by the court registrar and submitted to the file of the trial.[54]

During the trial, the prosecution stated its findings, as summarized in the Indictment Conclusions.[55]

Before the Military Court

The Sentence

The PE-1 trial opened in the Bucharest Regional Military Court on August 7, 1961, and the sentence was issued on August 19, 1961, as Sentence no. 58/19, August 1961. The main accusations in the PE trial were the undermining of the national economy; betrayal of the homeland; intensive counterrevolutionary activity against the working class; plotting against the social order; and the use of foreign currency for personal purposes, propaganda, and agitation against the regime.

The entire group of defendants was declared an anti-revolutionary bourgeois group of Jewish origin whose purpose was to overthrow the communist regime in Romania.

It is noteworthy that in this trial the prosecutor requested the death penalty for the first five defendants, which was the maximum punishment under the law for the crimes of which they were found guilty. A list of the charges for the main defendants follows:

- *Pavel Donath, Micu Mordehai Suzin, Alfred Schwartz, Viorica Vrânceanu* were found guilty of the following crimes and felonies:
    - The crime of undermining the national economy[56] combined with some mitigating clause.[57]
    - The crime of betrayal of the homeland[58] in accordance with Art. 194^2 (2) combined with Art. 194^4 and Art. 25 (1).[59]
    - The felony of plotting against the social order.[60]

Although the Prosecutor in the PE-1 trial requested the death penalty for the aforementioned charges, the request was denied by the members of the Military Court.

- *Pavel Donath* was found guilty, in addition to the previous accusations, of intense activity against the working class and the revolutionary movement.[61]
- *Milea Wulich* was found guilty, in addition to the previous accusations, of illegal handling (sale, purchase, transfer) of foreign currency, precious or semi-precious metals, or other valuables, in accordance with Art. 268[28a].

For all these crimes they were sentenced to life imprisonment.

The prison terms to which the convicts were sentenced were to be served concurrently. In addition, these five convicts were subject to some additional punishments, which included eight years of civic degradation and confiscation of all their property. The additional penalties would be applied from the date of release, or in the case of a pardon or amnesty, from the date it would go into effect.

The other two defendants, Radu Simion and Andrei Csendes were charged with almost identical charges, but their penalties were lower, because their implication in the company activity was less. However, Csendes was charged in absentia, as he passed away during his investigation, while being held at Malmaison, the Securitate prison.

The defendants who were merely connected with the PE-1 officials were sentenced to between 7 and 12 years of forced labor, as well as between 4 and 5 years of degradation and confiscation of all their property.

During the pronouncement of the Sentence by the president of the Military Court or his deputy, there was reference in the speech to the connection between the economic crimes committed by the accused and the fact that they were all citizens belonging to the Jewish ethnic group. This fact cannot be seen as a simple coincidence, because throughout the investigation and finally even by the judge, the representative of the Romanian law of the time, the defendants, who were all Jews, were considered to be intent upon causing damage to Romania's economic situation, denigrating the country, and in some situations, changing the social order. This approach by the authorities was clearly an unjustified anti-Semitic attitude, considering the long-time dedication of those people to the Romanian Foreign Trade, and the significant role they had played in its inception.

This event recurred during one of the trials that followed the PE one, namely that of the RE officials.[62]

The Appeal and the End of the PE-1 Trial

The agreement of the PE-1 trial convicts to confess to the crimes they were accused of, both during the investigation and before the appearances before the Military Court, was among the most significant achievements the Securitate could have hoped for, as it justified the convictions, allowing the prosecutor to request the death sentence for some of the defendants. Though his request was not accepted by the Military Court, the PE-1 appeal, filed on October 19, 1961, Decision no. 243, did not result in any change in the convictions.

On July 29, 1969, when the defendants in the PE-1 trial, except Donath, had already been released, Sentence no. 58 of August 19, 1961, of the PE-1 trial, together with the Appeal Decision no. 243 of October 19, 1961, was reexamined by the Supreme Court. Following this new appeal, the third charge against Pavel Donath in the aforementioned sentence and appeal was canceled.

Prodexport and Its Contracts with Foreign Agents

Romania's possibilities for the export of raw or processed food products to European countries during the 1950s and 1960s, were quite limited. Milea Wulich addressed this situation on several occasions, presenting the reasons for these difficulties in exporting meat, between 1948 and 1950. The causes were both internal and external. The situation changed gradually, but still it remained only a partly solved problem.[63]

Difficulties Arising from Internal Causes

Both slaughterhouses and meat product factories lacked modern refrigeration facilities for holding the meat during its processing and storage. The lack of compressors in slaughterhouses and factories made the meat production process slow by European standards, and the transport had to be done without refrigerated railroad cars. The quantities needed to meet Romania's export requirements for raw and processed products were difficult to meet, so on-time delivery could not be ensured. Under these conditions, Romania was forced to pass up some of the meat import propositions coming from some Western European states.

Milea Wulich, former director of exports at the MCE, and one of the main defendants in the PE-1 trial, refers during the investigation to the decisions of the time, leading to the purchase of refrigerator cars for transporting meat to the West. This acquisition, initiated by the manager Donath between 1949 and 1950, was criticized by Wulich during the investigation. These cars, which could not really be exploited, were considered in the ministry to be an unnecessary waste of money. They proved to be relevant some years later. Transport was not the only technical difficulty that hindered export from Romania to Western Europe. Because of this, investments were made to upgrade two of the main slaughterhouses in Romania.[64] The work plan called for the commissioning of compressors to operate the cooling systems used in slaughterhouses and meat production plants. Most of the offers were coming from Switzerland. Lacking currency, the Romanians favored businesses that could carry out barter transactions.[65]

Switzerland accepted this kind of trade with Romania, through which Romanian meat was exchanged for Swiss compressors. Thus, the ties between PE and the Swiss company "Frigaliment" began to strengthen, and the Swiss company started issuing letters of guarantee to other Western companies, which were to become the end buyers of the Romanian meat. "Frigaliment" remained an intermediary for the pork, poultry, and live animals exported by Romania.

Difficulties Arising from External Causes

In the early 1950s, the capitalist market showed restraint and a certain lack of confidence in the development of trade with socialist countries, including Romania (RPR).[66] The governments of foreign countries did not readily issue import licenses for any kind of products originating in Romania, including meat and its products.

At the same time, export approval in Romania was also not readily granted, and difficulties were often encountered in obtaining these documents. This situation, revealed by both the accused and the witnesses in the PE-1 trial, was a main reason that Romanian meat products had difficulty penetrating the internal markets of the Western states in 1951–1952, when most of the meat exports were destined for the markets of the Czechoslovak Socialist Republic and the German Democratic Republic.

Romanian meat export improved around 1955, with progress made in both production methods and means of transport.

A special meat export service was set up at PE around that time.[67] During this period, contracts for the sale of Romanian meat were first signed with Italy and later with France. Aside from the contracts for the sale of meat from Romania to Italy, contracts with other countries were limited, and even existing contracts were short-lived. Therefore, some signed contracts were never fully carried out, and not all the products reached their destination. The main agent who mediated the export of meat to Italy was Fischl Tibor, a Yugoslav of Jewish ethnicity, whom Milea Wulich met in 1955 while traveling abroad to find markets for Romanian products, with the help of one of the officials in the Romanian Economic Agency in Vienna. Since Western countries rarely approved import licenses, PE agents abroad very firmly requested exclusivity in meat sales on the Italian market. This was true in Fischl's case, but also elsewhere.[68]

In order to facilitate trade between Romania and companies in Western states, a front company was apparently involved, aided by the Romanian embassy, with the participation of some representatives of the local Communist Parties, who helped to mediate trade with potential local buyers. One such company was URE,[69] an Italian company, belonging to the Italian Communist Party. The front company was, on the one hand, involved in local political relations, thus sometimes managing to obtain import or export licenses, and on the other hand, if revenue was obtained, the trade partner (Romania in this case) paid a certain share to the company, eventually reaching the local Communist Party. According to Wulich's statements throughout the investigation, agent Fischl, a representative of the Italian companies, was an excellent connoisseur of the Italian meat market and in close contact with companies interested in buying meat. This was a good reason to keep in touch with him in order for PE to enter the Italian market.

Toward the end of the 1950s, an agent of the French company Collectorgane from Paris appeared in Romania, competing with Fischl for the representation of PE in Europe, mostly Italy. At the beginning of the connection between PE and Collectorgane, made through Regis Chomienne, the export of Romanian meat had been directed toward the Italian market only through Fischl, but later, in May 1959, this unwritten agreement was abandoned, and from January 1960, the Collectorgane agent tried himself to sell Romanian meat on the Italian market, in addition to the French market.[70]

Most of the meat contracts that were involved in the PE-1 trial were made through an intermediary, and sometimes another foreign company came into play, as a third party. After countless investigations made in the primary archival documents at ACNSAS, regarding the PE-1 trial, it can be assumed that some of the defendants had some illegal connections, prohibited by the law in force at the time. These were manipulations of illicit currency exchanges with representatives of foreign companies, and perhaps in few cases, one of these agents was granted preferential treatment. Even if it is true, it is difficult to equate this negligence in the service with a crime of undermining the national economy. The prosecution and the prosecutor's office were very categorical and decisive in their conclusions regarding the seriousness of the crimes committed, but despite this fact and a large number of primary sources identified as part of the criminal file P7955 of the PE-1 trial, it is still impossible to formulate an unequivocal position regarding the involvement of the defendants in any action aimed at damaging the economy of the Romanian state. Could it be that the PE officials put their own interest above that of their company and the task they had, in their position as civil servants, to represent the Romanian state?

The PE-1 trial, and to some extent all the other PE trials, obviously differ from the other Foreign Trade trials, in the repeated admission of guilt by almost all the defendants, sooner or later.[71] All 14 defendants admitted their guilt and confessed to the crimes they were accused of by the prosecutor's office through the criminal investigators.[72]

This attitude was rather different than that of defendants from other foreign trade enterprises, either earlier or later on. Some of the other defendants fought fiercely to prove their innocence throughout the investigation.

We can assume, among other things, that the physical and spiritual strength of the PE suspects, people who had passed their middle age, was limited and that they encountered real difficulties in maintaining a position of confrontation and denial of some allegations that came up during their investigation. Unfortunately, the existing documentation reveals to the historian investigating this trial, only the miserable world of those under investigation, who were constantly under the virtual "whip" of their investigators, often referred to as "executioners" in literature, even if they didn't actually have at their disposal the physical tool by which they could have killed.

I argue that the confessions of the majority of the convicts should be regarded as questionable, even if the absolute integrity or innocence of all the PE defendants could also be questionable. Although there are some doubts about the PE-1 defendants, they could not be accused of undermining the national economy or of plotting against its social order. The severity of the punishments to which they were sentenced is in no way justified in the context in which the trial and the whole series of actions that preceded it took place. The legal basis of the allegations was not proven or reinforced by the evidence analyzed in the investigations or subsequently in the gloomy reality of their appearance before the Military Court.

In 1964, the general prosecutor of Romania, Augustin Alexa, appealed to the Supreme Court on behalf of the PE-1 defendants. This time, the appeal was accepted and as a result, most of the defendants serving their sentences in Aiud prison received a significant reduction of the initial sentence (to half or even to less than half of the initially determined years of forced labor). Some of the convicts were released before their initial sentence was up, not only as a consequence of this appeal but also as a result of additional amnesties that were granted later, for example, in 1967 on the 20th anniversary of the establishment of the Romanian People's Republic, on December 30, 1947. The last convicts were released from prison in 1969 following the amnesties granted by Nicolae Ceaușescu, the party leader who succeeded Gheorghe Gheorghiu-Dej after his death in March 1965.

The Last Prodexport Trials (PE-2 and PE-3)

The details concerning the last two PE trials will be presented in a shortened form, due to the extensive amount of material related to the Foreign Trade trials.

I will share some representative details regarding the two women defendants involved in the PE-2 and PE-3 trials,[73] in approximate correspondence with the model used for analysis, but significantly abridged, as mentioned earlier.

Preliminary Stages

PE-2

The Warrant for initiating the PE-2 criminal trial was issued by the Criminal Securitate investigator, Captain Iosif Bistran,[74] on October 7, 1961. The defendants were

- *Ana Capitanescu Blum*, economist, head of the PE's oil import-export service; and
- *Pavel Donath*, the director of PE, who was already being held as a defendant in the PE-1 trial at the time of Ana Capitanescu's arrest.

PE-3

The Warrant for initiating the PE-3 criminal trial was also issued by Captain Bistran on May 8, 1962. The single defendant was

- *Otilia (Tutzi) Minzer (Schöner)*, an expert in the science of commodities. As head of a PE export service, she was responsible for the export of feathers and fresh or frozen poultry intestines and organs.

The Surveillance

PE-2

The pre-Surveillance file in the case of Ana Capitanescu's case was opened on August 26, 1959, following a request dated as early as December 1958. Among the documents to be found there is the report of her meeting with the Israeli ambassador in Romania at that time, Moshe Yager. In the telephone conversation I had with him in Israel, in 2012, regarding the time he served in Bucharest, Mr. Yager did not remember having had a meeting with Capitanescu, but neither did he remember having known anything about the trials, which were taking place then in Romania. In fact, while studying the correspondence between the Israeli Ministry of Foreign Affairs and the Israeli Embassy in Bucharest, at the Israeli National Archives[75] regarding that period, it was proven that the Israelis had a minimum amount of information regarding the foreign trade trials. This also attests to their secret character.

The pre-surveillance file became a surveillance file one year later, on November 18, 1960.[76]

PE-3

Although there have been countless written and verbal attempts to obtain Otilia Minzer's Surveillance file, the repeated requests addressed to SRI, by CNSAS, ultimately failed to yield results. And yet it is impossible that such a file was never opened, and it is quite likely that it had been opened years before Minzer was arrested. Moreover, in the Warrant for initiating the PE-3 trial, reference is made to it.

From the Opening of the Criminal Procedure to the Appearance before the Court

The Arrest

PE-2

Ana Capitanescu was arrested on October 7, 1961, and released from Oradea prison[77] on September 1, 1968. Pavel Donath was arrested on February 26, 1961, and released from Aiud prison on January 3, 1969.

PE-3

Otilia Minzer (Schöner) was arrested on May 8, 1962, and was released from Oradea Prison on November 21, 1968.

The Investigation

PE-2

Captain Iosif Bistran led the investigation of Ana Capitanescu. From the beginning, Capitanescu admitted most of the accusations brought against her. She admitted her participation in discussions that she herself defined as "hostile" to the Romanian state. Discussions of this kind took place in her office between some of the company's officials or between friends at home.

The other "crimes" of which Capitanescu was accused had been carried out in the professional field due to her being the head of the oil and sugar import-export service. Its responsibility consisted not only in choosing the commercial partner to whom it was to sell the products but also the decisions regarding transport, such as choosing the means of transport used,[78] which determined the necessary expenses (transport and insurance).

The foreign partner continued to sell Romanian oil and sugar in other states. Thus, among the companies that won the tenders and transferred the

Romanian goods further were Van Doorn & Co. from Rotterdam, Holland, whose representative was Visjman, and Primateria from France. In the opinion of the investigation, the establishment of links with these companies was not based on economic considerations in the interest of the Romanian state, but on personal interests. On January 14, 1962, Bistran ordered a financial assessment.[79]

Among those appointed as experts to execute the financial assessment was the legal adviser of the RE enterprise, Constantin Dobrescu.[80]

The financial experts appointed by the order of the Securitate presented a report of the material damages, following an analysis of the contracts for which Capitanescu had been responsible, The investigation of the second suspect, namely Pavel Donath, was carried out parallel to Ana Capitanescu's investigation. An attempt was made to highlight his lack of involvement and critical assessment in signing the contracts and his indifference and irresponsible attitude as director of the operations executed by his subordinate, Ana Capitanescu.

PE-3

Minzer's investigation began on May 10, 1962 and lasted for a long time with almost daily questionings until December 1962. After this date, and until October 1963, when the investigation ended, the frequency of the meetings was reduced.[81] During the investigation, Minzer tried to justify all her decisions and signed contracts, thus rejecting the allegations of the investigators regarding the damages to the Romanian state economy and to PE that she supposedly caused intentionally. Minzer gave plausible explanations for the relatively low prices charged at the time, in the field for which she had been responsible. For instance, among her claims, she sustained that poultry that was exported by Romania was considered on the international market to be of lower quality than that exported by other Eastern European countries, such as the Polish People's Republic and the Hungarian People's Republic. Consequently, several people working in the laboratories of the Ministry of Food Industry[82] confessed that the Romanian products were proven to be of lower quality by experiments that were carried out.[83] The inferiority of Romanian products was also known, through telegrams, telexes, and some officials' discussions and reports following their visits abroad.

It seems that Minzer's investigators were not very impressed by her statements and the reasons given for her decisions.

Some of the witnesses, who had worked at feather collection centers, claimed that Romanian feathers were of high quality and had a good sales potential on the European market. Despite this situation, Minzer determined that the German representative of PE abroad, Bickenbach-Handelsverkehr, would be the only one who brokered the sale of the feathers. The sales were made through this intermediary and not directly, which in the defendant's opinion had advantages, since the direct selling method was difficult to apply, due to Romania's problematic sales on the European market.

Minzer's investigation brought up the names of three foreign agents through whom she regularly sold products exported by PE. The investigation concluded that these persons offered her commissions in return for preferential treatment. These three agents are listed here:

- Kurt Dietrich, the representative of a German company that was the only intermediary of the sales of Romanian eggs and poultry on the German market for a long time.
- Isidor Gewurcz, an agent who brokered sales of internal organs and poultry.
- Bickenbach, the broker for the sale of feathers in Western countries.

Otilia Minzer was accused of receiving commissions from all three agents for the sales she coordinated for PE.

The investigation documents show a turning point in Minzer's attitude after she was confronted with the names of some foreign agents.

Until June 15, 1962 (the arrest took place on May 9, 1962), when the first Warrant of Indictment was issued, Minzer maintained her position, denying all charges and explaining the rationale of the decisions made during the period in which the incriminating contracts were signed. As the names of the agents were invoked, she gradually changed her position, acknowledging a different version, according to which she received certain monetary advantages from some of the foreign agents, in accordance with the sales made. In return, Minzer was obliged to ensure the continuous supply of Romanian goods and their distribution to those agents, sometimes based on preferential financial terms. They also sometimes received products of a higher quality than those paid for and specified in the signed contract. At this point in the investigation, Minzer stated that the money received from sales agents was deposited in certain bank accounts in Vienna and Berlin in her late husband's name. In fact, in the late stages of the investigation, Minzer admitted that she had received commissions from the agencies she worked with in the Western market. And yet, in addition to the somewhat confusing and blurred nature of the situation, the alleged procedure seems completely unlikely, as her husband was no longer alive at that time, and according to her declarations, the account nevertheless remained active.[84] On December 1, 1962, after eight months of investigation, a financial assessment was ordered.

Witnesses

In the PE-2 trial, as in all the others, the witnesses were only prosecution witnesses. Some witnesses spoke about the activity carried out by Ana

Capitanescu, explaining why the contracts through which she sold the products could be considered disadvantageous to the Romanian economy. Interrogation of witnesses under arrest in the investigation or in court was a technique often used during economic trials, some of which took place in parallel. Other witnesses who appeared in the PE-2 trial invoked the equivocal and especially subversive expressions used against the Romanian state. This was also one of the accusations brought against Capitanescu, throughout the trial.

PE-3

In the PE-3 trial, as in all the other trials, there were only prosecution witnesses, while the defense was not allowed to bring any witnesses who might contradict the prosecution's testimony. A number of prosecution witnesses emphasized Minzer's good conduct in the service, as well as the fact that she enjoyed the sympathy and admiration of her colleagues, that the decisions made over the years proved to be balanced and professional. At the same time, they reported that she used to receive small gifts from visitors from foreign companies, which was a common expression of gratitude and goodwill. Minzer asked for witnesses to be brought to court in her defense, such as Radu Abagiu, an official at the Romanian Economic Agency in Frankfurt, West Germany, and Andrei Csendes, accused in the PE-1 trial. She also requested the presentation of business documents from the PE, which could have served as favorable evidence in support of the repeated choice of the same sales agents, in the existing context. All her requests were denied, during the investigation as well as later, in the court.

Another notable incident that occurred during the PE-3 investigation was the suicide of the consultant Simion Cionca, who had been working at PE at the time.[85] His name is mentioned on some of the documents of Criminal file P14281. Minzer and Cionca worked together in the company. Probably, following the arrest of Otilia Minzer, Cionca, summoned to serve as a witness in the trial, was frightened by the prospect of appearing before the court, and by the possibility that he might be required to collaborate with the Securitate. There is no documentation on this subject.

It is difficult to understand and to analyze the reasons that made Minzer change her position by 180 degrees, as the investigation went on, so that at the end she confessed to all the Securitate's accusations, the same ones she totally denied at the beginning. The documentation of these changes in attitude is laconic, and the authenticity of the statements therein remains questionable. There is no additional evidence to validate or contradict this assumption, but such a drastic change in the defendant's attitude, and self-incrimination, required a very special intellectual effort and creative interpretation. To fully clarify this enigma, it seems that we should be in a detective story, in which logic and imagination should intervene to help each other, in order to create an overall scenario different from the official scenario, suspicious enough, which is reflected in the documents prepared only by one side, the prosecution, that is, the Securitate.

Formulation of the Indictment Conclusions

PE-2

On August 22, 1962, the criminal investigator Captain Iosif Bistran submitted the Indictment Conclusions, directed against Ana Capitanescu (Blum) and Pavel Donath. The indictment included two main parts:

1. Ana Capitanescu, in her position as head of service, acted in bad faith in the execution of the various contracts. The prosecution represented by the Securitate claimed that Ana Capitanescu did not submit appropriate reports on future acts of purchase to the director of the company or to the relevant sections belonging to the MCE. A greater number of requests and offers should have been analyzed and the available prices compared. The importer for PE should have been selected accordingly from a list of contenders.
2. A second issue raised involved the erroneous calculations made by Capitanescu for transport expenses, neglecting to take the transport taxes into account so the import prices on edible oil and other transport expenses appeared to be too high.

As for Pavel Donath, his main accusation in this trial concerned his negligence in failing to alert his superiors to the advantages offered by Capitanescu to foreign companies.

PE-3

On October 7, 1964, the same Bistran submitted the Indictment Conclusions, directed against Otilia Minzer.[86]

Before the Military Court

The Sentence

PE-2

The PE-2 trial began on September 18, 1962, and the sentence was pronounced on October 8, 1962, Sentence no. 57/18/10/1962. The sentences of the defendants in the PE-2 trial were presented in accordance with the CP-1960:

- *Ana Căpitănescu (Blum)* was found guilty of the following crimes and offenses:
  - The crime of undermining the national economy[87]
  - The crime of plotting against the social order[88]

She was sentenced to 20 years of forced labor. An additional penalty included eight years of civic degradation and the confiscation of all her property.[89] As for the punishments to which she was sentenced, they were to be served concurrently.

The application of additional penalties became active from the date of release, or in the case of a pardon or amnesty from the date on which it goes into effect.

- Pavel *Donath* was found guilty of the following offense:
  - The crime of negligence in office.[90]

He was sentenced to seven years of correctional imprisonment. This punishment was merged with the rest of the punishments to which he had been sentenced by Sentence no. 58/1961 issued in the PE-1 process.

PE-3

The PE-3 trial opened on December 3, 1963, at the Bucharest Regional Military Court.

The sentence of the defendant Otilia Minzer in the PE-3 trial was presented in accordance with the CP-1960; on December 16, 1963, Sentence no. 65/16/12/1963:

- *Otilia Minzer (Schöner)* was found guilty of the following charges:
  - The crime of undermining the national economy[87]

She was sentenced to twenty-three years of forced labor. An additional penalty included eight years of civic degradation and the confiscation of all her property.[91]

The Appeal

PE-2

The appeal of the PE-2 trial was held between the dates of November 9, 1962, and November 15, 1962, when Decision no. 287/15/11/1962 was issued. As was the case with the other economic processes, the appeal was rejected, and the original punishments remained unchanged. Ana Capitanescu served her sentence at the women's penitentiary in Oradea.

PE-3

The appeal of the PE-3 trial ended in Decision no. 33/22/02/1964 on February 22, 1964. As in the other trials, the decision rejected the appeal and reaffirmed the sentence determined by the Military Court of the Bucharest Region, not accepting any modification. Otilia Minzer served her sentence at the women's penitentiary in Oradea.

General Observations Concerning the Unfolding of the PE-2 and PE-3 Trials

PE-2

> Ana Capitănescu had a hostile attitude toward the democratic regime in Romania. She said that innocent people were convicted in Romania and that she would receive harsh punishments for just a few words.[92]

The aforementioned statement by Alfred Schwartz, one of the main PE-1 convicts, was given as part of his testimony in court before the Military Court, after he himself had already been sentenced to forced labor. These words can be seen either as an accusation against Capitanescu or, on the contrary, as an accusation of the authorities and identification with what is said earlier. Schwartz's remarks may raise one of two issues:

One is that Schwartz could consider himself a victim who had received a disproportionate punishment relative to his alleged guilt, which may have proven the truth of what Capitanescu had claimed, according to the quote mentioned earlier. The other is that Schwartz accepted the authorities' decisions, which were based on a policy of harsh treatment of those caught criticizing the regime, in which case the state tyrannically took innocent people into custody, and the witness himself could be considered an example of this type of tyranny.

As decided by the prosecution, Capitanescu was accused of signing 12 import contracts and six oil export contracts of different categories and qualities, offering advantages to certain foreign agents in exchange for commissions which she supposedly received and which were kept abroad. There was no real proof other than her own declarations, which were given under the well-known conditions of the Securitate investigation. In addition, she was condemned for undermining the national economy, as well as for slandering the social order and state institutions in Romania, during 1950–1960. Just as in the PE-1 trial, the general prosecutor of Romania at that time, Augustin Alexa, requested an appeal in the case of Ana Capitănescu addressed to the Supreme Court in 1964. The appeal was accepted and as a result, Căpitănescu's sentence was reduced from 20 to 12 years of forced labor, by Decision no. 2 of 2/4/1964.

PE-3

Otilia Minzer was the sole defendant in the PE-3 trial. In this trial, Pavel Donath was only a witness of the prosecution. As director of the company, Donath was informed about the trade relations Minzer maintained, about the proposals that she made or received, and also about the contracts that she concluded. Donath, who at the time of the PE-3 trial had already been convicted in the PE-1 and PE-2 trials and was serving his sentence in Aiud prison, was not found guilty in PE-3. It seems that Minzer's activity was much more independent than that of Capitanescu, and therefore she was considered solely responsible for the alleged crimes involved.

In 1964, the general prosecutor of Romania, Augustin Alexa, addressed an appeal to the Supreme Court, on behalf of Otilia Minzer, as he had done on behalf of the other convicts of the PE enterprise. As a result of the acceptance of this appeal, Minzer's sentence was reduced to 12 years of forced labor, by Decision no. 11/2/4/1964. Minzer was released from prison in 1968, before the end of her sentence, due to an additional amnesty, granted later, during Nicolae Ceauşescu's leadership.

Conclusions for all the (three) PE Trails

PE's activity was condemned by the three economic trials, during the decade between 1950 and 1960. At that time, meat products and other products sold by the company could not be considered to be of high quality compared to others on the European market, even those from other socialist countries. This reality was not taken into account in any way, neither by the prosecution nor by the investigation teams, nor by those who had supplied financial assessment in any of the trials. These facts were even acknowledged by some of the prosecution's witnesses in the trials as part of the context.

Among the documents carried out for PE officials' investigation, it can be clearly seen that the majority of the defendants confessed to the charges, including the very serious ones, such as the crime of undermining the national economy, betrayal of the homeland or plotting against the social order. Actually, the accusations referred only to conversations with foreigners or coworkers or to hostility toward the political system in power. The defendants' confessions nearly brought them to the gallows, but in the end, despite the military prosecutor's request for the death penalty, they were sentenced only to forced labor for life.

How could this phenomenon of self-incrimination, which characterized almost all the defendants of the PE trials, be explained? We certainly cannot underestimate the power of the physical torture and the psychological manipulations that were certainly inflicted upon those under investigation by both "bad" and "good" investigators. The accused had limited powers of resistance and these were weakened over time. The asymmetrical relationship between the two poles, the Securitate as an investigative division versus its subject, the defendants, was obvious in all phases of the trial, from the investigation to the appearance before the court. Lacking legal representation during their investigation and almost up to the end, being held separately, but living in detention cells with Securitate informants, being verbally abused, violently beaten, and deprived of sleep, in addition to the threats toward their relatives, left a heavy mark on the people involved, detained under Securitate arrest, before the Tribunal. This method of investigation seriously and directly influenced the mental capacity of the defendants, destroyed their resistance and paved the way to self-incrimination.

In the course of searching the archives for evidence, it has become apparent that the truth was never really relevant, given that any evidence contradicting that presented and prepared by the Securitate bodies, is almost entirely absent.

What was the real reason these people were convicted of such serious economical, but in fact political crimes? What was the true extent of the apparently illegal PE activity that could warrant such charges, and therefore such harsh punishments, and still be in accordance with the legislation of the Criminal Code CP-1960?

It mustn't be forgotten that all archival material held by the researcher had been prepared entirely by the Securitate authorities in order to serve their interests.

Where did Pavel Donath, director of PE, at a relatively advanced stage of sentencing, still in prison, manage to find the courage to protest against one of his convictions and why didn't he then ask for full acquittal but asked to be acquitted only of one single charge against him. It is likely that Donath requested this appeal due to the political change that took place in Romania after 1965, the year of Gheorghiu-Dej's death. A year earlier, in 1964, the Romanian government granted an almost complete amnesty to political detainees convicted of political crimes. The only political prisoners who were not included in this amnesty were those classified as counterrevolutionaries. All the foreign trade convicts, without exception, remained in prison.

Three years later, on the occasion of the twentieth anniversary of the declaration of the Romanian People's Republic (1947–1967), Nicolae Ceauşescu decided to ease the punishment of some of the political prisoners, and on this occasion granted an amnesty.[93] Shortly afterward, in January 1969, the last of the convicts in the PE trials was released. The arrest, the investigation and the years of detention left the people involved in these trials with deep scars that time could never heal. Many of them died in the early years after their release in the early 1970s, and fewer completed another decade of life, disappearing in the early 1980s. The tragic image of PE convicts, some of whom had the good fortune and the right to be parents in their youth, probably remained a distorted memory in the minds of their children who grew up in the meantime and are today, themselves, on the descent from this world, which has not since proven to be "a world of justice."

AGROEXPORT TRIAL

The field of activity of AE[94] was the export of special Romanian agricultural products, such as beans, corn, various cereals, oil production by-products, poppy seeds, reed stems, and sugarcane. The importers were companies from Belgium, the Netherlands, West Germany, France, and Austria. The reed was exported to Europe by two intermediaries, Leo Bauer and Müler, both from West Germany. Trade in reed stalks had begun in 1956. When a contract was first signed with Müler in 1956, it was discontinued at the initiative of the importer before the end of the contract due to complaints about the quality of the product. As a result, the German company stopped payments. At the end of the same year, the first contract was signed with the German company Leo Bauer, which agreed to take over the entire amount of reed intended for export. Bauer continued to import Romanian reeds for many more years, until 1961, the year in which the AE trial, whose sole defendant was Sami Edelstein, began. While Bauer continued to remain the customer of AE for a long time, other importers from Switzerland, France, and Austria were added, but they imported small quantities compared to Bauer. The German company was eventually granted exclusivity for importing Romanian reeds to Germany, initially only for a year. Another reason for granting Bauer this privilege was the connections he had in various European countries, which allowed him to obtain import licenses for the Romanian product from their governments. According to Edelstein, Bauer was a serious importer, considering the quantities he requested and the annual frequency. Due to the complaints of the importer Müler about the goods provided by AE, Edelstein, as coordinating director, preferred to strengthen the export-import link with Bauer, though he also had complaints. For example, the reed stalks that had been transported on the Danube to the port of Passau in Germany had rotted due to the excessive moisture on the boat during transport.[95]

Preliminary Stages

The warrant for initiating the AE criminal trial[96] was issued against one single person.

- *Sami Edelstein*, the manager of the Agroexport company

The Surveillance

Sami Edelstein's surveillance file[97] included, among other things, the accusation that he had committed a number of illegal acts and other actions to the detriment of the Romanian state. The report was based on information provided by some of the Securitate informants, colleagues, or employees of the Securitate, who worked with Edelstein or who were sent for various follow-up tasks. The Securitate used operational methods such as wiretapping the homes and offices of those under surveillance. All of Edelstein's correspondence was monitored, and the authorities used various means of interception[98] for his surveillance both in his office and his home.[99] During these overheard discussions, they heard about the difficulties imposed by the Romanian political system on Jews who wanted to emigrate to Israel or to other Western countries. It must be remembered that this was the period following 1958, when Romanian authorities had encouraged Jews to submit applications for emigration to Israel. Thus, learning about their intentions, Jews enrolled for emigration were removed from office and replaced by non-Jewish officials.[100]

An additional surveillance file was opened for Edelstein after his release from prison, immediately after he began working at the headquarters of the Jewish community. After their release, many former Foreign Trade officials who had been convicted in the economic trials worked at the Jewish Community in Bucharest, where Moses Rosen[101] was at that time the chief rabbi of Romania. This situation indicates, among other things, the uneasiness of the Securitate institutions and its constant, rather obsessive surveillance of these people, "redefined" as targets to be pursued, even after their release from prison.

From the Opening of the Criminal Procedure to the Appearance before the Court

The Arrest

The Indictment Warrant in the case of Sami Edelstein[102] was issued by Captain Stefan Nedelcu, a Securitate investigator, belonging to the Criminal Investigations Division of the Ministry of Internal Affairs, on August 30,

1961. Sami Edelstein was arrested on August 30, 1961, and released from the Aiud prison, on January 31, 1969.

The reason for opening the criminal trial against Edelstein was his "hostile" activity against the Romanian state, during the years 1957–1961 by granting priority to some foreign agents and companies, and "causing economic damages to the state."

b. The Investigation

Captain Mircea Onea began Edelstein's criminal investigation, which was later taken over by Captain Stefan Nedelcu. The investigation started on August 31, 1961, and ended on January 12, 1963. The extended period is evidence of the investigator's difficulty in obtaining the desired confessions from Edelstein. The prolongment of the investigation was especially unusual, considering that there was only one defendant.

An uncommon feature of the AE trial, which had also occurred during the CA trial, was that one of the accusations appearing on the first Indictment did not appear in the final Indictment Conclusions document, although a new charge was added during the AE trial, as will be mentioned further. Edelstein denied most of the allegations raised against him.

At a time when the PE trial had already ended with heavy convictions and the AE trial investigations were in full swing, Edelstein faced the allegations against him with great courage and boldness, both at the time of the investigation and later before of the Military Court. He presented some arguments regarding each of the two accusations brought against him at the end of the criminal investigation.

> Regarding the second accusation[103] contained in the Indictment warrant, I do not admit any guilt of having knowingly concluded commercial operations disadvantageous to the RPR economy, by favoring capitalist companies or merchants, in order to provide some personal material advantages. If we have concluded such commercial operations disadvantageous to the national economy and favorable to some traders or firms, they are due to mistakes or ease in dealing with those contracts.

During the investigation, the Warrant for a Financial Assessment was issued on March 12, 1962, in order to evaluate Sami Edelstein's work in the AE Enterprise.[104] At that time, Edelstein was allowed to write a document asking for clarification.[105] The preparation of the assessment lasted more than a year, and the investigator Nedelcu rejected most of Edelstein's requests through the 11 questions he submitted, agreeing that only 2 of them could be addressed back to the committee of experts. His request to propose an expert to the appointed group was also rejected.[106] As explained elsewhere, the experts appointed to prepare the financial assessment were not professionals in the field of foreign trade and had never held positions in this field. Confronting Edelstein with the recordings of conversations held in the apartment where he lived or in his office, the investigator accused him of plotting against the social order and the existing political system in Romania. Edelstein rejected this accusation as well, and in the end, Captain Nedelcu apparently had no choice but to accept this rejection and omit those accusations from the final Indictment. However, a new charge was added to the Indictment Conclusions, connected to dissemination of classified documents.

The Witnesses

As in all the other trials, there were only prosecution witnesses, among whom were two people, both involved in the activity of AE, and both non-Jews, Elena Reţegan, head of an export service, and Anton Sachelarides, deputy director of AE. Despite the fact that both held positions of great responsibility in the conclusion of the reed export contracts at the time of Edelstein's alleged misdeeds, they were not detained for investigation nor were they charged with any crime.

In addition to the prosecution testimonies, it is important to note Edelstein's own testimony made before the Military Court, on August 8, 1963, the opening day of AE trial. During the court session, the defendant Sami Edelstein exhibited rather unusual behavior, revealing his genuine state of mind during the investigation.

> After receiving the Indictment conclusions, I would like to make a statement. Before your interrogation, I would like to declare before the General Court that I do not maintain my admissions of guilt regarding the contracts signed between 1957 and 1958.
>
> During the investigation I was forced to accept the accusations, partly because some materials I was shown were only fragmentary. I did not remember some of the discussions I had with my coworkers who dealt with these contracts and I was not aware of everything that happened. When I read the material, I realized that I had drawn erroneous conclusions and this was also due to my mental state at that time, as follows: from the very beginning I was treated in the Investigation as a dishonest person and I was told that I had been dishonest not only in the reed transactions, but also in transactions of other products. I do not maintain the allegations I made in connection with the contract of December 16, 1957 and November 6, 1958.[107]

This remarkably bold speech accuses the investigation bodies, a rare phenomenon in communist trials in general, and in these economic trials in particular. Edelstein testifies that he went through an intense emotional struggle, but despite the physical and mental pressure exerted on him, upholds his views and position in court, and seeks justice for himself, although his earlier position was different. And he explains why. The testimony also raises one very serious issue common to all these trials, but difficult to prove—the false confessions made by most of the defendants during their investigations, when they were no longer able to hold their ground. Edelstein appears as a brave man standing before the Tribunal, as a voluntary representative of a group of defendants lacking a voice or any real defense, by his sharp revolt and personal truth, despite realizing the likely consequences of this courageous attitude.

Formulation of the Indictment Conclusions

On May 28, 1963, Captain Stefan Nedelcu submitted the Indictment Conclusions directed against Sami Edelstein, and all the material was handed to Edelstein to be studied and signed.[108] The indictment included the two accusations leveled against Edelstein, the undermining of the national economy and the dissemination of classified materials. These would later form the basis of the conviction and the sentence. As already mentioned, the accusation of plotting against the social order was erased, and the Security Investigator Nedelcu confirmed that there was no body of evidence that would support that accusation. The only similar case happened during the CA trial, with the defendant Octav Botnar, when one of the original charges was dropped.[109]

The indictment also attempts to hold Edelstein responsible for the execution of contracts to sell the reeds to the West German company, Leo Bauer, without considering proposals from other companies, which in the opinion of the Investigative Bodies might have been preferable in terms of the price offered.

The fact that Edelstein was abroad for a long time, as the official representative of Romania, and therefore absent from his position as director of AE, as well as the role of other colleagues, who had been approved by members of the ministry, in finalizing these contracts, raises serious questions regarding his alleged guilt. Certainly, his courageous testimony before the court, partly presented earlier, reinforces this assertion.

Before the Military Court

The Sentence

The AE trial began on August 8, 1963, and Sentence no. 32/15/08/1963 was pronounced on August 15, 1963. The sentence of the single defendant in the AE trial was presented in accordance with the CP-1960:

- *Sami Edelstein* was found guilty of the following crimes and offenses:
  - The crime of undermining the national economy[110]
  - The felony of spreading prohibited publications[111]

He was sentenced to 20 years of forced labor. An additional penalty included five years of civic degradation and the confiscation of all his property.[112]

The application of additional penalties became active from the date of release, or in the case of a pardon or amnesty, from the date on which it goes into effect.

The Appeal

The appeal in the AE trial, regarding Sentence no. 32/15/08/1963, was held on September 30, 1963, no. 261/30/09/1963. The appeal was heard in the same court and it rejected all the defendant's or lawyer's observations, so the sentence remained unchanged. Edelstein was first sent to Jilava Prison, and after the appeal he was transferred to Aiud prison for the rest of his sentence.

AE Trial Conclusions

Sami Edelstein, the sole defendant of the trial, climbed the ladder of management positions in the company, rising to the position held at the time of his arrest, that of coordinating director.[113] He was department director (1948), counselor (1950), and in 1957, he reached the position of director of the company.[114] Edelstein was accused not only in the context of contracts made for the sale of reeds but also for the conclusion of unprofitable contracts for the sale of cereal grains (e.g., corn and corn products). Unlike what happened in the PE trials, the defendant answered the investigators with self-confidence and denied the accusations. Other officials, even superiors, were involved in AE's activity during the period when the contracts under investigation were signed, but no one other than Edelstein was suspected of making mistakes or causing damage to the state. The others were, however, called to testify against Edelstein.

However, a fog enshrouded the charges throughout the investigation and the trial. During the persistent effort to obtain new material from the Romanian archives, a special document was found at CNSAS[115] referring to the AE trial. It is a memorandum written by Edelstein's wife, Gitla Edelstein, to the State Security Council, a second appeal for the reversal of the court's decisions, by which Sami Edelstein was convicted and sentenced. Ion Stănescu, director of this Council, appointed two officers to verify details brought to their attention regarding the case. The result of the investigation, probably undertaken in 1968, was the rejection of the request because the two concluded that the punishment was correct and justified. At the beginning of 1969, Edelstein was released following the amnesty of Nicolae Ceaşusescu mentioned earlier.

CONCLUSIONS

The chapter includes a brief description of the characteristics, conditions, and progression of the first Foreign Trade trials. The convicted officials in the three companies were mostly Jews. The trials took place at the Military Court because according to CP-1960, the crimes of which they were accused were considered political crimes and as such were judged according to the Romanian legal procedure of the time, by a Military Court. In reality, the Tribunal was entirely subordinate to the wishes and orders of the Securitate, which itself operated under the party's directives.

The defendants in these trials could be divided into two categories: the first includes those who confessed to the accusations made against them by the Securitate investigators from the initial stage of the investigation, without any attempt to prove their innocence; the second category included those defendants who, despite the pressures, terror, and conditions they were subjected to, struggled, with minimal means, to maintain their physical and mental resilience and their position of self-defense, by denying the charges and seeking to prove their innocence before the judicial authorities. The defendants in all the trials were at a disadvantage as they had no legal representation except in the final phase when the trial had already reached the court. No request to adduce evidence or witnesses to counter the indictment was accepted.

In the years 1963–1964, when most of the trials drew to a close, a dramatic event took place: the Romanian government decided to grant amnesty to the majority of political prisoners and there was a mass release from Romanian prisons. This was achieved by issuing decrees 767/1963, 176/1964, and 411/1964, decrees that were not published in official newspapers and therefore have never been exposed to the general public, remaining in the shadows. Prior to their release, the former prisoners had been warned not to disclose their place of detention or other information related to the conditions of their incarceration.[116]

The release of political prisoners took place in several stages. This situation came about as a kind of political consensus between the countries of the Communist bloc, including Romania, to release those considered "former victims of Stalinism," offering them the opportunity to rebuild their lives after liberation. In this context, Gheorghiu-Dej himself decided to enact this massive amnesty, an action that would also bring him political capital, by improving his position in the West as the following words point out:

> I would like to say—with a certain malice—that Dej agreed to carry out these interventions, because he realized that, as a result of this measure, he would increase his prestige abroad.[117]

Whatever the truth had been, the amnesty of such a large number of political convicts who were serving their sentences in Romanian prisons at the time was an event that was not only dramatic but also extraordinary in the political landscape of the Romanian state. This event also proved that the Foreign Trade defendants were given a "special" status, because despite the release of all the political prisoners, none of the Foreign Trade convicts who had been sentenced to long years of forced labor was included in this amnesty. And despite this situation, in the same year, 1964, another event occurred in the context of the above trials, an event already mentioned before.

Augustin Alexa, in his position as General Prosecutor, requested an appeal under supervision[118] regarding the reduction of sentences for convicts in the economic trials. Appeal under supervision was defined in the Code of Criminal Procedure,[119] and was a legal procedure carried out by the Supreme Court, through which it could reconsider any ruling of a lower court, in this case, the Military Regional Court of Bucharest. This legal procedure of the Romanian Code of Criminal Procedure of the time is difficult to perceive in a democratic state, where the prosecutor general would not have the power to challenge decisions made by an independent court. However, there was no separation of powers in the communist state.

How can this change of attitude be explained with the coming of 1964 and the mass release of political prisoners? It is the last period of Gheorghiu-Dej's leadership.[120]

Romania's tendency at that time was toward preferential treatment of the population of Romanian nationality compared to those of other nationalities. The Jews, among them the Foreign Trade group, were primarily targeted. Political amnesties, as already mentioned, included various political prisoners, among them a considerable number of former Iron-Guard members. But they did not include a single Foreign Trade official among those already in prison. The action taken by Alexa in 1964 can be seen as a kind of compensation for the convicts in Foreign Trade, after the Romanian government authorities had denied them any chance.

The events and facts presented during the economic trials are full of duality, leaving room for ambiguity during both the criminal investigations and, of course, in court. The existing documentation, unfortunately, does not facilitate compliance with Ranke's postulate that "things should be presented as nearly as possible to how they really happened." Despite numerous attempts to correlate and compare historical evidence, I often encountered a fog masking the truth, the result of the fact that the files were prepared by the repressive Romanian Securitate.

Ultimately, even if some of the evidence could be found to incriminate the representatives of the Foreign Trade companies, they claimed that the prosecution invoked the harshest articles in the Criminal Code of the time to punish some possible acts of negligence in service, or perhaps in currency transfers. The prosecution had predetermined the purpose and name of the charges against those to be investigated, before the investigation had even begun, involving serious crimes against the state, political crimes, for which the prosecutor requested in some cases even the death penalty. As it is known, the investigation was constantly accompanied by physical violence, harsh and violent expressions, beatings, and direct threats, not only to the prisoners themselves but also to their families. It is not surprising that under such conditions, most of the PE officials lost their strength of resistance and endurance. This constant torment and lack of defense crushed them, and thus they contributed to their incrimination even against their own will. Only a law enacted as late as 1967[121] led to the release of most Foreign Trade officials before the end of their original prison terms.

The Securitate continued to pursue them after their release. The last PE prisoners were released from prison in 1968–1969, following the amnesties granted by Nicolae Ceauşescu, Gheorghiu-Dej's successor as the head of the PCR. Less than a decade later, all the Jewish Foreign Trade officials, seriously ill after long years of inhumane prison conditions, had passed on to a better world.

NOTES

1. This refers to the CP-1960, Book II "Crimes and felonies in particular," Title I "Crimes and felonies against the State," Chapter II "Crimes and felonies against the Internal Security of the State," Section I bis, Art. 209[1], paragraph I.
2. According to the Criminal Code in force at the time, CP-1960, punishment for those crimes were either 25 years of forced labor, or the death penalty. The acronyms CP-XXXX and CPP-XXXX will stand for Criminal Code or Criminal Code Procedure, where XXXX represents the year of its publication.
3. CP-1952, CP-1955, CP-1958.
4. See chapter 3 for more details.
5. The file, describing the CA trial, is held at ACNSAS, under no. P7893 (7 volumes).
6. This warrant was issued on the April 25, 1960, by the Criminal investigator Nicolae Dumitrescu.

7. As an officer of the Ministry of Internal Affairs, it was understood that he held a position in the Securitate. As such, he had accompanied various delegations sent abroad.

8. The types of the former Securitate files held today by CNSAS can be seen in appendix III. Botnar's Surveillance file number is I211278 and it includes six volumes.

9. The arrest warrant issued by senior Lieutenant Iosef Bistran for Botnar is to be found at ACNSAS, P7893/Vol. 1/pp. 2–3, that of Perianu, issued by Colonel Nicolae Dumitrescu, is to be found at P7893/Vol. 1/pp. 259–260, that of Pantazescu, given by Lieutenant Anatolie Dulipovici, at P7893/Vol. 1/pp. 288–289. All these people were Securitate criminal investigators.

10. ACNSAS, P7893/Vol. 1/pp. 189–191.

11. Ioanid Group comprised five men and a woman, Jewish intellectuals, all members of the Romanian Workers' Party. On July 28, 1959, following an armed robbery, the members of the group were caught and arrested, the money was recovered, and the armed robbery was reenacted on camera. In the closed-door trial, the five men were sentenced to death and the only woman involved was sentenced to forced labor and a life sentence. She was later released and allowed to emigrate to Israel.

12. ACNSAS, P7893/Vol. 1/pp. 282–283.

13. ACNSAS, P7893/Vol. 1/p. 382.

14. PVI, in Romanian Proces Verbal de Interogatoriu, mentioned in chapter 4, Transcript of Interrogation, a reproduction of the Interrogation to which the defendant was subjected.

15. This is the period of the late 1950s and early 1960s, in which we can speak of a certain relaxation in the investigations conducted by the Securitate. However, the testimonies of some of the defendants in the economic trials, such as Adalbert Rosinger, in his personal memoirs, or Angelo Chinzbrunner, through talking to his wife, or others, claim that the brutality of the investigators continued to be harsh.

16. The reference is made to Samy Edelstein, the only person convicted in the AE trial.

17. ACNSAS, P7893/Vol. 1/pp. 431–440.

18. CP-1960, Book I "General Proceedings," Title III "Punishments," Chapter V "Punishments Referring to Rights," Section I "Civic Degradation," Art. 58 (2–4).

19. In Romanian, Ministerul Comerţului Exterior, henceforth the abbreviation to be used through the whole book is MCE.

20. ACNSAS, P7893/Vol. 2/pp. 1–4, the testimony of Isac Mincu about the difficulties encountered by Romania in concluding contracts with the West, or ACNSAS, P7893 / Vol. 2 / the PP. 47–52, Rufel Acatiu's testimony about Cartimex's request to maintain high-quality standards, following the requests of Atico, with which it had concluded the long-term carpet contract.

21. Maquis (Resistance) was a French resistance movement of partisan groups fighting the German occupation in France.

22. ACNSAS, P7893/Vol. 4/p. 35.

23. As there were three Prodexport trials, they will be named by PE-1, PE-2 and PE-3, according to their chronologic order.

24. The Criminal file, describing the PE-1 trial, is held at ACNSAS, under no. P7855 (32 volumes).

25. The methods used by Romania, in the exchange of goods at the time, were called compensation methods, and didn't involve the use of foreign currency, which was lacking. There were two basic compensation methods, "barter" and "clearing," and by their usage, Romania was not required to make payments in foreign currency. The difference between the two methods was the way the transaction was made and the amount of time that elapsed until the transaction was completed. Barter was a system used for exchanging goods of equal value, and the clearing was a system of exchanging goods, made by mutual compensation of debts and receivables. Balancing the debt of a commodity was performed during a whole year and the transaction could be executed between two or even three partners, so it could be concluded, even at the end of the year, by the transfer of goods, executed from one customer to another (or between three customers). After the actual execution of the goods transaction, if there were differences left, they could be counterbalanced and delayed, sometimes even by state intervention.

26. It was explained in chapter 4.

27. ACNSAS, P7955/Vol. 1/p. 26.

28. Data on Arrest Warrants of each defendant, belonging to the PE-1 Trial, will be mentioned in the footnotes accompanying each of their names. Most of them were issued by the Securitate investigator, Leutenant Iosif Bistran, and were based on the accusation of undermining the national economy, based on Art. 209[1]. Bistran took part as the main criminal investigator during almost all the defendants' investigations. Between April 1960 and December 1960, Bistran was promoted to the rank of captain. An important article on the biography of this Securitate torturer was written by the Romanian historian Dumitru Lăcătuşu, Iosif Bistran, Accessed November 11, 2020, https://www.contributors.ro/tortionarii-mor-in-somn-colonelul-iosif-bistran/.

29. Prior to the Surveillance file, the Securitate sometimes used to open a pre-Surveillance file (in Romanian mapă de verificare). This name will sometimes be used in the next chapters.

30. ACNSAS/DIE 20318 (in Romanian, DIE, Direcţia Informaţii Externe).

31. The Securitate organizational structure is briefly presented in appendix II.

32. The types of the former Securitate files held today by CNSAS can be seen in appendix III.

33. Surveillance file number, I195684, held at ACNSAS.

34. Surveillance file number, I257122, held at ACNSAS.

35. Surveillance file number, I235107, held at ACNSAS.

36. There are some data on arrests and releases, such as Pavel Donath, arrested on February 26, 1961, and released on January 31, 1969; Milea Wulich, arrested on November 30, 1960, and released in 1968, Micu Mordechai Suzin, arrested on March 16, 1960, and released in 1968; Alfred Schwartz, arrested on June 11, 1960, and released in 1968; Viorica Vrânceanu, arrested on March 16, 1960; released in 1968; Radu Simion, arrested on June 3, 1961, and released in December 1966; Andrei Csendes, arrested on March 16, 1961; died during his detainment at Securitate

Malmaison Prison. His death, which occurred during the harsh investigation, was documented as being caused by painful ischemic heart disease and acute circulatory and cerebral insufficiency.

37. ACNSAS, P7955/Vol. 6/p. 427.

38. Testimonies from Aiud penitentiary, at https://evz.ro/vladimir-tismaneanu-moartea-se-numeste-enoiu-456961.html, or Stelian Tănase, "*Anatomy of Mystification 1944–1989*", (Bucharest, Humanitas, 2009), which presents in an original form aspects of the Noica-Pilat, intellectuals' trial, that took place in 1959.

39. ACNSAS, P7955/Vol. 21/pp. 185–191.

40. Siguranţă was the name of the Romanian Intelligence Service until 1940. After this date, its name was changed to the Special Intelligence Service (in Romanian, Serviciul Special de Informaţii or SSI.) active until 1944. See also appendix. II.

41. Arad is a town in the southwestern part of Romania, called Banat.

42. The charge Donath tried to dismiss at the time was not among his main charges, but the third one, "intense activity against the working class and the revolutionary movement, during the period between the two World Wars," based on Art. 193 (CP-1960).

43. At that time, Nicolae Dumitrescu was the head of the Department of Criminal Investigations of the Securitate

44. The words are underlined in the original printed file to be found at ACNSAS, P7955/Vol. 21, p. 349.

45. ACNSAS, P7955/Vol. 21/p. 349–350.

46. The reason was that in 1967, President Ceauşescu, in service office at that time, issued an amnesty on the occasion of the 20th anniversary of the proclamation of the Romanian People's Republic

47. ACNSAS, P7955/Vol. 21/p. 364.

48. ACNSAS, P7955/Vol. 22/pp. 158–245.

49. This was done by finding his whereabouts through the LinkedIn network and contacting him in 2013.

50. A relative of Any Schwartz, apparently her uncle, was living at that time in Brazil.

51. ACNSAS, P7955/Vol. 6/pp. 426–491.

52. PE-1 trial opened on August 7, 1961.

53. ACNSAS, P7955/Vol. 20/p. 263v.

54. ACNSAS, P7955/Vol. 20 includes the Indictment Conclusions summary, meant for most of the defendants.

55. The prosecutor's plea in the PE-1 trial can be found in ACNSAS, P7955/Vol. 20/p. 270.

56. CP-1960, Book II "Crimes and felonies in particular," Title I "Crimes and felonies against the State," Chapter II, "Crimes and felonies against the Internal Security of the State," Section I bis, Art. 209[1] paragraph II.

57. CP-1960 Book I "General Provisions," Title VII "Cases that defend criminal liability or reduce it," Chapter II "Cases That Defend Criminal Liability or Reduce It" Section XIV "Mitigating circumstances," Art. 157.

58. CP-1960, Book II "Crimes and felonies in particular," Title I "Crimes and felonies against the State," Chapter II, "Crimes and Felonies against the External Security of the State," Section II "The Espionage." Art. 1941(2) and Art. 1944.

59. CP-1960, Book I "General Provisions," Title III "Punishments," Chapter II "Species and Degrees of Punishment," Section II "Complimentary Punishment," art. 25 (1), regarding civic degradation.

60. CP-1960, Book II "Crimes and Felonies in Particular," Title I "Crimes and Felonies against the State," Chapter II "Crimes and Felonies against the Internal Security of the State," Section I "The Attack and the Conspiracy against the Constitutional and Social Order of the RPR," art. 209(2a).

61. CP-1960, Book II "Crimes and Felonies in Particular," Title I "Crimes and Felonies against the State," Chapter II, "Crimes and Felonies against the CP-1960, Book II "Crimes and Felonies in Particular External Security of the State," Section II "The Espionage," Art. 1931, paragraph 2. Author's note: In CP-1960, this article appears to be repealed or nonexistent, as long as it appears in the form mentioned in the PE-1 Sentence (P7955, Vol 20/p. 296).

62. This was the opinion of Silvia Chinzbrunner, the wife of Angelo Chinzbrunner, one of the convicts, present during the trial, with whom I had several talks in her apartment, in Frankfurt am Main, Germany, between 2008 and 2011. Silvia passed away in 2014.

63. ACNSAS, p7955/Vol. 2/p. 115v.

64. The slaughterhouses of Salonta and Burdujeni.

65. Brief explanations about the trade methods used in Romania at that time, can be found earlier in the subchapter referring to PE trial.

66. Romanian People's Republic, in Romanian, Republica Populară Roman Republica Populară Română.

67. This can be seen from the investigations of some of the defendants, in particular Schwartz and Suzin.

68. Fischl acted as sales agent of some Italian companies that bought Romanian meat products. Among these were Silcas, Fratelli Zerbi, Manzotin, and Centin.

69. URE = Unione Representanze Estere or The Union of Foreign Representations.

70. ACNSAS, P7955/Vol. 14.

71. The previous subchapters mentioned the cases of CA defendant Botnar, also that of AE defendant Samy Edelstein, while the next chapter will relate the RE defendants' attitudes.

72. With the possible exception of Alfred Schwartz mentioned earlier.

73. The file of the PE-2 trial is held by ACNSAS, its number is P13116 (11 volumes). The file of the PE-3 trial is held by ACNSAS, its number is P14283 (14 volumes).

74. The name of Bistran was already mentioned earlier in connection with the PE-1 trial. Here he had already been promoted to the rank of captain.

75. In Hebrew, called Ginzah Hamedina, Department of Foreign Affairs/File 3/ No. 316/17.

76. ACNSAS, File I195681.

77. In Oradea, the capital of Bihor County in Transylvania, there was one of the Romanian women's prison.

78. The Romanian company that had been used for trade transport in many cases was Romtrans.

79. ACNSAS, P13116/Vol. 2.

80. Dobrescu was one of the main Securitate agents in the RE trial, his contribution to the gathering of information regarding the Jewish officials in foreign trade, and in particular, those of RE was of great significance. His name as an information agent was Horia Mihai. More references to this Securitate agent can be found in the next chapter on the RE process.

81. The investigation was conducted by the Criminal Investigations Division of the Ministry of Internal Affairs.

82. In Romanian, Ministerul Industriei Alimentare (MIA).

83. It was expected that the prices of products exported by those countries would be quoted at about 15% more than the prices of equivalent products exported by Romania. Therefore, the fixed price should have been considered an acceptable price, given the conditions of trade at that time. Moreover, a difference of $50 per ton of products between different suppliers was considered an acceptable difference in the conditions and date of sales (late 1950s).

84. In order to prove her claim, Minzer told investigators how she had arranged to receive the money. The relevant sales person had to open an account in the name of her late husband, at one of the big banks located in Berlin or Vienna. Presenting a document proving that she was his widow, Minzer was to receive the money. There is something doubtful in this statement. Therefore, I tried to verify whether, as it was written in the investigation file, accounts were opened in the name of Minzer's husband, at Dresdener Bank, AG, at one of the branches located in Berlin. This bank was bought by the German Bank Commerz Bank in 2009. I wrote to the new bank in mid-2013, still trying to find out this detail, that is, if there was an account in the relevant period of time, in the name of the deceased (although bank information is known to be top secret). The bank replied that the archives I was referring to are too old and not available to them. My assumption, in the case of Minzer, is that the story of the accounts and deposits was a personal invention, which ensured her release from the pressures of the Securitate during the investigation. The chance that the bank would let an account be opened in the name of a deceased man, and grant his wife rights to withdraw money from the account, does not seem logical or feasible.

85. The information about this sad event was received through oral testimonies, from persons who were involved in the MCE, or who had known personally about this case.

86. ACNSAS, P14281/Vol. 11 /pp. 448–471.

87. CP-1960, Book II "Crimes and felonies in particular," Title I "Crimes and felonies against the State," Chapter II, "Crimes and felonies against the Internal Security of the State," Section I bis, Art. 209[1] paragraph II.

88. CP-1960, Book II "Crimes and felonies in particular," Title I "Crimes and felonies against the State," Chapter II, "Crimes and felonies against the Internal Security

of the State," Section I "The attack and the conspiracy against the constitutional and social order of the RPR," Art. 209(2a).

89. CP-1960, Book I "General Provisions," Title III "Punishments," Chapter II "Species and degrees of punishment," Section II "Complimentary punishment," Art. 25 (1), regarding civic degradation.

90. CP-1960, Book II "Crimes and felonies in particular," Title III "Crimes and offenses against public administration," Chapter I "Crimes and offenses committed by civil servants," Section III "Negligence in service," Art. 242 (2c).

91. CP-1960, Book I "General Provisions," Title III, "Punishments," Chapter II "Types and degrees of punishment," Section II "Complementary punishments," Art. 25.

92. Alfred Schwartz was accused in the PE-1 trial.

93. MAN enacted Law 25/27 December 1967, regarding amnesty, pardon, and reduction of penalties, on December 25–27, 1967, accessed July 7, 2021, http://legislatie.just.ro/Public/DetaliiDocument/22098.

B.O. is the shortened name of the Romanian state official publication, Buletinul Oficial, where acts, laws and other decisions part of them belonging to the constitution, were published until 1989. This Gazette had stopped appearing after 1989, being replaced by the Monitorul Oficial (M.O.).

94. The Criminal file, describing the AE trial, is held at ACNSAS, under no. P8004 (eight volumes).

95. ACNSAS, P8004/Vol1/pp. 60–64.

96. The warrant for initiating the AE trial was issued by Captain Mircea Onea, a Securitate investigator belonging to Criminal Investigations Division of the Ministry of Internal Affairs, on August 25, 1961.

97. Sami Edelstein's Surveillance file has the number I195682, includes four volumes and can be found at ACNSAS.

98. They included telephone and mail interceptions, ambushes, street searches, or in various public places.

99. ACNSAS, I185686/Vol. 1/pp. 9–17.

100. The issue of Romanian authorities' attitude during the years 1958–1961 was commented in the previous chapter, based on the memoirs of Silviu Brucan, *The Wasted Generation: Memoirs of The Romanian Journey from Capitalism to Socialism and back* (Boulder, CO: Vestview Press, 1993), 73, from now on, Brucan, *The Wasted Generation.*

101. Moses Rosen (1912–1994) was the religious and spiritual leader of the Romanian Jewish Community between 1948 and 1994. He also held the position of president of the Federation of Jewish Communities of Romania between 1964 and 1994. He was the chief rabbi during the whole time of Communist Romania and maintained a good relationship with the Communist leaders. He was also a deputy of the MAN from 1957.

102. The Indictment and the Remand warrant against Edelstein, ACNSAS, P8004/Vol. 1/pp. 2–3.

103. Undermining the National Economy, as specified in Art. 209[1] of the CP-1960.

104. ACNSAS, P8004/Vol. 1/p. 149.

105. ACNSAS, P8004/Vol. 1/pp. 154–155.
106. ACNSAS, P8004/Vol. 1/pp. 156–158.
107. ACNSAS, P8004/Vol. 5 p. 22.
108. ACNSAS, P8004/Vol. 7 pp. 165–179.
109. ACNSAS, P8004/Vol. 7 pp. 178.
110. CP-1960, Book II "Crimes and felonies in particular," Title I "Crimes and felonies against the state," Chapter II, "Crimes and felonies against the Internal Security of the State," Section I bis, Art. 209[1] paragraph II.
111. CP-1960, Book II "Crimes and felonies in particular," Title VI "Crimes and offenses against public order," Chapter III "Incentives, instigations and other offenses against public order," Art. 325 (2).
112. CP-1960, Book I "General Provisions," Title III "Punishments," Chapter II "Types and degrees of punishment," Section II "Complimentary punishment," Art. 25.
113. Coordinating director was actually equivalent to that of general manager.
114. In the Foreign Trade scale of hierarchical positions, coordinator director was the equivalent of the general director.
115. It is a Documentary Fond (in Romanian Fondul Documentar), existing as part of the CNSAS archives and it includes documents, journals, online library, and documentary information of the Foreign Intelligence Service (in Romanian Serviciului de Informații Externe-SIE).
116. This information was provided to me by Ms. Gina Radu, employed by the Ministry of Internal Affairs of Romania, who has been in the IICCMER service in recent years. The correspondence with Mrs. Radu from 2013 is in the author's possession.
117. These are the words of Corneliu Mănescu (1916–2000), politician and minister of foreign affairs of Romania. Mănescu was elected president of the United Nations in 1967.
118. In Romanian, "recurs in supraveghere," "imported" in Romania from the former Soviet Union Code of Criminal Procedure. Some of this information can be found in the correspondence with Ms. Oana Axinia Soare, lawyer at IICCMER, in the letter dated December 5, 2014, in the author's possession.
119. CPP–1960, Art. 413.
120. Gheorghe Gheorghiu-Dej passed away on March 19, 1965.
121. These are the amnesties initiated by Nicolae Ceaușescu, the leader of the PCR: in 1967, on the occasion of the 20th anniversary of the founding of the Romanian People's Republic (December 30, 1947, following King Michael I being forced to abdicate).

Chapter 6

Românoexport Trial

On June 9, 1961, my deputy Rado Alexandru and I were picked up in the middle of the night and in the Securitate car, while putting on the black iron glasses, they told me:

"And now keep silent and speak only when asked"

In the car, on the way to Malmaison,[1] knowing well that no criminal act could be imputed to me, I hoped that the truth would come to light, as it was supposed to after Khrushchev's 1956 congress. I hoped that no Stalinist trials could take place any longer, and that I would soon be home, where my wife and my 9-year-old daughter were waiting for me.

"They did not bring you here in order for you to justify your actions, but to admit to their accusations, as soon as possible so as not to hold them up, that is their pleasure," said my cellmate, a former magistrate, convicted of bribe. How right he was I would understand much later.

Adalbert Rosinger[2]

INTRODUCTION

Chronologically, the RE trial is the last in the series of the Foreign Trade economic trials and the case study of the whole book. The nine people accused in this trial performed important duties on behalf of their country prior to their arrest. The criminal proceedings against the RE officials opened with the arrest of the first two suspects, Alexandru Rado and Adalbert Rosinger, on the night of June 8–9, 1961. From this date until the official opening of the trial before Bucharest Military Regional Court, three years would elapse. The trial opened on June 9, 1964, and lasted for nearly a month. The sentence was given on July 4, 1964. On January 26, 1965, the appeal was held, marking the end of the legal proceedings.

The analysis of the RE trial proved to be very complex for at least two reasons: first, because of the very large volume of data that constitutes its legal documentation, and second, because these documentary data represent, almost exclusively, the point of view of the prosecution. This reality did not allow a detailed description of either the pre-judicial stages or the course of the trial, especially regarding both parties involved. These limits must be taken into account when assessing the position of the judiciary under a totalitarian regime.

The RE trial was unique among the other previously analyzed trials due to the three and a half years, duration of the whole legal action.

According to the Criminal Code of the time, CP-1960, the accusations against RE officials fell into the category of political crimes, being classified as actions against the internal security of the state, as acts of undermining the national economy.

During the investigation and later during the trial, some of the defendants had the audacity and courage to oppose to some extent the charges raised against them, as had previously happened in the CA and AE trials. However, in the RE trial, the opposition of several defendants led to the extension of the investigation and furthermore, the oral or written arguments eventually led to a revision of the initial financial assessment, the main document claiming the value of the defendants' damages to the economy. The trial ended with the conviction of all defendants under severe sentences-long years in prison, large fines as debts to the State, and deprivation of rights.

The sources available for the investigation were the RE Criminal file P179,[3] which held a well-inventoried group of documents, from the beginning of the criminal procedure through the pronouncement of the sentence and the appeal. They related to all the stages of the trial, but they consisted almost exclusively of materials prepared by the investigation or the Prosecution. Apart from the Criminal file, other files, like informant and network files[4] regarding the people involved in the trial were also found at CNSAS. The material underlying the allegations was transferred from the SRI archive to the CNSAS archive in 2002. Additional sources were investigated through the Romania National Archives. Some information came from oral sources, through discussions with people who had been involved in the surroundings of the trial, like a few children of the defendants. Another primary source was the manuscript written by one of the main RE defendants, Adalbert Rosinger.[5]

The specialization of RE was mainly the import and export of raw or processed materials for the textile, leather, and building materials industries.[6] The accusations, based on economic business concluded during the years 1950–1960, claimed that huge damages had been caused to the national economy. But the damages, presumptive ones, were exclusively determined by the prosecution's opinion that higher sale prices and lower purchase prices should have been obtained at the conclusion of the contracts, and the designated financial experts calculated the damages accordingly. The prosecution decided to focus on a small number of contracts, which made up the company's imports and exports, namely cotton and cement.

The RE trial, like the other economic trials, remained unknown to all but the Foreign Trade officials, the involved party members, the Securitate, and last but not least, the circle of the convicts' families and those close to them.

It should be noted that all the contracts that were alleged to have caused economic damage to the state represented an extremely small percentage of the total number of contracts concluded by RE during the period of time involved. In order to demonstrate the contractual issue through this book, only one or two of the incriminating contracts were used to exemplify the procedure through which the contractual decisions were made and how the contracts were deemed to be detrimental to the State.

The analysis of the RE trial done later in this chapter will follow the structure already used for the other economic trials. But, as the RE trial basically serves as the case study of this book, this basic structure will be presented in more detail and with more specific data.

PRELIMINARY STAGES

The Structure of the Criminal Case P179

The RE trial focused on the activity of the enterprise between 1950 and 1961. The information was initially concentrated at the Securitate, in a file under the name SRI-53437.[7] After 1989,[8] the original SRI file remained with SRI, the legal heir of the Securitate after the fall of communism, later being transferred to CNSAS,[9] following my request in 2002. After its delivery to CNSAS, the whole file was redone, pages rearranged, receiving its new name and number: Criminal Case P179.[10]

The file consists of 59 volumes and was created under the tutelage of the Ministry of Internal Affairs,[11] written by Securitate officials at the Department of criminal investigation in the 1960s. The preparation of the file was done partially during the legal procedure and the rest after the final sentences and the appeal, in January 1965. At the beginning of the first volume, one can find its table of contents, under the name of "OPIS." The description of the P179 file contains the index of almost all the information found between its covers but not all of it. The detailing of the information in OPIS stops after the index of volume 37 and up to this place there are 18,000 pages. The reason remains unknown. Nine volumes out of the 59 represent the personal files referring to each of the defendants, during their whole period of imprisonment, either in Aiud or in Oradea.[12]

These last volumes, representing the defendants' prison files,[13] were drawn up for each convict, after the completion of the entire judicial procedure and start of their prison term. Each such file numbered around 100–150 pages. They contained, in particular, information added during the years of imprisonment, mainly testimonies about the state of health, the work of inmates, about personal difficulties, or requests, sometimes attempts to appeals to judicial authorities. Additionally, they contained specific personal data or assessments done by prison guards and also complaints from cellmates. The photo and fingerprints of the inmate are to be found on the first page of each personal file. The structure of personal files is not entirely uniform. Sometimes there is also a table of the inmate's working days, which in addition gave him the right to days off. This explains the fact that inmates whose health, physical capacity, or younger age allowed them to participate in various types of work managed to accumulate days or months, to be later deducted from the period of detention to which they were initially sentenced. But as most of the RE convicts were over the age of 50, they could not benefit from this situation, encountering difficulties with even the lightest of the required work assignments.

Most volumes out of Criminal Case file P179 contain around 500 pages.[14] The most complex parts of the Criminal Case P179 are the investigations of the accused[15] and the analysis made to the trade contracts by the financial assessments . Their single aim was to sustain the court's point of view regarding the future conviction of undermining the national economy, along with the crime of plotting against the social order of the state. These infractions were mentioned by the prosecutor's office as the basis of their indictment and arrest, which allowed the criminal procedure to begin. The financial assessment of the RE trial filled about 825 pages.[16]

RE Defendants and Their Positions Prior to the Trial

Angelo Chinzbrunner, ethnically Jewish, was born on January 14, 1917, in Bucharest. He graduated from the Bucharest Academy of Commerce. The last position in which he served was that of technical consultant for export at RE.

Alexandru Samuilă Costin, ethnically Jewish, was born on July 19, 1911, in Zabaltz, Lipova, Banat County. His last position was that of technical consultant at CA (from 1961), but the arrest occurred as a result of his activity as director of RE (1958–1961).

Mihai Crainic, ethnically Jewish, who had converted to Christianity, was born on May 16, 1904, in Bucharest. His last position was director of the export department at the "Confectia" Textile and Knitwear Factory. He was arrested in the past for his position in RE (1957–1949), as the head of the Textile Import Department.

Sidonia Grigoriu, ethnically Jewish, was born on April 1, 1916, in Bucharest. Her last position was as an expert in the science of commodities at PE. The arrest was in the context of her work at RE (1952–1958) as an export consultant and a coordinator for the trade of cement, textile, and glass products.

Gheorghe Manheim, ethnically Jewish, was born on September 9, 1924, in Poeni, Huedin, Transylvania. His last position was of department director at the Department of Wool Import. He also served as coordinator of the Leather Department.

Alexandru Rado, ethnically Jewish, was born on June 17, 1905, in Resita, Banat County. At times, he held several senior positions at RE, but his last position was of that of an import-export consultant.

Adalbert Rosinger, ethnically Jewish, was born on July 31, 1909, in Oradea, Transylvania. Between 1949 and 1961, he served as coordinator director, deputy director, and technical director at RE. His last position, at the time of his arrest (1961), was that of consultant.

Biniamin Schwartz, ethnically Jewish, was born on September 29, 1909, in Bucharest. His last position was that of director of the Cotton Import Department at RE.

Paul Ştefănescu, ethnically Jewish, was born on October 3, 1915, in Tulcea, Dobrogea. His last position was that of export director in the MCE. Most of the RE defendants were charged under Article 209[1] specifying the undermining of the national economy and the counter-revolutionary sabotage. Although this article served as the basis for all the accusations, depending on the circumstances, the investigators' assumptions and the positions they held in RE, the defendants were also accused of other criminal acts allegedly committed during the period in question (1950–1960).

It was impossible to obtain the personal details of all the Securitate investigators, though data regarding several of them are already cataloged in CNSAS catalogues. The signatures of both the investigators and those under investigation appearing on the filed pages were in most cases handwritten. As some of those pages had later been transcribed by typewriter, the signatures were no longer preserved. It is difficult to conclude from here if the original, written during the investigation, corresponded letter for letter with what was printed. I suppose that the equivalence of information between the two categories of documents, often filed together, was still preserved.

The number of investigators who participated in the investigations was quite small, given the large quantity of pages written during the long time devoted to each of the defendants. The reason for using a small number of investigators was certainly the complexity of the material they needed control of, in order to conduct the investigation in the desired direction. The main investigator of any trial finally wrote the document called the Indictment Conclusions, which was submitted to the Military Court, for the continuation of the trial and the appearance in court. Constantin Cenuse was the author of the Indictment Conclusions for the RE trial. During the investigation, the defendants were presented from time to time, with their up-to-date Indictment documents, and had the right to react in writing. Searching through all the archival materials regarding the trials, RE trial in particular, raised the issue of how the Securitate investigators manipulated the whole complex investigation procedure, in order to reach their goals. The Securitate Criminal Investigation Directorate, through its director,[17] encouraged those appointed to investigate the RE officials to make use of various methods of terror, blackmail, and other means of physical and mental pressure, by which to squeeze out the information needed to form the broad core on which the allegations were to be based. If in the early 1950s, the Securitate consisted mostly of uneducated people, with a low intellectual level, the situation had changed significantly 10 years later, when the Securitate selected employees[18] with a higher level of intelligence, perhaps even with some kind of higher education,[19] who also had the ability to conduct complicated surveys in economic and various sociopolitical fields. Thus, the new Securitate personnel may have had some intellectual abilities on the one hand but also had the necessary physical skills to carry out the "necessary" actions during the investigations, on behalf of the Securitate, with appropriate cruelty. This was also the case of the group of investigators in the RE process.

Criminal Surveillance of the RE Functionaries

In most cases, preliminary versions of Surveillance files were opened for the RE defendants around the year 1958. Their surveillance lasted several years, beginning with the opening of these files. Most of these files were turned into Surveillance files (in Romanian Dosar de Urmărire Informativă, referred henceforth as DUI),[20]and after processing the material they contained, it was decided to personalize and focus the tailing of the suspects by means of rules and procedures specific to the Securitate surveillance.[21]

Each of these files contains the names of those responsible for gathering information about each of the pursued, with as many details as possible, in order to facilitate the finalization of the reports and the final structuring of the DUI. The Securitate had agents and informants, who were all collaborators with varying degrees of commitment. The agents, having signed letters of commitment to service, were obliged to provide information regarding those people specified by their superiors. Other collaborators, who were less involved and under less obligations, were called informants. The Securitate recruited its people through various methods. Some of them were even employees of commercial enterprises, who were routinely in close proximity to those pursued. A study of the Securitate documents referring to the foreign trade trials reveal that a minority of the collaborators, who were identified by their real names, proved to be later, among the future RE defendants. Despite their previous service to the Securitate, they did not receive better treatment or the trust of their investigators. Some of them collaborated at the request of the Securitate, some out of their own initiative.

- Alexandru Rado had been pursued by the Securitate since the mid-1950s, but it was only on June 20, 1960, that a two-volume DUI was opened in his name.[22] Rado dealt with both sales and purchase contracts for the textile industry, in either of his positions, partly vis-à-vis German companies (as in the Bohumer Affair, to be discussed later in this chapter) but also many others (as Egyptian or Australian companies). A Securitate collaborator himself, he had been surveilled closely by many agents and informants.
- Sidonia Grigoriu had been pursued since September 1958, and her DUI, containing a single volume, was opened in November 1961.[23] She was arrested in July 1962. The source of the countless information, found in Grigoriu's file, were written notes offered to the Securitate by informants, whistleblowers or various agents, all this beginning in 1956. One of the reasons she was under surveillance for so long was her father and her sister's emigration to Israel. In this personal file, one can also find various testimonies of cellmates, who assumed the role of stool pigeons.
- Mihai Crainic's pre-Surveillance file was opened in June, 1957. The DUI file, containing two volumes, was opened shortly before his arrest, in September 1961,[24] under number I211279. The file contains statements by some Securitate agents and informants who had reported on his activities within the RE. Another part of the DUI documentation refers to events that had taken place in 1958, when Mihai Crainic was found guilty of foreign currency trafficking while working at Confecţia textile factory. He was convicted under Article 268/17c of CP-1960 and sentenced to four years in prison. Crainic's prosecution was resumed in 1961, when he became a defendant in the RE trial, and the prison term to which he was sentenced was to be concurrent with the term he was already serving.
- Angelo Chinzbrunner's pre-Surveillance file was opened on June 16, 1962, and was turned into a single-volume DUI, numbered I211280, on

November 3, 1962.[25] On October 19, 1962, the Securitate authorities approved the decision to issue his arrest warrant.

- Gheorghe Manheim's personal pre-Surveillance file was opened on October 21, 1961, and was turned into DUI no. I211281, containing a single volume, on December 7, 1962.[26] The information contained in this file included the written observations of a number of agents who had been given the task of getting Manheim to disclose information. Interestingly, the file reveals the unscrupulousness of the Securitate, which was preparing to open Manheim's DUI, and was simultaneously conducting negotiations to recruit him as an agent. This was not a unique phenomenon, as several other foreign trade defendants had been recruited by the Securitate, years before.
- Alexandru Costin's personal pre-Surveillance file was opened on October 21, 1961, and a year later, it was turned into a single-volume DUI,[27] under the number I211283. The file mostly contains photocopies of the contracts and reports signed by Costin, during the period in which he held the position of coordinator manager of RE between 1958 and 1961. In addition, it describes reports of following Costin almost constantly. As usual, informants and agents were the source of this information to be found in his DUI.
- Paul Ştefănescu's personal pre-Surveillance file was opened on April 11, 1959, but closed shortly thereafter for lack of evidence. Initially accused of treason and the divulging of state secrets, he continued to be followed, so when his DUI was opened on December 13, 1963, it contained three volumes.[28] In Ştefănescu's DUI, there is a document, dated January 15, 1963, which attests to the intention of the Securitate to consult with Foreign Trade minister, Marcel Popescu, regarding the question of the detention or release of Paul Ştefănescu, at a time when most of the RE employees were already under arrest in Malmaison.
- Adalbert Rosinger's personal pre-Surveillance file was opened on December 2, 1958, and two years later, on August 27, 1960, it was turned into DUI no. I257122, containing three volumes.[29] In Adalbert Rosinger's personal DUI, there are action plans, as well as surveillance measures prepared several years before the official opening of the file, and his surveillance, by various means, preceded the official opening of the file. Although there are no exact data concerning his being followed by the Securitate, Rosinger's file shows he had been under surveillance since the mid-1950s (more precisely 1954), and was carefully monitored, being one of those people marked by the Securitate. The file contains personal correspondence along with notes sent by agents and informants. The amount of information on Rosinger's work is immense, reporting every step he took. No doubt the suspicions surrounding him were very high, long before he was arrested.

In Rosinger's DUI, one can find references and informative notes, as well as personal letters of his and his family's. Moreover, there is a whole volume with the transcript of his telephone conversations from home and office. Rosinger's close pursuit, which spanned nearly a decade before the trial, continued after his release from prison, with surveillance extending into the 1970s, practically until he left Romania in 1978. His letters and all his correspondence with people, mostly childhood friends, some of whom lived outside Romania, were thoroughly checked, both the letters sent and those received. Some of the letters were copied or photocopied and attached to his DUI.

An entire army of whistleblowers was thrown at RE officials, so various people followed their coworkers, which sometimes led to situations where those who informed about their colleagues found out in time that they were, in turn, pursued by the Securitate.

After his release from prison in 1969, Rosinger appealed to various governments, parties, and judicial authorities to prove his innocence, and even called for the reopening of the trial, and a review of what had happened between 1961 and 1964. But none of these led to any positive result in his favor, proving the blatant injustice of the RE trial. After he was approved to emigrate to Israel in April 1978,[30] before leaving the country in September of the same year, Rosinger handwrote five letters to Israeli recipients in which the sender's name was fictitious. Although the sender didn't exist and although the letters were sent from various mailboxes in Bucharest, the Securitate captured them and added them to the DUI, that continued to be held in his name, the same file opened long before his arrest leading up to his accusation in the RE trial. The original letters in Rosinger's handwriting, in the original envelopes, but with their stamps meant to be sent to Israel, removed, were found by me in his DUI at CNSAS.[31]

From the verification of the Informative Follow-up Files of the persons involved along the way, it can be concluded that the Securitate's well-oiled machinery was mobilized to the maximum during the years after 1958, to allow the accumulation of the necessary testimonies and incriminating evidence to facilitate their prosecution. This process is as terrifying as it is impressive, but there is no doubt that, at least for some of the country's inhabitants at the time, it would not have been considered surprising.

Going over the Surveillance files of the RE trial defendants, it becomes obvious that the cases were carefully woven for the construction of the file in order to form a basis for the accusations. This statement is supported by the following quote:

> We need to investigate Rosinger in order to determine the degree of collaboration between him and Rado, and the reasons that made him prefer Toriel and

> Interglobe-Oberheide.[32] And if he does not recognize it, he will have to be set up, unmasking through documents and mutual confrontations. We will call 35 witnesses to prove the involvement of this group in hostile activities against the state.[33]

This quotation is intended to demonstrate the importance that investigators attached to the confession by RE officials that they had committed those acts of sabotage for which they were already in custody. If he "won't recognize it," as the investigator puts it, means: if he does not agree to acknowledge the evidence the Securitate had acquired or fabricated. Here is the right place to mention a conversation I had with Gheorghe Leuchter,[34] one of the prosecution witnesses and one of the few survivors of the trial who was still alive in 2010. In our discussion, which took place on August 24, 2010, in his home in Düsseldorf, Germany, he made it clear that he could not refuse the Securitate's demand that he testify at the trial. Any person who was requested to testify by the Securitate felt an unspoken threat hanging in the air, and its purpose was to persuade any potential witness to accept the request without resistance. This situation casts a heavy shadow over the credibility of most of the prosecution's testimony in the RE trial.

FROM THE OPENING OF THE CRIMINAL PROCEDURE TO THE APPEARANCE BEFORE THE COURT

The Arrest

According to the norms in force in Romania, Captain Onea Mircea, security investigator at the Department of Criminal Investigations within the Ministry of Internal Affairs, signed the Warrant for Initiating the RE trial on June 5, 1961.[35] The warrant's purpose was to initiate the legal action against various officials within the institution. As in other trials, all the legal clauses cited in the arrest warrants as the basis for indictment, remained in force as the official charges against the defendants. The investigator concluded that according to the information found in Adalbert Rosinger's, Alexandru Rado's, and other people's DUIs, they were all suspected of having undermined the national economy, according to Article 209[1] of CP-1960. The reason was their having given priority to companies from different Western countries, which supposedly caused serious harm to Romania's economy. This accusation justified the judicial procedure.

After the arrest of Alexandru Rado and Adalbert Rosinger, former directors who had already been degraded to the position of consultants at the time of the arrest, the hunt after the other senior RE officials began. The first seven persons, among them one woman, were arrested at different stages, the timing being determined by the importance of their testimonies to the ongoing proceedings, as well as by the level of their commercial involvement in the activity of RE. The investigations were conducted simultaneously and the last defendants were Costin and Ştefănescu, arrested on February 13, 1963.

The Investigation

The investigations of all RE officials took place between June 9, 1961, the date of the first arrests, and February 9, 1964, when the investigation of most of them was officially completed by handing over "the minutes of the notification of the conclusion of the criminal investigation," and preparing the Indictment Conclusions.[36]

A few months later, on June 9, 1964, the trial was opened at the Bucharest Regional Military Court. The Securitate department that dealt with the criminal investigation, identified in documents as the Direction Eight of Criminal Investigations, was led by Colonel Francisc Butyka between 1958 and 1963,[37] the years of the RE defendants' investigations. Butyka's name is well known to any researcher of the Romanian Securitate history. Colonel Nicolae Dumitrescu was responsible for the investigation. The written information referring to the investigation spans thousands of pages, being divided into categories of dialogues between the investigator and the one under investigation, minutes, and declarations made by the investigated person, at the investigator's request. As for the time of the interrogations, it sometimes lasted for many long hours or sequential days, but sometimes, the investigation was interrupted for weeks or even months. On the whole it took up to three years. Some of those convicted in previous Foreign Trade trials, already in jail, were re-interrogated, in order to testify against the new suspects. The RE trial investigation was the longest among the Foreign Trade trials.

Here are some of the details of the interrogations, from the perspective of the accused in the RE trial.

Sidonia Grigoriu

On September 5, 1962, the first Accusation Indictment against Sidonia Grigoriu was issued by Adrian König,[38] who led most of her investigation. Sidonia Grigoriu was arrested on July 28, 1962, which shows that the indictment against her was issued one month and eight days after she had been detained. From the beginning of the investigation, Grigoriu denied all the accusations against her, which referred to preferential treatment granted to the Toriel company[39] at the time of signing the contract. She even claimed that in terms of cement export, she preferred other companies she had worked with, in the past, Toriel not among them, and this was not because she had received any bribes from them. Following the investigation, Sidonia Grigoriu admitted that she had had a conversation with Leon Levy, Toriel's representative, whom she asked to inquire about the situation of her sister, Lola Helman, who had emigrated from Romania to Israel.[40] Though this was a violation of some clause in the Romanian criminal law, it could not have been considered such a serious crime under the relevant law, at the time of the trial. Her next indictment was handed over by Chief Investigator König three months later, on December 24, 1962.[41]

Upon receiving it, Sidonia Grigoriu did not confess to any of the accusations brought against her. She explained that she sometimes took part in conversations with her bosses, but despite the investigator's opinion that such expressions were not aligned with the policy of restricting the right of expression of government officials, considering the spirit of the time, they were merely innocent jokes regarding the Romanian reality of those days, which was not very promising.[42]

Grigoriu received the final Indictment Conclusions of the criminal investigation on February 10, 1964. This indictment included the initial allegations, as well as additional accusations that emerged during the investigation. Immediately afterward, she wrote two declarations, in which she explained her refusal to sign the indictment.[43] The arguments she raised, as well as her deep and serious analysis of the various contracts, represented a detailed and in-depth explanation of the situation of the RE undertaking in terms of trade relations during the period in which its employees were incriminated.

Gheorghe Manheim

Manheim was one of those who took part in the signing of contracts for the sale of cotton yarns of various kinds between RE and the Egyptian company Toriel in late 1955 and in 1956, mediated by Toriel's representative, Leon Levy. These contracts were tied to the cement export contracts with Toriel, one of which will be discussed later in the chapter. According to the testimonies submitted during the investigation, at the time of the transactions with Toriel, there were more advantageous offers on the market for the purchase of cotton yarn, such as the offer of the Belgian company Bermal.[44] A thorough investigation of this case would require the verification of documents, which should have been found in the RE archives. Unfortunately, according to the statements of the representative of the present-day private company, Românoexport Ltd., which held the same name and a similar economic profile, even after 1990, the documents were destroyed. While Manheim acknowledged during the interrogations that the RE consultants could have made different choices during that period that would probably have been more beneficial to the company, he stressed that the decision to select Toriel, even if the reasoning behind it was erroneous or poorly thought out, was in no way ever intended to sabotage Romania's economy.

Manheim specified during the investigation that the management of RE was sometimes forced to opt for what was called the "Optical Price."[45] This price complied with the minimum price recommended by CMEA, but despite this requirement, at times a lower price had to be accepted in order to conclude the transaction. For example, when purchasing fabric remnants for the textile industry as part of the compensation transaction with Seymour,[46] Romanians accepted a higher price for the remnants on account of the cement that was sold. If this system had not been applied, the remnants would have had to be bought from another company, and payment made in foreign currency.

The first indictment against Gheorghe Manheim was issued on April 3, 1963.[47] Faced with the accusations, Manheim expressed regret, but denied that he had given priority to any company during the years he worked at RE, beginning in 1948. He acknowledged to investigators that in his business dealings with various partners, he had received some personal or collective gifts, but this was a common practice in trade relations. At the same time, he vehemently rejected the charges of any intention to sabotage the national economy.[48] He further justified the RE purchase of cotton from Toriel in 1955–1956. According to him, the Romanian textile industry's demand for cotton necessitated the purchase from Toriel, as there were no other offers for a while. On November 11, 1963, the Indictment Conclusions,[49] accusing Manheim of complicity in undermining the national economy were delivered to him by Adrian König. On this occasion, Manheim noted his reasons for opposing the findings of the investigation, as part of the conclusion of the criminal investigation.[50] Analyzing Manheim's two statements in depth, we can see that on both occasions, he presented justified, serious arguments explaining why the second transaction with Toriel had been concluded.[51] On February 9, 1964, Manheim received the final Indictment Conclusions, which again he rejected, stating his reasons for not accepting the charges against him.

Angelo Chinzbrunner

On April 2, 1963, only two months after his arrest, the first indictment was issued against Angelo Chinzbrunner[52] by Ion Sima, the Securitate investigator responsible for his investigation. Most of the investigations focused on the cement contracts with Toriel (C120, C150)[53] and on the amounts in foreign currency that the investigator claimed would have reached a relative of the accused in Paris, who would have been intended to support Chinzbrunner and his family, should they have chosen to leave Romania. Chinzbrunner makes a very interesting statement about the cement contracts, regarding a conversation at the MCE in the presence of Deputy Minister Valentin Steriopol. During this conversation, it emerged that the minister categorically requested that the signing of contracts include transportation by means of either the Cost, Insurance and Freight (CIF) or the Cost and Freight (C&F) systems, instead of the Free on Board (FOB)[54] system. The deputy minister admonished him for two things:

- First, for the failure of the production plan (probably related to cement) stemming from the rigid RE system, which failed to comply with the requirement to establish contracts based on the sale of large quantities, due to market conditions.
- The second concerned the stubborn attempts of RE to sign contracts for cement at "unachievable" prices.

With regard to transport systems, the minister was of the opinion that only CIF and C&F would manage to help the seller move the cement stock (or any other goods). As the transfer of the goods is under the sales agent's responsibility, he has the main interest in bringing the consignment of goods to the target country in the shortest possible time. The minister's position was totally contrary to that of the investigators, who showed that the preferred option would have been FOB transport, and especially regarding the determination to obtain the highest possible prices, without concessions, while according to the ministry, the essential objective was the volume of sales necessary to fulfill the export plan. Chinzbrunner received the Indictment Conclusions on November 21, 1963, from Ion Sima, and unlike the other RE defendants, Chinzbrunner accepted the conclusions of the financial assessment on his concern, and acknowledged the charges specified in the investigation, as well as his share in the signing of the two cement contracts with Toriel. He declared he had no claims against the prosecution and no objections to the findings of the investigation.

Alexandru Costin

Costin's investigation was led by Lieutenant Major Traian Lefticaru and Captain Ion Marin.[55] The main accusations referred to the period in which he was the coordinating director at RE (1958–1961), in connection with the selection of certain companies with which Romania signed contracts for the sale of textiles in exchange for the purchase of cotton fiber or cellofiber (fiber made from recycled cellulose derived from wood or cotton).[56] During the investigation, a comparison was made between prices of Romanian textile versus those of the Hungarian company Hungarotex of Budapest. Officials who had been involved in the sale were accused of selling at a lower price. Although this opinion proved to be unfounded, the documents showing the opposite with regard to prices later disappeared from the Criminal file P179. It was not an isolated case. Costin signed the first Indictment Conclusions on March 30, 1963, but later at the final Indictment Conclusions, received on November 9, 1963, he used the opportunity to supplement the "objections" paragraph, opposing part of the investigator's accusations with which he had been charged.[57]

Mihai Crainic

Crainic received the Indictment Warrant on March 14, 1962, from Lieutenant Major Cenuse Constantin.[58]

Ion Sima, the Securitate investigator, handed him the first Indictment Conclusions on November 14, 1963, to which he answered by issuing a declaration stating his observations and his opposition to the conclusions of the financial assessment, which he had been given for perusal.[59] Mihai Crainic received the second Indictment Conclusions, on February 9, 1964, after the report that followed, the second financial assessment was approved to be perused by the defendants.

Biniamin Schwartz

Schwartz was investigated by Major Lieutenant Traian Lefticaru. In one of his declarations, Schwartz agreed with investigator Lefticaru that Paul Ştefănescu, his director in the MCE, had said that the RE company was obliged to purchase cotton and cotton fibers for the textile industry in Egypt. This directive of Ştefănescu was based on the order sent to the RE officials by the representative of the ministry and it is possible that Ştefănescu himself, as director of the import department, was linked to its adoption. Acceptance of this directive was based on the fact that at that time Romania had a financial credit in Egypt that had to be used through purchases from Egypt, especially of cotton and fiber, and these transactions could be made on the basis of the clearing system.[60]

The first part of Schwartz's investigation took place between July 28, 1962, and September 5, 1962, the date on which the first Indictment Conclusions was handed to him. At the time of its receipt, unlike some of the suspects under investigation, Schwartz admitted that the charges against him were true. Biniamin Schwartz received the last document of the Indictment Conclusions, from Cenuse Constantin on February 10, 1964.[61]

Paul Ştefănescu

The investigation was led by Lieutenant Major Cenuse Constantin. On April 2, 1963, Ştefănescu received the first Indictment Warrant, which referred in particular to his collaboration with employees who held management positions within RE, as well as to the fact that he had approved the conclusion of contracts that had damaged the country's economy, according to the conclusions of the investigation. The investigator claimed that he had not analyzed the reports that had been submitted to him in sufficient depth, before his approval of the contracts.

Upon receiving his Indictment Conclusions from Cenuse Constantin on November 12, 1963, Ştefănescu refused to accept the charges and wrote a notice challenging the allegations in the indictment, as well as the findings of the first financial assessment. On February 9, 1964, he received the final Indictment Conclusions, and after verifying the second financial assessment, Ştefănescu partially approved the indictment, which referred mainly to the contracts with Toriel (C120 and C150).

The investigations of Adalbert Rosinger and Alexandru Rado were the longest among those of the RE employees. While each investigation covered around 400 pages, theirs spanned about 750 pages. The reason was likely that they were the first to be arrested, long before the other RE defendants, and the fact they held higher positions than the others.

Adalbert Rosinger

Adalbert Rosinger received the first Indictment warrant, on January 31, 1962, about six months after his arrest and investigation. Though Rosinger was forced to sign the order, he had the right to oppose its content.[62] He denied the allegations and instead of signing it, he wrote with his own hand on the document: "there is no connection between me and the accusations brought against me."[63] Following the investigation, he took a position contrary to that of his investigator. He challenged most of the charges against him. Throughout the investigation, there was a war of nerves, which was waged against Rosinger for three years, the duration of his investigation. The interrogations were sometimes daily, but there were interruptions of a few weeks, or, toward the end, even of a few months. The interruptions depended on the investigations of other people involved. He was confronted several times with his deputy from RE, Alexandru Rado, and sometimes completely contradicted Rado's testimony. The Indictment Conclusions were received on November 9, 1963. Shortly before that date, between September 23 and October 6, Rosinger was granted the right to study the survey material as well as the first financial assessment results.[64] On October 11, 1963, after studying the material received, Rosinger noted his observations and prepared the notes on which he intended to base his defense. For this reason, Ion Marin issued another decision on November 25, 1963, relating to Rosinger's arguments. Although it rejected most of Rosinger's comments, a few of them were, however, accepted and in the end, also due to the opposition of other defendants, it was decided to carry out a second, additional financial assessment.[65]

According to Rosinger, the investigation was conducted under inhuman conditions, and the chief investigator Cenuse had done his best to break the defendants' spirits, forcing them to confess. The treatment included beatings in sensitive parts of the body, crushing fingers with boots, swearing, and applying other means of physical and mental pressure. Not surprisingly, no evidence could be found in the investigation files of this violence, which took place there in the cellars of Malmaison.[66]

The commission of specialists that prepared the financial assessment claimed that in his commercial relations with some of the defendants, Levy offered them commissions in exchange for their future support of continued trade relations between RE and Toriel.

Some other defendants immediately avowed their connections with Levy, but others denied it, like Rosinger and Grigoriu, who had denied any relationship with him for a long time. A rather unusual situation took place during Rosinger's investigation, in which, at a certain moment, after almost two years since the beginning of his investigation, he made a statement, that he had indeed collaborated with Toriel representative Leon Levy, a person often mentioned during the RE trial.

As Rosinger confessed, he eventually succumbed to torture at the end of March 1963, accepted that he had collaborated with Leon Levy and Lily Oberheide, and had received commissions from both.[67] But after giving this statement, he retracted it the next morning. Rosinger described the conditions under which he agreed to sign the statement as "the known conditions of the investigation and my special state of mind at that time," and that was why he had withdrawn the declarations the very next day. Later, while writing his objections to the Indictment Conclusion (the one submitted to him on November 9, 1963, the final one was submitted on February 11, 1964), Rosinger also claimed the same.[68]

Other objections Rosinger registered on the occasion of receiving the first Indictment document referred to what he considered the investigator's erroneous and dishonest work in manipulating the investigation and the indictment decisions, as well as that of the team named to prepare the first financial assessment.[69] Upon receipt of the Indictment, on February 11, 1964, after the publication of the data of the second financial assessment, it could be observed that the estimate of damages had decreased by 20.4% compared to the initial estimate.

During Rosinger's interrogations, as in others' investigations as well, the defendants were asked the same questions, regarding their intention to deceive the State, time and time again, being forced to answer and talk about the same topics over and over. Rosinger ceaselessly opposed the accusations brought against him, stubbornly claiming that none of the contracts, which he had signed or approved, had resulted in losses to the Romanian economy, and none of them had caused any damage, intentionally or unintentionally.[70]

Alexandru Rado

Rado's investigation was different from the others. It was organized mostly as a collection of declarations, unlike the investigations of the others, which were dialogues of questions and answers between investigator and respondent. Among his multiple declarations, there were many details about various topics related to his position and his activity over the years, but especially about the activity of the other defendants. Sometimes the answer to a single question from the investigator was a long one, written on many pages. It is difficult to conclude from his statements, which of the written testimonies portrayed a true picture of his work. From the very first days, Rado seemingly spoke freely about all sorts of alleged betrayals and conspiracies that he had taken part in during his years in the service of the RE enterprise. Given the way in which the investigation was conducted, the truth of his statements is questionable. Rado received his second indictment warrant on February 2, 1962,[71] from Lieutenant Major Cenuse. Rado signed the Indictment Conclusion without objecting. On November 9, 1963, he received the last Indictment Conclusions from the same Lieutenant Major Cenuse.[72] In accepting the decision, unlike many others, Rado did not deny the allegations against him or the accusations of the financial assessment. In addition, he confessed in an absolutely unusual way, both during the investigation and before the Military Court, that, during his working years, he had committed various acts, either giving preference to certain foreign companies or giving priority to agents of clients with whom RE had concluded commercial contracts, in exchange for various advantages or commissions the agents could have offered him.

In conclusion, the investigation strategy in the RE trial, as in all the trials, was violent and full of traps set for the defendants. In their official position within the enterprise, the defendants were sometimes forced by circumstances to make decisions that were not always in accordance with the written regulations or the optimal conditions. The investigators presented these isolated cases as if they were the daily working routine. The defendants were accused of working without in-depth analysis, without sufficient attention to details, as well as with premeditated sabotage of Romania's national interests. The intensive and painstaking tracking of their activity during a whole decade as well as the focus on specific decisions, without taking into account any other activity carried out over the years, created an alternative reality that investigators created by dismissing everything else, an alternative reality based on a network of false accusations. In this frightening reality, of exhausting interrogations that included psychological manipulations, the investigators managed to destroy the defendants' self-confidence, so that all their professional successes collapsed overnight, like a house of cards.

Warrants Issued during the Investigation

- Warrant for execution of a Financial Assessment

On January 16, 1962, the Criminal Investigation Division of the Ministry of Internal Affairs, which was the department in charge of conducting the investigation in the case of RE, under the leadership of investigator Cenuse Constantin, initiated the appointment of a commission of "experts."[73] They were supposed to conduct an in-depth analysis of a large number of transactions carried out by RE officials, some with the relevant directorates within the MCE.[74] Some of the transactions under investigation involved the import of cellofiber in 1951, the import of cotton between 1954 and 1957, the export of cement between 1955 and 1956, and the export of different types of textiles between 1956 and 1961. It should be noted that their monetary value represented only a tiny fraction of the financial total of the transactions carried out by RE between 1950 and 1960.

In the financial assessment, with reference to these transactions, the commission found a number of mistakes and some irregularities, which in its opinion had caused damages to the Romanian economy. As already specified, both from the testimony of Adalbert Rosinger and from other documents,[75] that after analyzing the professional backgrounds of the appointed financial experts, it may be concluded that none of them had ever held positions related to foreign trade, and therefore their ability to assess trade and transactions was minimal, almost nil.[76] The first version of the assessment was completed on December 30, 1962.[77] As a consequence of appeals and objections raised by some of the defendants,[78] a new warrant was issued for carrying out a new assessment, which was published more than one year later, on February 4, 1964.

This alternative assessment raised the question of how all these estimates were made in the first financial assessment. In addition, the new estimate, which held the extent of the damage to be over 20% less than was previously stated, was not the last. As will be seen further, the final assessment adopted by the court was even lower, and it was the one mentioned in the final decisions of the trial, as a total expression of damages (tables 6.1 and 6.2).

Both tables present the values of the two assessments. Table 6.1 lists the financial damages as established by the First Report of the Financial Assessment in December 1962.[79]

Table 6.1 Damages According to the First Financial Assessment Report

Operations and Products	*Value in Lei*	*Value in Dollars*	*Conversion rate (Lei/$1)*
Cellofiber import Bruno Hasner	7,520,320	474,615	15.84
Cotton Import (1951–1956)	15,270,479	324,666	47.03
Cotton yarn import from Egypt	9,761,982	281,464	34.68
Fabric export transactions with counterparties	34,655,606	557,146	62.20
Cement export to Toriel	44,871,000	443,921	101.08
Total	112,079,387	2,081,812	

Source: Compiled by the author from data in the volumes, ACNSAS/P179/Vol 32 and ACNSAS/P179/Vol 28 where the RE Financial Assessments were published.

Table 6.2 Damages According to the Second Financial Assessment Report

Operations and Products	*Value in Lei*	*Value in Dollars*	*Conversion rate (Lei/ $1)*
Cellofiber import Bruno Hasner	7,520,320	474,615	15.84
Cotton import (1951–1956)	10,938,327	253,379	42.33
Cotton yarn import from Egypt	7,825,703	234,950	33.30
Fabric export transactions with counterparties	27,515,362	436,632	63.01
Cement export to Toriel	35,410,000	347,025	102.03
Total	89,209,712	1,751,601	

Source: Compiled by the author from data in the volumes, ACNSAS/P179/Vol 32 and ACNSAS/P179/Vol 28 where the RE Financial Assessments were published.

Table 6.2 lists the damages established by the second financial assessment, whose data are significantly different from those in table 6.1 reflecting the damages according to the first financial assessment. The value in lei in the second table represents 79.6%, of the value in lei according to the first, and the one in dollars, 84.14% of the value of the amount from the first table. The exchange rate is not the same, and was itself arbitrary in all those computations.

The fact that the figures for the second financial assessment were significantly different from those for the first and that ultimately the final figures were further reduced shows, in a way, that the claim of some of the defendants, namely that the calculated damage was artificial and without any real basis, was based on fact. These essentially fictitious damages were calculated using a comparison between sale or purchase prices agreed in the contracts concluded by RE officials, and prices that the financial experts determined could have been obtained under the same contracts by choosing other companies. So, the accusation brought against the defendants, the causing of damages, originated from the accusation that they had agreed to sell at a lower price and buy at a higher price than could have been obtained. Another very problematic issue was the totally arbitrary dollar-leu[80] exchange rate, determined by the so-called financial experts with no apparent logical basis.

After the two reports, another assessment of the damages was made, which amounted to a total of 76,197,547 lei for all RE defendants.[81] This value, which refers to the total in lei, of the alleged damages, remained the final value, as set by the Sentence on July 4, 1964. It represents 68% of the value established in the first table[82] and 85% of the second one.[83] The damages are, as we have already mentioned, presumptive damages, derived from the Securitate investigators' manipulations of product prices and currency exchange rates.

- Warrant of Final Closing of the investigation (Indictment Conclusion)

Toward the end of the investigation, it was customary to bring the warrant for the closing of the criminal investigation to the attention of the defendants. As previously specified, a warrant was issued for each defendant, sometimes more than once, and another for the completion of the entire criminal investigation. The Indictment Conclusion required the signature of the defendant, and in most cases, they agreed to sign, having the right to register some observations as a personal point of view.

According to CPP-1960, the Indictment Conclusions had to be written and submitted to the Tribunal by the Investigating Body, in the RE case, the Securitate. They had to be approved by the prosecutor who was to bring it before the court, in this case, the Military Court. The reactions of the defendants in the RE trial were different, although most agreed to sign the indictment. It should be noted, however, that Sidonia Grigoriu, who was arrested on August 28, 1962, received the first Indictment Warrant on January 31, 1963, and the last one on February 10, 1963. She refused to sign the Indictment Conclusions, and instead wrote her refusal at the bottom of the document.[84]

In the same context, another defendant in the trial, Adalbert Rosinger, was handed the first Indictment Warrant on January 31, 1962, by Cenuse Constantin.[85] Like Sidonia Grigoriu, Rosinger Adalbert refused to sign the Indictment Conclusions, stating that he did not acknowledge any of the charges against him.

Confrontation between Defendants and Prosecution Witnesses

Direct confrontations took place during the investigations, either between defendants in the same trial,[86] with defendants in other trials, or between defendants and prosecution witnesses.[87] Sometimes so-called "indirect" confrontations took place when a defendant was confronted with a declaration written by another defendant. Rosinger, for example, was confronted with statements made by Alexandru Rado, who was being investigated in parallel. Rosinger rejected Rado's statements.[88]

These confrontations took place between December 1962 and August 1963. They demonstrated different approaches of the defendants. For example, while Rado and Schwartz agreed to testify against fellow defendants under the investigators' pressure, others, such as Costin, Rosinger, and Grigoriu, totally refused to collaborate. It is difficult to analyze the dynamics of life and people's harsh behavior toward one another at Malmaison. It was a unique experience, and it is impossible to know what conditions and what kind of promises or verbal assurances persuaded some defendants to make statements against others, so any attempt to formulate a position in this regard is doomed to failure.

Cellmates Working as Spies for the Investigators[89]

These reports were intended to reveal the reactions of the defendants in various situations, ranging from daily life, to the eve of investigations, or especially their mental states before the daily investigation hours, or upon their return after a whole day of torment.

The reports of the informants, imprisoned in the same cells with the RE defendants, were used as evidence against them during the investigations in Malmaison. These reports revealed the defendants' moods, feelings, strictly personal events, and psychological problems. Some examples will be presented here.

Sidonia Grigoriu

Sidonia Grigoriu revealed to her cellmate how members of the Ministry of Commerce unleashed against the staff of the cement department a kind of verbal terror whose purpose was to achieve, at almost any cost, the quotas for the sale of cement abroad. Reading Sidonia's statements, one can understand the pressure on officials employed in the sale of cement during those years:

> Sell, why don't you sell cement? The task for which you have the functions you have in the company, is to sell cement. So why don't you do it?[90]

For instance, Sidonia's cellmate reported an unusual situation when, returning from the investigation, Sidonia was overcome with hysterical weeping, because pages she had seen in the past, dated December 1962, had disappeared. Their disappearance significantly hindered the preparation of her own defense in the relatively short time allotted for this purpose. This was not the first time the disappearance of documents was reported.[91]

Alexandru Rado

Even if the statements made by the stool pigeons ("cell agents") cannot provide reliable evidence of what happened, they still shed light on the personalities of the RE suspects, who were often discouraged and, having been deprived of any hope of proving their innocence, reached the verge of despair. It is interesting to note, in the words of the stool pigeon reporting about Rado, the lack of veracity of the repeated and almost obsessive statements he made, affirming his intentions to deceive the company and the state, through a conspiracy involving the Jewish Egyptian agent, Leon Levy.[92] His statement made to his cellmate raises the suspicion that his confession of cooperation with Levy was only the result of the humiliation and pain inflicted on him by the Securitate investigators.[93] During his investigation, Rado repeatedly admitted that he had agreed to receive a commission from Levy, Toriel's representative, in exchange for promising to help maintain the continuity of trade relations between Toriel and RE. Quoting what Rado said, it could be understood what was referred to, aforementioned text:

> I'm very sorry, Rado said later, I haven't really done any foreign exchange business, although I've had many opportunities. In addition, when I was in Egypt in 1957, I could not have returned to Romania. I could have brought my daughter to Egypt, as well as my brother, who lived then with his daughter, in Timisoara.[94]

Although Rado felt close to his brother, the latter knew nothing about any money that Rado held abroad.

"I don't keep any money abroad," Rado's cellmate quoted him as saying:

"After all the statements, the investigator still does not believe that it is true and, along with death threats, continues to threaten that he would lose all money outside Romania, but Rado was very calm, because the truth was, he had no money abroad."[95]

Various notes sometimes appeared in red on the margins of the reports, such as "for Comrade Cenuse," or "be careful not to promise something we cannot fulfill."[96] A short dialogue in Rado's cell with his stool pigeon follows:

Rado told his cell mate:

"The investigator told me not to believe that by acknowledging everything, I would receive better food, but that I should have no desire to keep any secrets hidden from the investigation." At which the cellmate continued:

"He does not know whether the investigators, on the contrary, will not appreciate his sincerity, so he might get more years of detention and never be released."

The cellmate tried to encourage him, saying that he would be rewarded for the sincerity of his testimony, after which Rado continued:

"I doubt it, they probably want to use me to incriminate the other defendants, who probably won't admit any allegations against them, and then leave me high and dry."

The cellmate tried to calm Rado and persuade him to continue acknowledging the "facts" the investigation was trying to attribute to him.[97]

Paul Ştefănescu

Reports regarding Paul Sefanescu were written by a stool pigeon in the same cell who barely knew the Romanian language.[98]

Gheorghe Manheim

In the cellmate's reports about Manheim, one can see his insistence on trying to convince the cellmate about his innocence and also the hope that the other officials would keep the same attitude of resistance, rejecting the accusations brought against them. The stool pigeon reported that Manheim had mentioned the torture he was subjected to during his investigations, like slapping, poking fingers in his eyes, and of course swearing and verbal abuse. Reports of Manheim show a freely expressed, stronger opposition than that shown by other defendants through their cellmates' reports. Manheim also mentioned during the investigation that all the defendants were Jews who had been singled out by the Securitate to stand trial.

Adalbert Rosinger

The reports written about Rosinger fill more than one volume (around 700 pages) because of the importance ascribed to his case.[99]

The stool pigeons' reports, assuming that the information was reliable, give a picture of the respondents' state of mind, either after investigation sessions or on days off, as well as the emotions they shared with their cellmates in times of distress, concern, or sometimes even hope. Their thoughts, intentions, and doubts in those hard times of suffering spent in Malmaison can sometimes be vaguely discerned through the reports sent to security investigators. The conversations held by the defendants reveal the fog surrounding them, the relentless emotional load, but especially the uncertainty of tomorrow. The human image these reports let us glimpse at is one of people who until recently had fulfilled their duty to the state, had enjoyed the trust and appreciation of their directors for many years, and were even rewarded for the quality of their work and publicly praised for their achievements. And one day, they were framed and thrown into the "pit" of the prison, where the Securitate investigations took place. Reading the words that the stool pigeons managed to record, one can relive that mixture of hope and despair, which probably emerged in the souls of the prisoners.

The Witnesses for the Prosecution

As already known from previous chapters, all witnesses in the trial were exclusively prosecution witnesses, and no defense witnesses were admitted. The prosecution's rejection of any testimony on behalf of the defendants, in violation of the law guaranteeing the right to defense,[100] is proof of the deliberate elimination of any chance for the defendants to express their views in order to defend themselves. This was not only a gross violation of the law but also the deliberate prevention of the interrogation of witnesses who could have brought the prosecution's accusations into question.

Witnesses used in the RE trial belonged to different professional backgrounds. Some were themselves officials of foreign trade enterprises or MCE officials, others were people who gave in and were compelled by the Securitate either to work as informants or simply to testify against the defendants. It can also be said that in the conditions of detention, the testimonies of the detainees or of the prosecution witnesses were given under the oppressive influence of Securitate representatives. The pressure could be direct, but sometimes it was indirect, being applied to other family members. In most cases, if one member of a couple was arrested, the other was always summoned during the investigation to give their own testimony.

THE COURT SESSIONS

Testimonies before the Court

On June 9, 1964, the RE trial began. The trial ran from June 9 to July 9, 1964. The defendants' testimonies in the presence of the Military Court were complex, but their exact content can only be partially known. All the documentation in the volumes of the P179 revealing the proceedings of the court hearing was based on the daily court recording, made by the tribunal clerk. This method of documentation, common in the Romanian Courts, differed from those used in the trials of Stalin's time in the Soviet Union and in the political trials of Eastern Europe.[101] The protocols and discussions that took place in court were included in the Conclusion[102] document. It also included the short daily official recordings of the trial sessions. Thus, we see that the registration of events that took place during the hearings as well as the protocols were only partially written by the court clerk.[103]

Between June 9 and June 18, the nine defendants, followed by the prosecution witnesses, testified before the Military Court. On the morning of June 20, following the defendants' requests, a brief meeting with the lawyers was approved. As already mentioned in a previous section, meetings between lawyer and client had never been allowed during the investigation. When defenders appeared before the court, they had a short time to express their requests. During this time, they tried to insist on the approval of defense witnesses, who might testify in their favor, supporting their arguments, in order to mitigate the harsh allegations established through the Indictment Conclusions.[104]

As their request was rejected, the defenders expressed their views in one single day, June 22, 1964, when they presented their arguments, and each in turn asked the court to admit evidence supporting the reduction of their alleged guilt in accordance with the applications they had submitted. Prior to the final deliberations of the court, the prosecutor spoke again and rejected all of the defendants' requests, expressed through their lawyers, to bring new documents and witnesses before the court and to appoint a new commission of experts to carry out an independent financial assessment, parallel to those which led to the assessment used by the prosecutor and presented to the court.

In the end, the second judge of the appointed Military Court gave his approval for additional evidence in favor of the witnesses, such as documents kept in the RE or MCE offices, or various reports. He also agreed that the experts should clarify some of their arguments regarding the assessment. They appeared in court and responded to some of the defendants' and lawyers' statements. On June 22, 1964, the representative of ISCE RE civil party[105] spoke about the damage established by the financial experts, and accordingly requested that the court order the defendants to pay the damages.

In the end, the prosecutor took the floor again. This time he proposed changing the punishment for undermining the national economy, which was to refer to each of the accused: rather than applying Article 209[1] (paragraph 2), which demanded the death penalty, Article 209[1] (paragraph 1) would be applied, reducing the punishment to "only" 5–25 years of forced labor. Thus, the prosecution showed his "generosity" toward the defendants.

Attempts continued to persuade the court to mitigate the verdict of undermining the national economy, even to the point of eliminating it. Defendants argued that the charge of undermining the national economy should reasonably be replaced by a charge of negligence in office, in accordance with Article 242 of CP-1960.

The court accepted the prosecution's position in full.[106] Prior to the verdict, the defendants were asked to state their views on the court decision. The reactions were very different. While Grigoriu, Manheim, Rosinger, Costin, and Ştefănescu were eager to plead total innocence, rejecting all charges against them, Chinzbrunner and Crainic asked that the decision be left to the discretion of the court, without insisting on their guilt or innocence, and Schwartz and Rado fully accepted the accusations brought against them during the investigation.

The Sentence

The documents that were issued at the end of the trial, after the Conclusion, were the Minute and the Sentence.[107]

As soon as the defendants' positions were heard, the members of the court withdrew in order to formulate the final sentence. The discussion was thus closed on June 26, 1964, in order to reopen for the pronouncement of the Sentence, on July 4, 1964.[108] The document preceding the Sentence, the Minute,[109] essentially comprised the court's decisions on the appropriate punishments for all charges in the RE trial, in accordance with CP-1960. The last part of the RE session at the Military Court was arrayed[110] like a play on the open stage: the accusers face to face with the defendants, the audience composed of the relatives of the accused, opposite the Securitate representatives, and last but not least, the members of the judiciary, those who in the heat of July 1964, decided the fate of the group of Jewish RE officials, actually for the rest of their lives. In reality, the whole play-trial was manipulated from behind the curtain by its initiators, of the Department of Criminal Investigation of the Securitate, under the unambiguous leadership of the PCR.

- *Alexandru Rado* was found guilty of the following crimes and felonies:
  - The crime of undermining the national economy[111]
  - The felony of plotting against the social order[112]
  - The crime of disclosing state secrets[113]

He was sentenced to ten years of forced labor and subjected to five years of civic degradation and the confiscation of all his property.[114]

- *Adalbert Rosinger* was found guilty of the following crimes and felonies:
  - The crime of undermining the national economy[111]
  - The felony of plotting against the social order[112]
  - The crime of disclosure of data not intended for publication[115]

He was sentenced to 15 years of forced labor and subjected to 8 years of civic degradation and the confiscation of all his property.

- *Mihai Crainic* was found guilty of the following crimes and felonies :
    - The crime of undermining the national economy[111]
    - The felony of plotting against the social order[112]
    - The crime of disclosing state secrets[113]

He was sentenced to eight years of forced labor and subjected to five years of civic degradation and the confiscation of all his property.

- *Paul Ştefănescu* was found guilty of the following crime:
    - The crime of undermining the national economy[111]

He was sentenced to five years of forced labor and subjected to three years of civic degradation and the confiscation of all his property.

- *Biniamin Schwartz* was found guilty of the following crimes:
    - Complicity in the crime of undermining the national economy
    - The crime of disclosing state secrets[113]
    - The felony of plotting against the social order[112]

He was sentenced to six years of forced labor and subjected to three years of civic degradation and the confiscation of all his property.

- *Alexandru Costin* was found guilty of the following crime:
    - The crime of undermining the national economy[111]

He was sentenced to 10 years of forced labor and subjected to 5 years of civic degradation and the confiscation of all his property.

- *Gheorghe Manheim* was found guilty of the following crime:
    - Complicity in the crime of undermining the national economy
- He was sentenced to five years of forced labor and subjected to three years of civic degradation and the confiscation of all his property.
- *Sidonia Grigoriu* was found guilty of the following crimes and felonies:
    - The crime of undermining the national economy[111]
    - The felony of plotting against the social order[112]

She was sentenced to 10 years of forced labor and subjected to 5 years of civic degradation and the confiscation of all her property.

- *Angelo Chinzbrunner* was found guilty of the following crimes and felonies and misdemeanor:
    - The crime of undermining the national economy[111]

- The felony of plotting against the social order[112]
- The misdemeanor of non-compliance with legal obligations regarding the execution of operations with foreign means of payment[116]

He was sentenced to eight years of forced labor and subjected to five years of civic degradation and the confiscation of all his property. The punishments for each defendant's different convictions were to be served concurrently, resulting in the prison terms listed earlier. The application of penalties regarding the civic status of the defendants would go into effect from the date of release, whether that date had been changed by a pardon or amnesty.

In addition to the severe punishments mentioned earlier, each defendant was obliged to pay the costs of the trial to the state treasury, according to the severity of the punishment received. Sentence no. 31 / 4.07.1964 was read before the Military Court of the Bucharest Region, before the RE defendants who had already been convicted. They were given the right to submit an appeal to the Military Court within three days.

Thus ended the first part of the RE trial, after three years of sustained investigation, the conviction of all those brought before the judiciary, and heavy sentences of years of detention and forced labor. The fact that all the defendants were Jewish was mentioned as a factor in their alleged crimes against the state during the reading of the sentence, but this mention, as well as other parts of the speeches given in court, was not recorded by the clerk. The financial damage, finally established for the third time during the procedure, remained set at the value of 76,197,547 lei.

The Appeal

The Sentence of the RE trial remained unchanged even after the appeal, held on January 26, 1965, by Decision no. 4/26.01.1965. Some minor changes were however accepted, one for all the convicts and two for specific persons:

The general amendment was to change the status of the charge of plotting against the social order of the State based on Article 209 (2c),[117] to the same charge based on Article 209 (2a).

In addition, two other changes were accepted regarding two defendants:

- *Mihai Crainic*, whose punishment according to Sentence no. 31/4.07.1964 was merged with an older punishment, Sentence no. 1446/18.08.1958. Consequently, his years of detention were counted from 1958.
- *Angelo Chinzbrunner*, whose charge of illegal foreign currency transactions established by Sentence no. 31/4.07.1964 in the RE trial was reduced from four to two years. However, since his maximum sentence had been set at eight years, the actual period of detention was not shortened.

THE ANALYSIS OF SOME INCRIMINATING CONTRACTS

After three years of investigation, the Securitate authorities presented the Indictment Conclusions to the Military Court gradually, adding each defendant to the group in turn, and presenting more and more evidence. Each person's investigation lasted a year or two, depending on their position at RE, while the investigation of some, who held senior positions in the company, continued for as long as three years. The written material compiled during the investigation comprised a very wide range of facts, not only in terms of the events on which the trial was based but also particularly extensive documentation and databases that were created over time, in an endeavor to describe and explain what led to the eventual conviction. The subject, as already known, was the conclusion of various contracts between Romania and foreign countries either for purchase or for sale, which were carried out by the employees of RE. The operations spanned the entire decade between 1950 and 1960. The largest part of those contracts were either for the sale of Romanian products, like textile or leather articles, or construction materials (cement mostly), whereas the purchases were mostly of cotton and cotton yarn. The financial value of the contracts that were identified as criminal during the RE trial represented only about 2% of the total RE turnover during the decade considered. Out of the many incriminating contracts specified by the financial assessment, two of them will be further chosen for a broader analysis of the situation and an attempt to establish whether the RE officials' decisions had indeed been incorrect and detrimental to the national economy. The selected contracts were very significant contracts, concluded between RE and the Egyptian company Toriel in the years 1955–1956, and will be discussed in more detail. The contracts with Toriel are related to each other and represent two of the main contracts on which the prosecution based its argument during the trial, especially as these contracts concerned the largest group of defendants.

These contracts will be approached using the information contained in the Criminal Case file P179, and partly using the personal Informant Files of some of the persons involved.[118] All will be done within the context of the economic and commercial norms of the time. My choice to discuss these two contracts for the sale of cement concluded between RE and the Egyptian company Toriel (hereinafter referred to as C120 and C150) was due, on the one hand, to the need to limit the presentation of countless data, and limit my analysis to a small number of transactions between RE and foreign companies, and on the other hand, due to the representative nature of these contracts, because of their complexity and the variety of points of view from which they were regarded by both the investigators and the defendants. These contracts represented a turning point in the construction of trade relations between Romania and its trade partners in the mid-1950s. Based on these two contracts with the Egyptian company Toriel, one of the main suppliers of cotton to Romania at that time, as well as a buyer of cement, a product exported by Romania to various world markets through intermediaries such as Toriel, I will try to explain which context led to the preparation of the economic trial against the senior officials of RE who were involved in the Toriel transactions.

Cement and Cotton Contracts Concluded in 1955–1956

General and Administrative Aspects

In the first years after gaining power, the new regime paid special attention to initiatives in the development of foreign trade, as Romania's foreign trade ties were partly lost after the end of World War II, and their resumption was imperative.[119]

Most of the activity of RE was related to the import and export of products like textile, leather, and construction materials. Carrying out transactions was a complex process, begun by establishing contacts, mostly made indirectly, through intermediaries, agents or buyers. It is also worth mentioning that many of the agents sent to Romania were former Romanian citizens who had adapted to life in Western countries, after leaving the country during the interwar dictatorial regimes, when Jews were persecuted by various means, or toward the end of the 1950s, when the communists came to power in Romania. Through them it was customary to establish the price, the type of transaction, the method of payment (barter, clearing or exchange of compensation in foreign currency), and the modes of transport. How the efficiency or profit of some transactions was assessed often depended on the attitude toward the product in question. For example: Was it better to sell the entire quantity in stock, but at a lower price, or on the contrary, to get a better price, but without being able to sell the intended amount, thus remaining with unsold merchandise? Was it better to maintain collaboration relations with certain important companies, allowing Romanian products to penetrate the markets of countries to which the products had not yet been introduced, despite poorer conditions for the sale and purchase of the products in question, or should higher prices be maintained in any case, at the risk of losing trade relations with suppliers with good potential for future business? Although procedures and working methods were officially established, contracting opportunities often emerged unexpectedly, through last-minute decisions made by a senior official. Moreover approvals were sometimes granted through unofficial verbal exchanges with the relevant director or deputy minister, which more than once took place in private. Consequently, decisions were often based on a personal trade relationship, that had developed over the years. In this way, a new trade connection could often be established when an official managed to form a relationship with a potential trade partner, even in a less formal way.

The RE foreign trade plan, as well as that of the other enterprises belonging to MCE was derived from a provision issued by the CSP,[120] which set the annual quotas on all import-export trading enterprises. After receiving these quotas to be achieved, enterprises published some tenders and requests to foreign suppliers, some of which were mentioned in trade magazines, in an attempt to open negotiations. The information was found either directly or through the Chamber of Commerce of Romania, which published lists of foreign magazines categorized according to fields of activity, or types of products. Sometimes, the names of agents who mediated in the various fields of trade were also published. In the event that some future contractual relations began to form, it was necessary to inform the representatives of the MCE, or more precisely its Import or Export Directorate, depending on the type of transaction in question, so that the buying or selling activity could be coordinated with the Plan Directorate[121] of the MCE. The communication of these reports was made together with the monthly or quarterly comparison of the requested quota with the number of transactions achieved. In addition, the execution and volume of the transport, either by sea or by land, was monitored and reported. The reports were forwarded by the Plan Director to either Rosinger, the RE coordinating director, or in his absence, to Klein[122] or Rado, who were also deputy directors, whose signatures were required for the implementation of those transactions.

After the decisions were made within the relevant Directorate, the implementation plan was transferred to services responsible for the next phase of concluding the contract. Officials in the MCE were further notified of the progress of the negotiations only if the offers were too low (for sale) or too high (for purchase), or when there were significant changes in delivery dates. Sometimes the report to the ministry about the final conclusion of a contract that had been under negotiation for a longer time was limited to personal phone calls between the RE staff, who participated in the negotiations, and the ministry officials, either directors or officials holding key roles.[123] The conduct described earlier, which represented a usual way of proceeding, was later used by the Securitate against the accused officials.

During the discussions held by members of the RE, either with traders or with representatives of foreign companies, before concluding sale or purchase transactions, a report was prepared addressed to the MCE. This procedure took place in particular for goods sold at the Stock Exchange, such as cotton or sugar. The purpose of the report was to show what offers had been received for the products to be traded. The main sections that were included in the report reflected the relevant offers received during the negotiations for the conclusion of the contract, as well as certain relevant data, such as the estimated price of the product, the quality and quantity in question, the country of origin, and delivery dates provided by companies in coordination with possible transport mechanisms.[124] The paper also aimed to indicate alternative proposals made at the same time. Usually, a Report of Principle could be submitted first and only later, after the approval in principle had been received, the report could be sent to be signed. The signature was a green light for concluding the transaction with the customer. Based on the approval in principle, the negotiating team (which could sometimes include only one person) in essence had the approval necessary to close the deal. If a contract was amended, the negotiating team had to obtain a reapproval, at least verbally by phone. The conclusion of the transaction was accompanied by the final version of the report, which was to be sent for final approval to the appropriate Directorate of the Ministry of Import or Export. The approval was usually given by a deputy of the minister of Foreign Trade and was based on the approval of the director of the trading company.[125] In addition to the signatures mentioned, the signatures of the Directors of Payments and Relations also appeared on the report. The approval of a transaction followed a discussion with the consultant[126] of the relevant department, after which it had to be forwarded to the corresponding directorate in the MCE.

Because the appropriate director in the ministry was not always available for signing, consultants were sometimes entitled to sign the final version of the contract. The approval of the MCE was still necessary. The following measures had to be taken into account toward closing any contract:

- Planning of data set by the CSP
- The proposed terms of auction proposals or other offers if any were submitted
- Careful examination of the quantities and quality of the contracted product, its delivery time, and the MCE's ability to make the payments
- Information on the delivery of the product (conditions of transport, sea, rail, or road, as well as the associated payment system)
- Methods of action in the event of a litigation between the parties involved, or in case of a breach of the terms of the contract
- The offer or the receipt of guarantees related to the delivery of products or to compliance with the accepted terms of payment

RE had the duty to ensure the quality of the products upon receipt, in accordance with what was stipulated in the contract. Even if, according to the defendant Alexandru Rado, the direct trading method would have been preferable to the use of intermediary services, this could not be easily achieved, due to Romania's isolated position in international trade during the years 1950–1960. Western companies had difficulties at the time, in obtaining licenses to import goods from Romania, and it was also difficult to find suitable and reliable commercial agents. Still, representatives of Western Europe were sent to Romania to try to promote commercial business, and this was growing significantly during the 1950s.

These representatives had a personal interest in promoting transactions with Romania, since they received a certain commission upon completion. The defendants' testimonies unequivocally proved that granting commissions was common practice in international trade, even if it resulted in a certain increase in price.

The Cement Contracts, a Contractual Model of the 1950s

In the 1950s and 1960s, Romania was known in Western Europe as a major exporter of cement,[127] Poland[128] being its only competitor in the Communist bloc at the time.

In 1954, RE was unsuccessful in meeting the quota of cement exports imposed by the CSP. One year later, in 1955, CSP increased the cement export requirement to five times that of the previous year, and the quantity imposed by CSP amounted to 1,222,000 tons.[129] The need to find buyers was particularly urgent. Although Romania would have preferred payment in currency for the products it sold, this was often impossible, so barter or clearing methods were usually used. These methods had developed especially in times of economic instability, in the absence of liquidity in international trade and when there was no collaboration between the different countries' banking systems.

One of the compensation methods is barter and the other is clearing. Barter is the simplest method of compensation. Clearing, unlike the barter system, uses the global payment method, in which for all sales and purchases that take place within a set time period, the actual payment is made after the transactions have been completed, sometimes a year or more later, and between two or more partners. Clearing is similar to barter, in that payment is made in goods, but different from it, in that the barter system involves direct one-on-one transactions, while in the clearing system, the remaining financial balances from deliveries that have not yet been carried out are settled only at the end of a period agreed upon by the relevant parties. Compensation methods have often been used in trade between CMEA countries, sometimes with multilateral arrangements among several countries. In the 1950s, about 60% of international foreign trade was achieved through clearing methods, even between Western European countries.

Other terms related to foreign trade practices are the terms that describe types of cargo transport services, namely FOB: free on board; CIF: cost, insurance, freight; or C&F: cost & freight.[130] Negotiations on freight transactions have always included the type of transport to be used. The choice of a method of transport was made according to the considerations of importers or exporters: for example, using the FOB method, the exporter is not responsible for the arrival of the goods or for the means of transport, so the exporters would usually prefer this method that eliminates their responsibility for the transport of the product. Of course, this method involved a discount for the buyer, and sometimes this choice could determine a transaction's profitability, so the subject of transportation costs and the division of this responsibility were both complex issues.

In accordance with these transport methods, which referred here to clearing transactions, the payment due to Romania for the sale of cement became a credit for future purchases. The credit was opened in the country where the transaction was made, and RE was entitled further purchase products, for example, cotton or cotton yarn for the Romanian textile industry. Such transactions were made between two or sometimes even three partners.[131]

In the early 1950s, cement exports to Western markets gradually declined as different countries began to cover their own domestic cement needs. At the same time, some of the customers buying cement in Romania withdrew, partly because their governments refused to issue import licenses. Hence, the young socialist state had to promote trade relations through intermediaries in order to market the cement in Western countries or in the third world. It was sold to either local companies in the agent's country or to companies in other countries. Selling through intermediaries lowered the price, because a share of the sale price had to be paid to distributors. Carrying out sales through intermediaries, or allowing the resale by the intermediaries of the original Romanian products, were considered by the investigation to be serious accusations against the officials from RE.[132]

Romania-Egypt Cement Contracts of the 1950s

The trade relationship between the two states was started by the sale of Romanian wheat in exchange for Egyptian cotton through a barter transaction initiated by Adalbert Rosinger during a visit to Egypt in 1951.[133]

Until 1951, RE purchased the quantity of cotton needed for the textile industry from the USSR, supplemented as necessary with cotton purchased from markets in Western Europe (France, Italy), with the payment being made in currency. Romania's very low foreign exchange reserves and the need for cotton increased the interest in signing barter contracts with countries with great potential for cotton sale, such as Egypt. The supply of cotton and cotton yarn had various options, and payment could be made in Egyptian pounds, which were not considered a strong currency.[134] As a result of

Rosinger's visit, in the spring of 1951, Egypt (probably the MISR Company) sold 5,500 tons of cotton yarn to Romania, paid for with the credits earned from the previous sale of 64,000 tons of wheat.[135]

During Rosinger's visit to Egypt in late 1953–early 1954, a commercial link was established between RE and the Egyptian company Victor Toriel (hereinafter Toriel). Toriel was an Egyptian company that had the potential to fill Romania's cotton and cotton yarn demands.

In December 1953, following the establishment of links with various Egyptian companies, a quantity of cotton yarns was purchased from MISR[136] and later, in 1954, the acquisitions from MISR continued. Romania went on with the purchases from Toriel as well, although the delivery of the cotton was not on time. Thus, a letter of guarantee from the buyer (especially the companies Toriel or MISR, the main Egyptian cotton suppliers) began to be included in some of the transactions with Egyptian companies.[137] These contracts involved payment via compensation methods, exchanging Egyptian goods purchased by Romania for Romania's sales in Egypt.[138]

According to Rosinger's testimony in court, several Egyptian companies[139] had begun contracting with RE to sell cotton yarn at the time. During his stay in Cairo, in 1954, Rosinger served as chairman of the official trade commission of Romania. The purpose of the visit was to persuade Egypt to buy processed wood, oil, and various other Romanian products in exchange for the purchase of cotton and cotton yarn. On this occasion, the first contact was made with Leon Levy, a Jew of Egyptian nationality, the representative of Toriel company who held the position of buyer of the company.

Levy arrived at the Romanian Embassy in Cairo, in January–February 1954, requesting to meet Rosinger, the head of the delegation, in order to establish the basis of a bilateral trade relationship between Toriel, whom he represented, and RE.

Toriel had many branches all over Egypt and owned a lot of cotton spinning mills that had the ability to create various types of yarns among those requested by the Romanian textile industry. RE maintained its commercial contact with Toriel, sending Alexandru Rado to Egypt for new cotton purchases. In those years, Rado was an import-export consultant and played an important role in analyzing the cotton market and pursuing important offers in Egypt. He sought suppliers and possible contractors in order to export various Romanian products to Egypt. During his investigation, he admitted his preference for Toriel, probably as a result of threats he had been subjected to by the Securitate, whose investigators managed to manipulate him. Alexandru Rado admitted most of the charges brought against him, for instance, that he collaborated with Toriel's agent, Leon Levy, in exchange for a commission that Levy was supposed to pay him, following the increase in trade between the RE company and Toriel.

However, in a conversation with a colleague in the prison cell and also after his release from prison in a conversation in the house of another former foreign trade official, who had moved to Germany,[140] Rado presented a version that contradicts the statements he made during the investigation, when he could not withstand the three years of physical and psychological pressure to which he was subjected. It should be remembered that Rado and Rosinger were the first two people arrested in the RE trial.

At the end of 1954, Romania opened the Romanian economic agency in Cairo, under the leadership of Vasile Dinu. There had been disagreements between the Cairo economic agency and the management of the RE company in Bucharest, and arguments sometimes developed regarding the choice of suppliers for the RE transactions in Egypt. It should also be mentioned that Vasile Dinu would be one of the key witnesses of the prosecution against the RE defendants. Despite the fact that Romanian economic agencies all over the world were coordinated by MCE,[141] under the conditions of the partnership and in accordance with the direct instructions from the RE management in Bucharest, Cairo's economic agencies had some independence. Thus, the agency had the right to reject local offers and offer alternative proposals, sometimes overturning RE decisions. These conditions were also the causes of the tensions that arose in the reciprocal ties.

CMEA used to impose a price range for all countries in the Communist bloc, which was considered to be within reasonable limits. In addition, a recommended minimum price was decided. As will be observed in the case of cement operations between 1955 and 1956, the price used in the Romanian cement transactions was not the one established by CMEA, nor by any other authority, but only on the basis of supply and demand per product, or determined by other possible constraints.

According to study reports, in the early 1950s, the lower price limit for selling one ton of cement was set by CMEA at $9.2. In order to sell the cement at a lower price, a legitimate reason was needed. However, according to Rosinger, who served as the coordinating director of RE at the time, the price set for the product was ultimately, despite CMEA's recommendations, determined by the constraints, in the context of other obligations such as general requirements imposed by the CSP.[142]

CMEA's price recommendation ($9.2/ton), under the CIF delivery, had some flexibility, because in 1954–1955, the prices varied between $8.5 and $9.5 per ton, under the FOB delivery condition.[143] For the seller, the price corresponding to the "FOB delivery condition" was lower than the "CIF or C&F delivery condition," as it included transport costs only until the transfer of the goods to the buyer's means of transport. Therefore, the price under the FOB condition included neither the cost of insurance nor the cost of loading the goods onto the buyer's ship, nor further transport costs to the destination.

The difference between the two methods allowed the MCE to sometimes agree to lower the price of cement transactions. In conclusion, was it possible to accept a price below the lower limit set by CMEA?

It is very likely that in practice, the price set by CMEA was used only as a reference price. It should not be ignored that in all those years Romania maintained a degree of independence in its economic policy, which was true both in cement transactions, and in other transactions made by RE, especially with Western or third world countries. The fall of the price below the limit set by CMEA was more problematic when the payment was not negotiated in internationally accepted currency but rather in local currency, as in the transactions with Egypt, where the payment was calculated in Egyptian pounds.

Toward the end of 1954, some significant events took place in the RE export of cement. Toriel became not only an important trading partner for cotton versus cement transactions but also an intermediary seller of Romanian cement to new markets, to which Romania would not otherwise have had access. In addition, one of the events that tipped the scales in favor of the business partnership with Toriel and its agent, Leon Levy, was the Bohumer Affair.

The Bohumer Affair

Bohumer was a West German company producing various types of steel. During those years, Romania was attempting to promote cement sales in markets in the Persian Gulf region, including Saudi Arabia, areas without trade relations with Romania.

At the end of 1954, RE sent Alexandru Rado to Berlin, as an import-export German speaker consultant, to discuss possible transactions with Bohumer. The transaction with Bohumer had to be made through compensation between RE, the Romanian foreign trade enterprise Tehnoimport and the Bohumer company itself. During the transaction, the Germans were to make payments for Romanian cement by supplying various rolled steel products or other iron products manufactured by Bohumer. At that time, Romania had a significant deficit in terms of fulfilling the cement export plan set by the CSP. The price of cement in use was about $11 (approx. 79s.)[144] using the FOB method through the port of Constanta,[145] but this price was relevant only for the export of a small quantities of cement.[146] The cement demand on the world market had diminished, whereas the competition had intensified[147] and sales of surplus Romanian cement had become problematic.[148] During his stay in Germany, Rado received instructions to sell as much cement as possible, even if the price per ton would be below that set by CMEA. These were communicated to him through the cement export adviser, Sidonia Grigoriu, who was also a defendant in the trial.[149] Rado, who was fluent in German, established connections with other local companies besides Bohumer that had begun selling cement to various markets. In this way, an impression was created on the world market that there were numerous cement exporters, when in fact one of the few sources was Romania, trying in different ways to sell cement, as part of its own export needs. That was the reason that the general downward trend in prices continued. The false impression that was created on the world market that hundreds of thousands of tons of cement were to be sold did not reflect reality. At the same time, Greek and Yugoslav exporters also reduced their prices. Following these events, and the rumor of cement sales, the price of cement began to fall in the Persian Gulf and African markets, from $9.30 to $9 (from 64.49s. to 64s.).

At the beginning of January 1955, there was a discussion between Rosinger and Rado, during which it was agreed to require each state that would purchase Romanian cement in the future not to lower the price below a certain minimum sale value, which was to be established by intermediary companies. Even though in the first stage of negotiations with Bohumer, the Romanian side's asking price was $11 (79s.) per ton, using the FOB delivery condition, via Constanţa,[150] eventually, Rado's negotiations with the other German companies led to a drop in the price of cement to $9.5 (71.65s.) per ton, in part due to the multitude of competing suppliers. In January, 1955, some RE officials were invited to the office of MCE deputy minister Ana Toma[151] in the presence of the export director. At that meeting, Sidonia Grigoriu, the head of the cement export service, received the approval of the ministry, to convey to Alexandru Rado that the sale of the cement could be concluded by lowering the price to $9.20 (64.29s.). Following lengthy negotiations, Rado finally managed to sell Bohumer 150,000 tons of cement at a price of $9.23 (66s.) per ton, FOB Constanta.[152]

The most important fact in the clear favor of all RE members involved in concluding the contract with Bohumer was that despite the difficulties and the relatively low price, issues which had been known both by the management of the RE company and the MCE, not only did the leadership not reject the contract but also proceeded to sign it, finalizing it when Rado received approval.[153] The most important thing was to comply as much as possible with the cement export plan set by the CSP. Thus, the compensation could be achieved with the steel and iron products, which were to be supplied through the sale of cement, without the need to pay in foreign currency. Also, during her investigation, Grigoriu pointed out more than once that there was a document in the volumes of the financial assessment, according to which Rosinger, then director of RE, gave an express order to Rado, located in Berlin, namely to offer Bohumer an additional commission of 2%–3%, if the deal was completed. This type of commission, although not common at the time for similar business, was proposed in this case, because it was very important to keep the transaction. Grigoriu stressed that Rosinger could not have made such a proposal to Rado, on March 18, 1955, without the direct involvement of the relevant leadership in the MCE. Such a proposal would have been impossible, Grigoriu claims, without the approval of his superiors.[154] Moreover, Rado was offered a reward of $200 in appreciation of the signing of the contract.[155] All these statements had the role of emphasizing the importance and correctness of the decisions taken then by the RE management and senior officials involved in the Bohumer Affair. But despite all the measures taken and the events that Rado and the RE went through, in the end, the contract with Bohumer was terminated, for the following two reasons:

A. Once the contract was concluded, the association of cement exporters from Germany opposed its development because the relatively low price for sales on various markets would determine a future disadvantage for German cement exporters themselves.
B. On the other hand, cement importers such as Saudi Arabia refused to buy cement of Romanian origin, although it was sold at low prices. There were even more convenient offers at that time, for example, from the Greeks and Yugoslavs.

Consequently, the transaction with Bohumer was canceled. After its cancellation, the agency in Cairo persisted for several months, and through countless attempts, to sell the Romanian cement on different markets, through various intermediaries. But despite negotiations with several Egyptian companies and mediators for possible sales to Saudi Arabia or Sudan, no contract was concluded. During this period, another sale-purchase relationship began to materialize, between RE and the Toriel company, conducted through Leon Levy. After many failed attempts to trade cement through direct links made by the Cairo economic agency, the RE leadership asked it to stop any attempt at negotiation, in order to move directly to negotiations held in Bucharest. According to reports from Berlin during Rado's stay, Leon Levy was to become the potential buyer of cement in Romania in 1955.

The Cement Contracts between RE and Toriel—C120 and C150

According to the prosecution's argument, among all the cement contracts, these two caused the main financial damage. The actions taken by some convicts were presented by the investigation as having the intention and purpose of extracting personal benefits through the Toriel agent. In the following discussion, the two contracts will be referred to as C120 and C150. These terms refer to the quantity of cement in thousands of tons established in the initial contracts (120,000 and 150,000 tons of cement). The C150 contract was a barter transaction, the sale of cement in exchange for the purchase of cotton or certain cotton yarns. For this reason, the contract for the purchase of this cotton is considered in the trial, as part of the C150 contract. With regard to this addition of the purchase of cotton, as a component of the C150 contract, Romania had not undertaken through the transaction, to purchase this cotton, necessarily, from Toriel. If cotton-supplying companies selling at a more convenient price had been found, the purchase could have been made from those companies. Toriel would have priority only if it sold cotton at a better price than the others. However, the RE officials involved in signing this contract were accused of making the transaction in favor of Toriel primarily for reasons of personal, ethnic, anti-state interests. Unfortunately, because of the space limitations of this book, only one of the two, the C120 contract will be analyzed in depth.

The Contract for the Sale of 120,000 Tons of Cement to Toriel (C120)

The period when the C120 contract was concluded was a very difficult period in terms of the international conditions for selling cement. There were few opportunities and few customers until the third quarter of 1954. No attempt, made either directly by the RE representatives or by the Cairo economic agency, led to the conclusion of any contract. No reliable and firm offers from any company were received.

Besides the fact that the export objectives imposed on the RE were impossible in terms of quantity, other conjunctural conditions contributed to this situation. For example, in 1955, large quantities of cement remained stored in the port of Jeddah[156] without reaching their final destinations, and prices were lowered by the Yugoslav and Greek competitors. In addition, countries such as Sweden and Bulgaria reduced their domestic needs for cement imports. All this led to a decline in cement prices in all the world markets. Among other circumstances, Kuwait, Iraq, and Saudi Arabia stopped granting entry visas to Romanian citizens, so direct negotiation or completion of business had become almost impossible. This situation finally determined the completion of a transaction for the sale of cement between RE and Toriel's consultant in 1955.

When, at the beginning of 1955, the Bohumer contract was canceled and the Romanian market was flooded with cement due to the grandiose export program set by the CSP, and while Rado was still in Germany, Leon Levy's proposal to purchase a quantity of 120,000 tons[157] of cement was accepted.

The purpose of the transaction with Levy was the resale of the cement to Saudi Arabia, a market inaccessible to Romania at that time. Levy, who had already met some members of the Cairo Agency, was asked to come to the RE headquarters in Bucharest.

A previous contract for the sale of 5,000–10,000 tons of cement, at a price of $11.20 (80s.), signed with Levy in 1954, was not carried out due to Levy's failure to open a letter of credit,[158] as promised, by the agreed deadline. However, due to the market conditions already explained, RE was interested in the contract made with Levy. After his arrival in Bucharest in April 1955,[159] negotiations were concluded with a contract for the sale of 120,000 tons of cement, signed on April 14, 1955. The signatories of this contract were Rosinger, the coordinating director; Grigoriu and Chinzbrunner, cement export consultants; and Ladislau Ilies,[160] the head of the cement export service.[161]

Following are a few characteristics of the C120 contract:

1. *The cement price in the transaction and the method used for the transport*

The price of the cement in the C120 transaction was set at $16.38 (117s.) per ton, and the delivery condition was C&F, via Jeddah Port.[162] If the business had been concluded under the FOB delivery condition, via Constanta port, the price would have been set at $9.8 (70s.) per ton. From here it can be understood that the difference in transportation costs is the difference between these two prices, that is, about $8.5 (47s.) per ton. The FOB delivery condition is preferable for the seller, as the RE company was responsible for the goods only until delivery to the first means of transport. Thus, the price of the goods is not influenced by any changes in the cost of transport that may occur during the execution of the contract. This was one of the reasons why Leon Levy would not accept the FOB method of transport. If he had agreed to FOB, the payment of the supplementary transport cost by the Romanian side would have been avoided. Toriel's refusal of the FOB method, commonly used at the time, couldn't be rejected, especially at the beginning of the relationship with a new client. Toriel's representative attributed his disagreement in accepting the FOB maritime delivery condition to the fact that Toriel did not have any transport company, while the Romanian side had such a facility.[163]

2. *The fulfillment of the contract and the delays in the cement delivery*

The C120 contract was to be carried out in a few stages, so that the period of fulfilling the entire contract was to span eight months, from April 30, 1955, until December 31, 1955. The cement transport began only in July 1955 and continued until April 1956. The contract was not concluded by the end of 1955, and the quantity supplied to Toriel by then reached only 40,600 tons, 33.85% of the total.

Levy opened the letter of credit a few days later than the date agreed upon, and for a minimum amount of cement, the equivalent amount of

1,000 tons, instead of opening for an amount that should have been the quantity delivered in the first load. In October 1955, when it became clear that the letters of credit would be postponed, and because the contract also stipulated a penalty in case of delay, the Romanians considered implementing a penal procedure against Toriel and Leon Levy. However, the signatories of the RE contract did not consider it necessary.[164] The decision not to penalize Toriel was cited by the prosecution as an example of the negative attitude of the defendants, interested in causing damage to the national economy. In a letter to RE, Levy reiterated the original terms of the contract and made some significant remarks as to the delays in the supply of the cement, due to difficulties encountered by Romtrans in finding transport ships, required by the buyer's demanded C&F conditions.[165] As the seller was the one responsible for transporting the cement, Romania suffered the damage caused by delays in obtaining vacant ships for the transport of cement. The Romanians claimed, instead, that Toriel's failure to open the letters of credit on time caused the delay in supplying the cement. However, this statement was contradicted by the statements given by Sidonia Grigoriu at the end of her investigation.[166] On the other hand, Romtrans, which transported cement, was able to benefit from the increase in freight prices.

In conclusion, the reasons why the C120 contract cement supplies did not take place on time were the late opening of the letters of credit, and especially the inability of Romtrans to acquire the vessels needed to transport the cement to its destination.

3. *About non-inclusion of the penalty clause in the contract*

- The payment of the Toriel company for C120 was to be made half in pounds sterling and half in Egyptian pounds. The value of the Egyptian pound, inserted as a clause in the contract, was set in accordance with its market value at that time.
- Although the financial assessment claimed that it there should have been an agio[167] clause in the contract, Sidonia Grigoriu, one of those who decided on the signing of the C120 contract, denied[168] Toriel's obligation to reimburse the Romanian party for currency differences. This was because the difference between the Egyptian pound and the pound sterling in commercial transactions was negligible, therefore, the clause of the payment of an agio by Toriel was not necessary.[169]
- The C120 contract did not include a commitment by RE for future purchase of any type of cotton with the credit created at Toriel as payment for the cement.

4. *Granting exclusivity to Toriel*

The Romanians granted Toriel exclusivity in the sale of the cement to eleven potential customers, in areas inaccessible to Romania, like the Persian Gulf, the Arabian Peninsula, and West Africa. The exclusivity was offered only for the duration of the contract.

Problems Arising after the Signing of the C120 Contract and during Its Implementation

1. *Difficulties faced by RE in fulfilling the requirements of the contract*

The C120 contract was not completed, and not all the cement shipments were transferred to Toriel. Although this can be attributed to the company in charge of the transport, Romtrans, it must be taken into account that during May and June, the transport of goods to Saudi Arabia and Jeddah was interrupted due to the pilgrimage to Mecca. The eight-month interval provided for the execution of the contract was not respected, and the finalization of the contract continued into the following year.

Returning to Romania's export objectives, regarding countries outside its realm of accessibility, like Persian Gulf countries, it should be emphasized that the association with Toriel was justified in the context in which Romania's goal was to expand the cement sales market. To do this, Romania had needed intermediaries.

2. *Shipping costs*

The C120 contract was not completed and there was also a significant delay in the transport of cement, during which shipping prices increased. Although from July 1954 until the beginning of 1955, the transport expenses from Constanţa to the Port Sudan decreased, after the beginning of 1955 the prices stabilized. The shipping price, calculated in April, 1955, had been set at 47 shillings per ton for the distance between Constanta and Jeddah, but immediately after the start of the transports, prices began to rise, reaching up to 65 shillings per ton, over the same distance. In accordance with the C&F delivery condition of the contract, it did not provide for division of the transport costs, so only the Romanians suffered from the price increases.

The investigation included losses caused by the transport of cement in the damages to the Romanian state for which the defendants were considered guilty. However, the investigators deliberately ignored two things: first, the fact that all the defendants involved in setting the terms of the contract clearly pointed out that transport costs could not be shared due to the adamant refusal of the buyer, and second, Romtrans, the transport executor, exacted the price increase for the transport from RE, and did not absorb any of it.

In conclusion, at that time, Levy absolutely refused the FOB delivery, which would have represented an advantage for RE, nor did he agreed to share the expenses that might result from an increase in the price of transport between RE and Toriel.

3. *Non-inclusion of the penalty clause in the contract*

The non-inclusion of the sanction clause in the contract, for cases in which the parties do not comply with the terms of the contract (e.g., failure to open letters of credit on time, or significant delays in the supply of goods), was considered by both the investigators and the court as a serious infraction, proof of negligence and poor training of RE officials. Toriel's refusal to include the penalty clause in the contract was cited by all of the defendants who had been involved in the C120, both during the investigation and during the trial (Rosinger,[170] Manheim,[171] Grigoriu,[172] Chinzbrunner[173]). During the early 1950s, it was unusual to add such a clause, although there were isolated cases when it had been accepted by companies or their agents. In the case of Toriel, a new trade relationship, RE couldn't really oppose the omission of the clause, if the target was promoting the new trade relation. Starting in 1957, Romanian enterprises could introduce the penalty clause for instances of non-compliance with conditions in contracts signed with foreign companies. Another argument against the inclusion of the penalty clause in the contract was the statement of Sidonia Grigoriu, who recalled that the procedure was such that the clause was included especially in those contracts that were to run for a year or more. The C120 was scheduled to end after only eight months.[174]

It will be shown further that those involved in the decision-making process for the signing of the C120 contract made their decisions based on relevant economic considerations at the time of the transaction, and on facts, arguments, and the existing collection of comparative data, as partly already shown. Consequently, their incrimination concerning the conclusion of the C120 contract, as well as the others, which are not presented here due to space limitations, was unjustified. Next, some of these arguments will be discussed by taking into account the following three aspects:

A. Cement sale price, payment, and obligations of contracting parties
B. Conditions of cement delivery by sea and related costs
C. The position of the MCE relative to the Toriel transactions

A. *Cement sale price, payment, and obligations of contracting parties*

Hundreds of pages out of the Criminal Case file P179 file are devoted to the discussion on the prices of the C120 cement transaction. These are either part of the financial assessment or of the personal investigations of defendants involved in the C120 contract conclusion. Here are some aspects regarding the sale price of the cement during the time when C120 was concluded, and how the price issue was reflected in the accusations against the RE officials:

- As already mentioned, cement prices in early 1954 continued to fall. This drop in price was due, on the one hand, to the emergence of cheap deals on the cement market (Greek and Yugoslav), and, on the other hand, to the interruption of cement demand, following the Bohumer Affair. Toward the beginning of 1955, the international cement market was again rattled by Romania's agreement to reduce its cement price for Bohumer, to \$9–\$9.5, giving other sales people the opportunity to sell Romanian cement at lower prices (e.g., the Romanian agency in Cairo). The MCE supported the transaction with Bohumer mainly due to the need for steel products that were part of the deal. Bohumer tried to sell Romanian cement in Kuwait to the Dutch company, Jasumi-Java Sumatra, even cheaper than the sale price initially set by Romania.[175] Therefore, Romania failed to sign any contract for the sale of cement after September 1954, when it maintained the original price of \$11.41 (81.42s.) per ton.[176]
- The financial assessment tried to give the impression that before the attempts to negotiate the C120 contract, Romania could have obtained prices between \$10.5 and \$11.5 per ton for the sale of the cement, under the FOB delivery condition. At the end of the investigation, Sidonia Grigoriu tried to use other arguments to justify contracting as in C120. At that time, none of the negotiations carried out, by either the Cairo agency or by the members of RE themselves, had led to any transaction for the sale of cement, not even for small quantities. And it must not be forgotten, that around 1955, RE was under the pressure of the CSP's high export demands.
- All the defendants involved in concluding the C120 contract raised the same objections against the accusations brought by the investigation, through the financial assessment. These objections provided reasonable explanations concerning the C120 conclusion and should have been used as arguments in their favor, that is, under the circumstances of 1955, their decision had been the correct one. Therefore, the transaction also received the MCE approval, as well as that of its export department. Additionally, Paul Ştefănescu, who served as director of Import in MCE, stated in his testimony before

the court that during the considered period of time, RE was obliged to buy cotton yarn from Egypt, in accordance with the guidelines that he himself had received. His testimony also contradicted another argument, which had been put forward against the defendants, which erroneously claimed that RE could have approached other companies for the purchase of cotton.

- In the final stages of the investigation, Sidonia Grigoriu analyzed the circumstances that characterized the world cement markets in the first half of 1955, as the most important factors in determining the low cement prices during the time of C120. Grigoriu's criticism of the financial assessment concerned both the "experts'" attempts to hide the details of some commercial offers made at that time, which, in practice, could not have been certain until the late signing stages of the contracts, and the false presentation of selling through intermediaries as a disadvantage.

B. *Conditions of cement delivery by sea and related cost*

As already known, the C120 contract was signed with the condition of C&F delivery, and according to this, the transport of cement was to be by sea, the seller being responsible for insurance and transport. This will demonstrate how the contract not only did not affect the national economy negatively but also brought certain benefits.

- During the period when the C120 contract was concluded, Romania wanted to penetrate the markets in Saudi Arabia, as already explained, so it was entirely understandable that it would have accepted the buyer's conditions for transport costs in order to secure the transaction. Also, as in the last months of 1954, and by February 1955, transportation costs had gradually increased, a stabilizing trend was expected. It was therefore unlikely that from April 1955 onward, there would be a significant increase in transport costs.[177] These data are recorded in the pages of the financial assessment. Another reason to strengthen the consensus on the acceptance of transport was that the entire execution of C120 was expected to be completed within eight months. The division of any changes in the cost of maritime transport was a common practice only in the case of contracts with a delivery time of at least one year. This point did not appear to be crucial, and moreover, it would have been totally unacceptable to require it in a first contract, even if was warranted due to fluctuations in transport costs.[178]
- Levy intended to sell Romanian cement in Jeddah, so that once the contract was concluded, Toriel and Levy received exclusivity in Romanian cement sales in markets to which Romania did not then have access. Hence, exclusivity, as a consequence of the ratification of the contract, was fully justified and was practically an advantage obtained by RE. As a result of this clause,

Adalbert Rosinger, in his capacity as coordinating director of RE, ordered the Cairo economic agency, through Sidonia Grigoriu, to avoid concluding new contracts without consulting the RE offices in Bucharest. This measure was applied in order to ensure the exclusivity stipulated in the contract.

- Sidonia Grigoriu's testimony before the court also unveiled facts of crucial importance for understanding some of the factors that contributed to the increase of transport expenses. Romtrans addressed a request to all companies that dealt with the rental of transport ships, for a large number of ships to transport a variety of goods. In this way, the increase in demand for rental vessels, as stated by Grigoriu, had led to a significant increase in the rates of transport costs. As such, one of the reasons for the increase of the freight was the Romanian transport policy practiced by the Romtrans company itself. These facts, brought to light by Sidonia Grigoriu, show a criticism of the directors of Romtrans and other directors of the departments of MCE, people who, at that time, were not incriminated in the Romanian export proceedings.

C. *The position of the Ministry of Foreign Trade relative to the Toriel transactions*

Paul Ştefănescu's testimony in the court revealed some aspects of the relationship between foreign trade enterprises (ISCE),[179] economic agencies outside Romania (the economic agency in Egypt in this case) and MCE.

The Egyptian economic agency carried out certain independent actions, such as concluding cotton contracts or selling Romanian products, as well as negotiating and determining prices. However, when C120 and later C150 were signed, the intervention of the Cairo agency was limited, due to the exclusivity granted to Toriel. Ştefănescu's testimony upheld the proof that this was done with the approval of the ministry.[180]

- The same testimony brought up the inclusion of the penalty clause in the contract. In accordance with the Romanian Constitution from 1952, the Council of Ministers, the Romanian legislative body, approved the decision,[181] which allowed the inclusion of the penalty clause in commercial contracts, for when the conditions of the contract were not met. But, as was already shown, the suppliers of many countries objected to the inclusion of this clause in the contract. Therefore, excluding the clause from C120 was a condition for continuing the negotiations for the Toriel contract.
- The problem of the Egyptian suppliers, who sometimes delivered cotton late, was also known to the MCE, and yet the cotton had to be from Egypt, so the inconvenience resulting from the delay in supply had to be overcome.

- Paul Ştefănescu's testimony also contradicted the information provided by Biniamin Schwartz during the investigation, when he accused Rado and Rosinger of not provided him with the necessary data for setting prices in some transactions.[182]
- The requirements for the export of cement of 1954, as well as those of 1955, were not met, being excessively high. According to a financial report published in the second volume of the financial assessment, it was stated that by April 1955, only 17% of the quantity of cement designated for export had been exported, while the Securitate investigators had claimed that 63% of the export requirements imposed by the CSP had been met. During the investigations, incorrect, falsified data were used, as Sidonia Grigoriu demonstrated. In her testimony, she pointed out the inaccuracy and lack of coordination of the information provided by investigators. Grigoriu requested additional documents, as evidence before the court, but her request was denied by the Securitate.

Next, two pieces of evidence would be brought by two people, both non-Jews, prosecution witnesses who were involved in ratifying the cement contracts. The first was the engineer Mihail Ciobanu, the director of the export department between 1954 and 1956, the years when the C120 contract had been concluded. In his testimony before the court, he denied that he had been among those involved in the ratification of those contracts, but the approval of the export directorate was a necessary condition for the conclusion of any contract with foreign companies. The second person was Petre Toma, a director of the export department between 1959 and 1960. Their involvement in finalizing the contracts with Toriel was inevitable. Ciobanu justified his authorization of the contracts by signing the approval, by citing the discrepancy between the formulation of the initial report presented to the ministry and the final version of the contract. These two people, Ciobanu and Toma, who were important officials in the ministry and were involved in the RE trial only as prosecution witnesses, both held the most decision-making power during the period in which the contracts were finalized. However, no guilt or responsibility was imputed to them, the charges being brought only against the Jewish officials.

The Contract for the Sale of 150,000 Tons of Cement to Toriel (C150)

Despite the economic difficulties that prevented the full execution of the C120 contract, the RE cement export department decided to complete another transaction in November of the same year, 1955. This new contract consisted of the sale of 150,000 tons of cement to Toriel, a contract that will be called C150. Unfortunately, due to space limitations and the complexity of this contract, with several new features as compared with its analogue, C120, its analysis will not be included in this book.

Sidonia Grigoriu's Objections to the Financial Assessments Regarding the Cement Contracts

1. *On the Bohumer Affair*

The reason why, at the beginning of 1955, the MCE supported the pursuit of a contract with Bohumer was that due to RE's difficulty in managing very large quantities of cement for export, the transaction was practically the only one obtainable, despite its low prices. Therefore, the approval of all the ministry directorships was finally obtained[183] and Rado received the go-ahead for concluding it. During the investigation, as well as according to the observations from the financial assessment, it was found that the Bohumer contract was not an objective in itself. If this contract wasn't signed, the technical equipment that was part of a triple deal in the sale of cement to Bohumer would be lost.[184]

2. *About transportation costs*

In her testimony in front of the court, Sidonia Grigoriu claimed that starting at the beginning of 1955, worldwide transport costs had registered a downward trend, and that they were expected to stabilize after February 1955.[185] This was one of the factors that led to the signing of the first contract with Toriel, where the transport costs reached 47 shillings/per ton. When the second contract with Toriel, C150 was signed in November 1955, the MCE knew about the upward trend in transport costs, reaching 64 shillings/per ton. However, RE agreed to pay for these expenses, as this time, Levy agreed to share possible increases in transportation costs. Moreover, because the transport was provided by Romanian ships, the ministry even agreed to pay a 5% fee to Romtrans.[186]

3. *False data included in the financial report*

Among some of the false data included in the financial assessment was the claim that in April 1955, when the C120 contract was signed, 63% of the mandatory annual quota of RE cement export had already been achieved. However, according to Sidonia Grigoriu's claim, the investigation had fabricated this figure and it did not reflect the truth. Her request for the original RE or MCE documents to validate her claim was rejected. In the same context, Grigoriu pointed out that the delay in the delivery made by Romtrans during the C120 contract was caused by the C&F delivery conditions, requested by Toriel, to which RE could not object at that time.[187]

4. *MCE involvement in allowing the C120 contract to proceed*

After the meeting of October 1955 at the MCE, a senior ministry official who had attended the meeting opted not to interrupt the C120 contract, deeming it unnecessary. (By December 31, 1955, 33.8%, or 40,600 tons, had already been transferred, while transport costs appeared to have stabilized by the end of the same year.) It should be noted that the ministry was aware that during this period there were no other buyers of large quantities of cement, at a time when the textile industry had to import cotton yarns from Egypt immediately and urgently. (The Toriel company remained the main supplier, both due to the promise of keeping the price low, but also due to the balance of credit still available for payment.) Therefore, the directors in charge of RE, Rosinger and Rado, recommended that the sale of cement be continued, despite the late deliveries. The MCE gave their consent to this decision.

5. *Alternative proposals available during the conclusion of contracts with Toriel*

The financial experts argued against the defendants that during the conclusion of the contracts with Toriel, RE had alternative proposals for the sale of cement, citing as an example the Egyptian company André Riches, which they claimed would have proposed the purchase of 60,000 tons of cement in order to transport it to different destinations. In practice, there had been no possibility of entering into any agreement with this company, as Riches did not have import licenses.[188] In addition, Riches was not considered reliable and its proposals were uncertain; the clearest proof of this was that a year later, the company André Riches went bankrupt.[189]

6. *Continuation of trade relations between RE and Toriel after 1956*

Even after the conclusion of the C120 and C150 contracts and despite difficulties that had arisen over the years due to delays in delivery, or even a decline in the quality of imported cotton, the Cairo economic agency itself maintained its policy of buying cotton from Toriel.[190] This proves that despite the accusations brought against the RE officials, Toriel continued to be a business partner for RE, many years forward.

7. *Romanian trade relations with other companies*

Sidonia Grigoriu repeatedly pointed out that other existing proposals for the sale of cement, received by RE close to its contracting with Toriel, were made only in principle, were tentative, and did not represent any real commitment from the potential buyers. She also demonstrated through concrete examples how some of the transactions that had been considered by the Securitate investigators to be alternatives for cement sale, accusing the RE officials of not taking them into account, had proven to be practically impossible to carry out. The rejection was not due to any specific interests of either of the parties involved but had reasons related to the companies themselves and the lack of seriousness of the offers.[191]

8. *Promoting Romanian trade through intermediaries*

According to Sidonia Grigoriu, the system of trade through intermediaries practiced by Romania in the mid-1950s was a common business practice in many other countries, especially when its purpose was trade with countries of Western Europe. This system, in the Romanian experience, proved to have clear economic advantages, succeeding far beyond the initial expectations.

9. *Cement prices obtained by Romania, versus prices in other countries*

None of the offers received for the sale of cement by CMEA countries, used to compare prices with the ones obtained by RE, had indeed led to a completed contract. So the idea of relying on such a comparison was not realistic, considering the long-term business relationship established between RE and Toriel. The so-called experts who prepared the financial assessment misused these figures in favor of the Securitate investigation.[192]

10. *Romtrans and other transport issues*

Romtrans' policy of renting cement ships created a kind of panic in the markets of shipping companies.[193] By the second half of 1955, as well as after the opening of letters of credit by Toriel, Romania remained responsible for the transport as a result of the C&F delivery condition in C120. So, when there were requests from Romtrans for ships to transport cement to Saudi Arabia, prices went up, creating the impression of a far greater demand for ships than there actually was. Shipping prices reached up to 65–68 shillings. As mentioned earlier, following the meeting at the MCE in October 1955, the director of the MCE Export Department, Mihail Ciobanu,[194] together with representatives from Romtrans and RE, decided that despite the increase in transport costs, deliveries should continue. The conclusions of that meeting were recorded in a protocol document (Minutes of October 29, 1955), which showed, inter alia, that the conditions existing at that time were known and that they had also been approved by the ministry.[195] In conclusion, one of the main causes of delays in deliveries and increase in transport costs were caused by Romtrans itself. As for the non-inclusion of the clause of sharing in transport costs, the fact that this clause could not be introduced in contracts, any contract, before 1957, was cited, independently, by almost all the defendants.

11. *The C150 contract terms that favored the seller (RE)*

The clause for the reexamination of cement prices was inserted in contract C150 six months after the beginning of its implementation. The main reasons for inserting this clause were the significant delays in the supply of cement, compared to the original plan. Such a clause could not be included in the C120 contract, due to the categorical refusal of Toriel's agent, Leon Levy.

In conclusion, and in accordance with the highly reasoned and well-documented comments made by Sidonia Grigoriu, which were presented both during the investigation, under its harsh conditions and pressure, and later in court, RE did not have any other firm customers for the huge quantities of cement designated for export by CSP. Sidonia Grigoriu refused to sign her Indictment Conclusions, presented to her by the Securitate investigator, on February 10, 1964.[196]

The outstanding courage and resolve shown by Sidonia Grigoriu, under the circumstances of her detention, were completely extraordinary, and her arguments and written claims, as a series of objections to the investigation, can be considered a unique case. The explanations and comments made by Grigoriu could help justify other defendants in their fight, often doomed to failure from the outset, both in front of the Securitate and later, before the Military Court.

Conclusions Regarding the C120 and C150 Contracts

Cement sales contracts C120 and C150 were among the most complex contracts analyzed within the RE trial. The intermediate stages between signing and execution were extended beyond the time initially provided, due not only to bureaucracy but also to the political events that took place in the Middle East,[197] which made it difficult to transfer goods. Under these conditions, however, the cement contracts were partially fulfilled, even if some offers made by other companies seemed preferable to Toriel's. The economic conditions that existed on the international market—the price fluctuations and the lack of credibility of the alternative proposals that appeared preceding the contract with Toriel—were the reasons that no other contract could have been signed. Although all the defendants in the RE trial, on every occasion, rejected the suspicion that the business relationship with Toriel was made to promote personal interests, they were accused that this had been their real intention in favoring this company and the agent who represented it.

The prosecution claimed that the defendants responsible for the C120 and C150 contracts did everything to mislead the leadership of the MCE, choosing options that expressed personal preference and an interest in obtaining personal benefits. Being Jews, they preferred Jewish contact agents, in order to fulfill a "hidden" desire to emigrate, attempting to secure some material assets that would be at their disposal abroad. The difficulty in obtaining permits to import goods from Romania was a serious obstacle to trade in many foreign countries. These conditions led to the establishment of connections either with agents of foreign companies or with intermediaries who facilitated the trade. The prosecution in the RE trial did not accept this fact as an integral part of the opening of Romanian foreign trade to the Western countries. The argument of the prosecution that during the same period other countries in the Communist bloc would have obtained better prices than the prices achieved by the RE representatives was denied by both Sidonia Grigoriu and Adalbert Rosinger in their statements.

Defendants who were involved in the contracts with Toriel stated that until 1957, it was not possible to include a penalty clause in contracts with foreign countries, especially in contracts with third world countries (Grigoriu, Chinzbrunner, the consultants of the cement contracts).[198]

Chinzbrunner confirmed through his testimony that all RE contracts with Toriel had the approval of the MCE before the conclusion, and moreover, there was no objection regarding the price. This fact was stated independently by the other defendants (Rosinger, Grigoriu, Manheim), who were the signatories of the contract, and the existing conditions at Malmaison certainly wouldn't have allowed them to coordinate their positions.

According to all the defendants' depositions, the signing of a contract with a foreign country required the approval of the Directorates of the ministry and finally the signature of the directors themselves. The ministry was also responsible for carrying out the contract and making the payments. The same was declared by Paul Ştefănescu,[199] the Import director in MCE, by Rosinger, the coordinating director of RE at the moment of the transaction, and also by Manheim,[200] the interim consultant to the cement service, during the signing of the C150 contract.

Although the contracts with Toriel opened the way for Romania to new markets in the Middle East and the Persian Gulf, the Securitate investigators did not consider this an achievement. Another argument was the existence of alternative offers, both for the export of cement and for the import of cotton yarn, disregarding, for example, the order given by the MCE to import cotton exclusively from Egypt.

It is almost impossible to overcome the differences between the defendants' testimonies and the documents used as proof of the imaginary amounts of financial damages attributed to them.

During the investigation, accusations emerged regarding the period of institutionalization of trade relations between the two countries, which raised the issue of disclosing secret information to representatives of foreign companies regarding Romania's trade requirements for exports. In reality, such information was published in specialized economic journals, such as those of the Chamber of Commerce of Romania,[201] and the arguments put forward by the Securitate investigators were irrelevant. The reasons why Sidonia Grigoriu refused to sign her Indictment Conclusions are of great importance in exposing the irregularities that emerged during the investigation proceeding the RE trial.

> I refuse to sign the above, as it does not clearly reflect what I have argued during the investigation. I consider myself innocent, I reserve the right to defend myself in court. I do not recognize the damages mentioned in both the assessments and I did not take any hostile actions towards the State.[202]

She was not the only defendant to refuse to sign the indictment at the end of the investigation. Adalbert Rosinger also refused to sign the first indictment presented by the Securitate,[203] thus rejecting their conclusions. There were other RE defendants in the RE trial who objected to the allegations, although they did so orally only. The reason was easy to understand, because they were possessed by fear and despair, both for themselves and for family members.

The main accusation brought against the officials from RE, that of undermining the national economy, was based on their alleged favoritism toward some foreign companies, but especially toward certain agents, either to obtain benefits that would help them should they emigrate from Romania or to offer small token gifts to strengthen bilateral relations between the two sides. The subject of gifts was also discussed when in practice the daily allowances of these officials when abroad enabled them to buy small items that were almost nonexistent in Romania at that time.[204] Actually, the practice of giving small gifts was an international custom in trade, and a regular occurrence among the parties involved in the negotiations. The Securitate, both during investigation and later in court, preferred to ignore this, referring to gift-giving as unacceptable behavior, with criminal intentions toward the state.

Summarizing the analysis of the C120 and C150 contracts, we must remember the words of Sidonia Grigoriu, which ended her investigation, namely the fact that not only did the C120 contract cause no damage to the national economy but, on the contrary, brought benefits (as mentioned in the investigation, in her comments on the financial assessment, and in front of the court).[205] We must not forget that the idea of issuing accusations against Foreign Trade officials, especially against those from RE, was the consequence of the meeting of Foreign Trade workers with the party secretary of Bucharest and other members of the Communist Party, which took place in 1958 in Bucharest. Like the other trials, discussed in the previous chapter, this RE trial was set up and orchestrated from the very beginning by the Securitate, which worked tirelessly to find sufficient reasons to indict some of the Jews employed in various branches of the economic sectors, especially in Foreign Trade. In the case of the latter, the Securitate members involved in the criminal investigation, manufactured a virtual reality in which the real-life protagonists were cast in the role of criminals whose intentions were to undermine the economy of their country.

CONCLUSION

The criminal proceedings, which led to the trial of the Jewish RE officials, began on June 9, 1961, and ended three and a half years later, after the final verdict was handed down (Sentence no. 31/4 July 1964 and subsequently the decision of the appeal, on January 26, 1965).

In this chapter, we presented the development of the main events of the trial as well as the arguments used by the court, the Bucharest Regional Military Court, against the RE employees. In my endeavor to confine this book to a reasonable length, I decided to present the analysis of one single contract out of the incriminating ones, which were not a few, but still represented a very small percentage of the total number of transactions the RE company concluded in the period in question (1950–1960).

Because the accusations brought by the Securitate fell into the category of political crimes, the trial was judged by a military court. The existing documentation unilaterally shows the position of the Securitate, as the investigative body, and that of the Prosecution, which was represented by the Military Prosecutor's Office. Very rarely could documents written by the defendants in their own favor be found in the many volumes of the trial file. For instance, there are only a few statements showing opposition, or critical remarks on the Indictment Conclusions written by the investigation body, to illustrate the adamant opposition of some of the defendants and their determination to convince the court of their innocence.

The real situation of RE could not be determined solely on the basis of the indictment documents. It should be noted that RE, which continued its commercial activity under the same name, but as a publicly held company even after the December 1989 revolution, destroyed the entire archive of internal documents, consequently the one referring to the period of time relevant to this work.[206]

All the damages found by the investigation to have been caused by the RE defendants as a result of the conclusion of the contracts were presumptive damages only, and not real ones. The damages were artificially conceived by the financial experts in the Securitate's service, who claimed that the defendants had harmed the Romanian state, by selling at lower prices than could have been obtained, or by making purchases at prices that were too high. Some of these allegations were rejected by the defendants, in different phases of the investigation. The so-called experts, in dealing with the execution of sales or purchases, manipulated the currency, invoking false exchange rates, different from case to case, depending on the circumstances.[207]

The judiciary deemed the amount of damages, an expression of the crime of undermining the country's economy, to be 112,079,387 Romanian lei (or $2,081,812, using random conversion to dollars), as claimed by the first financial assessment, spread over more than 800 pages. Some defendants' written objections led to the execution of a second assessment, and in the end, the third and final evaluation, reached 76,197,547 lei, which evaluates to 1,465,337,[208] representing 68% of the initial value. This debt was considered to be shared by the defendants in the trial, depending on the role played by each of them in the activity of the enterprise.

If there had indeed been a financial loss during the operations analyzed, it could have been verified through the balance sheet of the annual financial statements of RE, which showed a cumulative overall profit, to which of course those defendants also contributed, through many other transactions. The financial loss in question was considered exclusively to be caused by most of the company's Jewish officials, while non-Jewish officials, some with official positions, were not implicated, coming out "clean," and were never indicted.

According to Adalbert Rosinger's testimony, the financial value of the incriminating contracts represented 2% of the financial value of the contracts of the RE company realized during the analyzed decade.[209] The financial value of the RE contracts, in its commercial relations with the Western countries, was on the order of tens of millions of dollars and implicitly, in favor of Romania. Although there were officially established Foreign Trade working practices and procedures, last-minute decisions were often made in some operations. It happened more than once in order to make a quick decision under pressure or in an emergency, and it could have turned out to be crucial for those who had to set the priorities involved in the negotiations. During the investigation and the trial, the Jewish representatives of the RE enterprise understood that the state had given up its responsibility for them, as citizens who had served their country. The esteem they had held for years as government representatives not only did not give them any additional rights, but they were ultimately destined for exclusion.

At the time of the trial, the political leadership had already formulated its national policy,[210] and the criminal law was also used in order to eliminate "the unwanted" from society. Centralization, the method employed by the political system to run the economy, a phenomenon attributed to the communist period, was undoubtedly reflected in the foreign trade sector, as well. The severity of the sentencing in the economic trials sometimes led even to the prosecutor's request to apply the death penalty.[211] The conditions under which the defendants were investigated, as well as the torment they were subjected to, bordered on physical and mental terror. This could explain why some of the defendants accepted the accusations brought against them without hesitation.

Some of the security investigators continued to live without any pursuit or punishment on the part of the new Romanian government, even after the 1989 revolution. There were and still are groups that continued to fight, even after the change of political regime in Romania, for the conviction and punishment of those people who should have been charged with crimes against humanity,[212] to which no statute of limitations applies. The economic trials of Romanian Foreign Trade of the early 1960s can be considered a communist variation of the traditional process of demonization of Jews in the pre-communist period. Perhaps only in this way can the removal and impeachment of Jewish officials from the MCE be understood, despite their major contribution to Romanian foreign trade development.

NOTES

1. Malmaison was the Securitate building where future prisoners were held.

2. Adalbert Rosinger, one of the main RE defendants, wrote these words as part of one of his essays, which are in the author's possession.

3. P signifies penal (criminal), also in Romanian, penal. This is one of the file types existing in ACNSAS. See appendix III.

4. See appendix III.

5. *Cartea neagră a Comerţului Exterior românesc*. Between 1978 and 1981, Adalbert Rosinger, my father, wrote a manuscript meant for being published as a book, supposed to be entitled Cartea Neagră a Comerţului Exterior Românesc (in English "*The Black Book of the Romanian Foreign Trade*"). He wrote an extended summary of the 36 chapters, supposed to be included in the book, but only 12 of them were completed, as Rosinger passed away in September 1981.

6. See chapter 3.

7. SRI, Romanian Intelligence Service (in Romanian Serviciul Român de Informaţii), actually the successor of the Securitate.

8. Year 1989 is the time of the Romanian Revolution, when civil unrest movements started in several towns of the country and led to the fall of dictator Nicolae Ceauşescu and the end of the communist regime in Romania.

9. The majority of CNSAS documents are held in the small town of Popeşti-Leordeni, in a space known as "The National Reserves," which was made available for CNSAS, as a place to store archive documents.

10. The Criminal Record of the RE trial is held by CNSAS, under the number P179 (P represents Penal).

11. The Securitate was subordinate to the Ministry of the Interior.

12. The women accused in the economic trials were imprisoned in Oradea's women's prison.

13. Criminal Case P179 consists of the 59 volumes, each of them being part of file P179. Among those volumes are the nine personal files of the convicts, made during their incarceration at certain jails.

14. 50 × 400 = 20,000 pages (approximately) are to be found in the complete file of the RE Criminal Case, P179.

15. Volumes 1 and 2 include the investigations of Rado, Rosinger, and Crainic; volume 4 contains the investigations of Grigoriu and Schwartz; volume 29 contains the investigations of Stefanescu and Costin; and volume 30 contains the investigations of Chinzbrunner and Manheim. These volumes include, in addition to the investigation documentation, the Indictment and arrest warrants of all the defendants.

16. The first financial assessment contains around 725 pages, the second one around 120 pages.

17. During one period of the course of the investigation, this director was Francisc Butyka, while at another time, it was Colonel Nicolae Dumitrescu.

18. In this case, it refers to Securitate investigators.

19. In a discussion with Mr. Florian Banu, principal researcher and historian at the CNSAS Archives, he explained about the changes that took place over time, mostly toward the 1960s, among the investigators and in general within the Criminal Investigations Directorate of the Securitate.

20. These files will be referred to, using their Romanian name, Dosar de Urmărire Informativă, shorten to the acronym DUI. The various files used by the Securitate will be explained in appendix III.

21. Listening to telephone conversations, physical tracking of the person and tracking of correspondence.

22. The personal Surveillance file of Rado Alexandru is located at CNSAS under the number I211282.

23. The personal Surveillance file of Sidonia Grigoriu is located at CNSAS under the number I211285.

24. The personal Surveillance file of Mihai Crainic is located at CNSAS under the number I211279.

25. The personal Surveillance file of Angelo Chinzbrunner is located at CNSAS under the number I211280.

26. The personal Surveillance file of Gheorghe Manheim is located at CNSAS under the number I211281.

27. The personal Surveillance file of Alexandru Costin is located at CNSAS under the number I211283.

28. The personal Surveillance file of Paul Ştefănescu is located at CNSAS under the number I211284.

29. The personal Surveillance file of Adalbert Rosinger is located at CNSAS under the number I257122.

30. The emigration approval of Adalbert Rosinger and his wife was the consequence of Presidential Decree no. 131 of June 8, 1978, issued by Nicolae Ceauşescu, following his visit to President Jimmy Carter in April 1978. At one breakfast that took place in the presence of various American and Romanian officials, the acting foreign minister, George Macovescu, was handed a letter, written by Rosinger's daughter, author of this document, addressed to Nicolae Ceauşescu, at the time President of the Socialist Republic of Romania, requesting the waiving of the presumptive damages and permission for Rosinger to emigrate to Israel. Rosinger left Romania on September 30, 1978. Both the letter and the Decree were found at the National Archives of Romania.

31. ACNSAS, I257122/vol.1/pp. 136–142v—this information will be referred to henceforth as "The letters."

32. This was an Italian import-export company for textiles and other consumer goods, owned by Lily Oberhide, henceforth Interglobe will be used for the name of the company.

33. ACNSAS, P179/Vol. 42/p. 179.

34. Gheorghe Leuchter's testimony in the RE trial can be found at ACNSAS, P179/Vol. 5/ pp. 149–151.

35. On the cover of Criminal file P179 Volume One, it was mentioned that the criminal procedure was directed against Alexandru Rado and all the others.

36. In February 1964.

37. Several documents concerning Francisc Butyka can be found on the CNSAS site, www.cnsas.ro, in Romanian. Accessed August 2, 2021. http://www.cnsas.ro/documente/cadrele_securitatii/BUTYKA_FRANCISC.pdf

38. Adrian König, accessed on November 23, 2020. http://www.cnsas.ro/documente/cadrele_securitatii/KONIG%20IOAN%20ADRIAN.pdf.

39. Toriel was one of the principal Egyptian clients of RE, regarding selling of cement in exchange for cotton. Later its name turned into Cofiltra.

40. At the time, there were no postal or telephone connections between Romania and Israel. It can be deduced from this that she had no means of communicating with her sister, or making any kind of connection.

41. ACNSAS, P179/Vol. 4, p. 191.

42. The author's opinion.

43. ACNSAS, 179/Vol. 4, p. 274. At the bottom of the page, one can see that she wrote that she refused to sign and under this statement, her signature can also be found.

44. Rosinger claimed that Bermal's offer was not taken into account due to the uncertainty of their proposal that emerged during the correspondence and discussions they had with Bermal representatives.

45. An "optical price" was a price set to satisfy the CMEA's request for a minimum value for the price of any given product. ACNSAS P179/Vol. 30, p. 264v.

46. A Canadian textile company.

47. ACNSAS, P179/vol30, pp. 332–333.

48. ACNSAS, P179/Vol. 30, pp. 334–343

49. ACNSAS, P179/Vol. 30, p. 394.

50. ACNSAS, P179/Vol. 30, pp. 395–400.

51. ACNSAS, P179/Vol. 30, pp. 396–397.

52. ACNSAS, P179/Vol. 30, p. 122

53. These terms refer to the quantity of cement in thousands of tons established in the initial Toriel cement contracts (120,000 and 150,000 tons of cement). These are the two-phase cement sales contracts, the first for 120,000 tons, referred to in the following pages as C120, the second for 150,000 tons, henceforth referred to as C150.

54. See appendix V for the explanation of the three sale and delivery systems for goods FOB, CIF, and C&F).

55. Ion Marin, accessed on November 23, 2020. http://www.cnsas.ro/documente/cadrele_securitatii/MARIN%20A%20ION.pdf.

56. Among these companies were Suntex owned by Max Salama, Interglobe owned by Lili Oberheide and Atlas led by Kurt Klarman.

57. ACNSAS, P179/Vol. 30, p. 444.

58. Cenuşă Constantin, accessed on November 23, 2020. http://www.cnsas.ro/documente/cadrele_securitatii/CENUSA%20CONSTANTIN.pdf.

59. ACNSAS, P179/Vol. 3, pp. 546–464.

60. See appendix V.

61. ACNSAS, P179/Vol. 4, p. 510.

62. ACNSAS P179/Vol. 2, p. 226.

63. These are the words that appear in the Indictment of January 31, 1962, ACNSAS/P179/Vol. 2, p. 226v.

64. The material available to Rosinger consisted of 8 volumes of the RE defendants' inquiries, 22 volumes of the first financial assessment, concluded on December 20, 1962, ACSNAS, p179/Vol. 3, p. 181.

65. The differences between the results of the two financial assessments will be presented in the next pages through data tables.

66. They were described over the years by former defendants after their release from communist prison. http://www.procesulcomunismului.com/marturii/fonduri/gcaraza/aiud/docs/cap7.htm or Rosinger, *Cartea neagră*, found in the author's possession.

67. ACNSAS, P179/Vol. 2, pp. 258–259.

68. Rosinger's declaration, while standing trial, ACNSAS, P179/Vol. 2, p. 248.

69. ACNSAS, P179/Vol. 29, pp. 183–214.

70. ACNSAS, P179/Vol. 2, p. 263.

71. ACNSAS, P179/Vol. 1, p. 285.

72. ACNSAS, P179/Vol. 2, p. 86.

73. The persons appointed to the commission did not have any experience in the field of foreign trade, see subchapter referring the warrants for the execution of financial assessment.

74. Although most of the transactions were related to export, I did not get the impression that anyone from the head of the export department of the MCE was among the suspects. MCE organizational chart can be seen in appendix IV.

75. See the details concerning the occupation and positions of the financial experts in appendix VI.

76. It must be mentioned that despite the collection of personal data of most financial experts from economic processes, CNSAS archive did not provide any of the personal files of these people selected by the investigators of the Department of criminal investigation, of the Securitate, though it should be certain, that such files could not be missing from the old SRI archive. More pressure had to be put on the actual Romanian SRI in order to get that information (author's opinion).

77. The first volume of the financial assessment, ACNSAS, P179/Vol. 32, p. 1.

78. Following the results of the first assessment, Adalbert Rosinger, Sidonia Grigoriu, Mihai Crainic, Alexandru Costin, Gheorghe Manheim objected. The results had been handed over to all RE defendants, together with the investigation material to be studied, for a limited period of time.

79. ACNSAS, P179/Vol. 33/pp. 386, 399, 410, 411.

80. Leu, plural Lei, was the currency used in Romania at that time.

81. ACNSAS, P179/Vol. 35/p. 32.

82. The damages in lei (Romanian currency) in the first table were assessed at 112,079,387 and the final amount of damages was 76,197,547. The final amount of damages was 68% of the original amount.

83. The damages in lei (Romanian currency) in the second table were assessed at 89,209,712, and the final amount of damages was 76,197,547. The final amount of damages was 85% of the second amount.

84. ACNSAS, P179/Vol. 4, p. 274.

85. ACNSAS, PA79/Vol. 2, pp. 226–226v.

86. ACNSAS, P179/Vol. 31, A confrontation that took place on December 21, 1962, between Alexandru Rado and Biniamin Schwartz, director of the cotton and cellofiber import department ACNSAS, P179/Vol. 31/p. 278.

87. ACNSAS, P179/Vol. 5.

88. ACNSAS, P179/Vol. 1/p. 415.

89. Another name used for these people was "cell agents."

90. ACNSAS, I211285/p. 302.

91. ACNSAS, I211285/p. 267, the same situation is reported by Adalbert Rosinger, in the same period of time and regarding the missing pages from the Criminal file P179.

92. ACNSAS, P179/Vol. 45/p. 23, Rado's testimony on May 16, 1962.

93. After his release from prison, Rado repeatedly visited another Foreign Trade official at Fructexport, Geza Kornis (1914–2019), who used to live in Bad Homburg, Germany, before whom he repeatedly confessed his constant fear during the investigation, due to the inhumane conditions in which he was held, being forced by beatings and threats to accept the statements of the investigator. This information, told by Kornis, was handed to the author as a letter dated October 26, 2009.

94. ACNSAS, P179/Vol. 45/p. 226.

95. Cell mate agent quotation, ACNSAS, p179/Vol. 45/p. 226.

96. ACNSAS, p179/Vol. 45/p. 235, on May 15, 1963.

97. It is clear from this exchange of statements, found in the archive file that Rado collaborated extensively with Securitate during his investigation, author's opinion.

98. Vol. 3/pp. 3–137/211284ACNSAS, the reports were written by an ethnic German, Baltes Hansof, living in Sighişoara, la ACNSAS, I211284/Vol. 3/pp. 3–137.

99. Tudosie Butoi's reports (400 pages), ACNSAS, P179/Vol. 41, Radu Motancea's in ACNSAS, P179/Vol. 43.

100. According to the Constitution of the Romanian People's Republic from 1952, Art. 69 provides that "the accused is guaranteed the right to defense."

101. The trials of Stalin's time, known as the Great Purge, or the trials of Rajk or Slanski, were covered by the media, their development being broadcast on the radio. This fact was verified during the discussions I had in 2008 via email, both with Prof. Peter Solomon, professor of Soviet Criminal Law in Toronto, and with Dr. Barbara Falk.

102. In Romanian, Încheiere.

103. Chapter 4 presents a description of each of these documents.

104. ANCSAS, P179/Vol. 35/pp. 1–29.

105. The injured party exercising civil action is a party to criminal proceedings and is called a civil party.

106. Except for what was previously mentioned.

107. Chapter 4 presents a description of each of these documents.

108. ACNSAS, P179/Vol. 35/pp. 33–233.

109. ACNSAS, P179/Vol. 35/pp. 30–32.

110. Conclusion, in Romanian Incheierea, ACNSAS, P179/Vol. 35/pp. 1–29.

111. CP-1960, Book II "Crimes and felonies in particular," Title I "Crimes and felonies against the State," Chapter II "Crimes and felonies against the Internal Security of the State," Section I bis, Art. 209[1] paragraph I (paragraph I was switched to from paragraph II, which stipulated the death penalty if the deeds were considered very serious).

112. CP-1960, Book II "Crimes and felonies in particular," Title I "Crimes and felonies against the State," Chapter II "Crimes and felonies against the Internal Security of the State," Section I "The attack and the conspiracy against the constitutional and social order of the Romanian People's Republic," Art. 209(2c).

113. CP-1960, Book II "Crimes and felonies in particular," Title XIII "Felonies against persons," Chapter II "Felonies against individual liberty," Section IV "Classified Information Violations," Art. 506, para.1.

114. CP-1960, Book I "General Proceedings," Title III "Punishments," Chapter V "Punishments referring to Rights," Section I "Civic Degradation," Art. 58 (2-4).

115. CP-1960, Book II "Crimes and felonies in particular," Title XIII "Felonies against persons," Chapter II "Felonies against individual liberty," Section IV "Classified Information Violations," Art. 506, para. 4.

116. CPP-1960, Book I "General Proceedings," Title III bis "Some crimes against the economic system of the RPR," Chapter I "Economic Misdemeanors," Art. 268(28a).

117. The meaning of Art. 209, paragraph 2c of the CP-1960, referred to slander, or defamation of the social order of the state, while paragraph 2a referred to propaganda, agitation, or any action to change the existing social order in the state, or the democratic form of government that would result in a danger to state security. It's clear that paragraph 2c relates to a less serious felony than paragraph 2a.

118. Called DUI in accordance with their Romanian name, Dosare de Urmărire Informativă.

119. ACNSAS, D11514/Vol. 5/pp. 25–32. This file, held in the CNSAS Documentary Fonds, refers among other things, to the serious problem, which had existed in cotton imports, in 1946. The interest in the development of trade relations with Western countries is emphasized. Next, on pp. 33–48, the difficulties encountered by the communist authorities upon taking power, in the development of these relations are mentioned. Cotton was among the raw materials of the textile industry.

120. The CSP functions were explained in the subchapter about Romania's economic position after World War II.

121. MCE organizational chart can be seen in appendix IV.

122. Andrei Klein, known also as Bandi Klein was among the witnesses in the RE trial.

123. Some of this information was provided by Mrs. Suzette Profeta Stoenescu, who at that time held the position of director of a department at Tehnoimport, and with whom I had innumerable discussions in her apartment in Bucharest, during 2010–2012.

124. ACNSAS, P179/Vol. 29/p. 113v, Gheorghe Manheim's testimony during the trial.

125. For example, RE and PE.

126. Consultants were hierarchically superior to the heads of services.

127. The cement industry started to develop in Romania in the eastern part of the country at the end of the nineteenth century, when cement factories were built near the Danube Delta, in Brăila and Cernavoda.

128. Poland was known as the biggest cement exporter among the East European socialist countries.

129. ACNSAS, P179/Vol.28/p. 58. This is the second volume of the financial assessment through the Criminal Case. The second assessment was initiated, after the defendants' observations following the first financial assessment.

130. These concepts referring to freight transport and insurance schemes are explained in appendix V.

131. Such a type of transaction will be analyzed in one of the next pages under the name Bohumer Affair.

132. ACNSAS, P179/Vol. 28/p. 58.

133. In 1951, Adalbert Rosinger made his first trip to Egypt as the official RE representative of RE, with the aim of concluding the barter transaction of selling wheat and buying cotton.

134. Though the value of an Egyptian lira at the beginning of the 1950s was close to that of a pound.

135. ACNSAS, P179 / Vol. 5/p. 74, a declaration made by the person in charge, Ion Georgescu, who was a Romanian staff member in Egypt at the time.

136. The company whose name was MISR—Filature Mehalla Misr, in Arabic (المحلة - مصر), was among the first with which RE closed contracts for cotton purchase after Toriel; MISR, in Arabic, means Egypt.

137. ACNSAS, P179/Vol. 34/p. 64.

138. This refers to selling products to companies in Egypt, such as different types of processed wood and kerosene, ACNSAS, P179/Vol. 2, pp. 434–435.

139. United Egyptian Commerce, Alexandria Cotton Trading, Riches-Alexandria, MISR, Filature Mehalla Cl Kobra.

140. Reference is made to a letter, now in my possession, written by former Fructexport employee, Geza Kornish (1917–2019) who lived in Frankfurt am Main.

141. ACNSAS, P179/Vol. 34/p. 94v, Paul Stefanescu's testimony in front of the Military Court.

142. ACNSAS, P179/Vol. 2/p. 447.

143. ACNSAS, P179/Vol. 2/p. 448v.

144. The Shilling (abbreviation s.) is an English coin used until 1971. Its value in terms of the English pound (£) was the following: 1 pound /20 = 0.05s. A complete table of conversions can be found in appendix V.

145. Constanța is the most important Romanian port to the Black Sea.

146. ACNSAS, P179/Vol34/p. 122, out of Sidonia Grigoriu's investigation.

147. ACNSAS, P179/Vol.2/p. 447, out of Adalbert Rosinger's investigation.

148. CSP had planned to sell 1,220,000 tons of cement, but in practice, RE had only started selling cement in the third quarter of 1954, an additional reason for the situation created by the cement events on the world market.

149. ACNSAS, P179/Vol. 2/p. 448. Despite CMEA prices, Romania used to make its decisions based on what was right for itself in the context of its commercial transactions.

150. ACNSAS, P179/Vol. 34/p. 122, during Sidonia Grigoriu's investigation on June 17, 1963.

151. Ana Toma, who held the position of MCE deputy minister, was mentioned in chapter 3.

152. ACNSAS, P179/Vol. 34/p. 122v.

153. ACNSAS, P179/Vol. 34/p. 122v, a well-documented statement with explanations on the subject can be found in ACNSAS, P179/Vol. 4/pp. 215–219.

154. ACNSAS, P179/Vol. 4/p. 213.

155. ACNSAS, P179/Vol. 2/p. 448, and about the $200 bonus in, ACNSAS, P179/Vol. 4/p. 80.

156. In Saudi Arabia.

157. C120.

158. A document issued by a financial institution and used for the commercial financing of a business. It was one of the main forms of settlement in the socialist economy, consisting of a document by which a credit institution offers a commercial institution the obligation to pay after certain obligations are fulfilled. The specified

amount of money is previously secured at the bank. Letters of credit are used primarily in high-value international business transactions between a supplier and a customer.

159. In the case of the C120 contract, The MCE approval report existed and was referred to, during the RE investigation, as no. 05216/31/01/1955.

160. Ladislau Ilies, whose Surveillance file holds the number I195690, held the position of head of the cement export service from 1954. He served as a prosecution witness in the RE trial.

161. Angelo Chinzbrunner's testimony to be found in ACNSAS, I21280/p. 25.

162. The cement was meant for sale to Saudi Arabia, through Jeddah harbor, in the western part of the peninsula.

163. Romtrans was the Romanian maritime transport enterprise, which used either its own ships or chartered ships from other countries.

164. ACNSAS, P179/Vol. 34/pp. 124–124v.

165. Romtrans was one of the companies that belonged to the MCE in the 1950s and 1960s. It was the Romanian transport company, engaged in the transport of goods. The ships that carried out the transports were both Romanian and also rented from foreign companies.

166. ACNSAS, P179/Vol. 4/pp. 224–225.

167. Agio is the difference between the official value of a currency and that used in commercial transactions. This difference is sometimes added to the price in transactions where changes in currency values are expected over the course of execution of a long-term contract.

168. ACNSAS, P179/Vol. 34/p. 130.

169. There was no significant difference between the two currencies, 1 pound sterling (£) = 0.975 Egyptian pounds.

170. Rosinger's testimony during the investigation, ACNSAS, P179/Vol. 3/p. 103 v and his PVI of December 22, 1962.

171. ACNSAS, P179/Vol. 4/p. 113v.

172. ACNSAS, P179/Vol. 4/pp. 130–131.

173. ACNSAS, P179/Vol. 34/p. 133v.

174. ACNSAS, P179/Vol. 4/p. 221.

175. ACNSAS, P179/Vol. 2/p. 457.

176. This was the last sale price, in September 1954, to the Jasumi, Java Sumatra Company in Rotterdam.

ACNSAS, P179/Vol. 2/p. 457.

177. ACNSAS, P179/Vol. 34/p. 69v, Rosinger's testimony in the court.

178. ACNSAS, P179/Vol. 34/p. 130v.

179. ISCE in Romanian means Întreprindere de Stat pentru Comerţ Exterior.

180. ACNSAS, P179/Vol. 4/pp. 92–97.

181. H.C.M 587/1952, *H*otararea *C*onsiliului de *M*inistrii., in English, *A Decision of the Council of Ministers*.

182. ACNSAS, P179/Vol. 4/p. 95v, the question of transport expenses (navlu in Romanian) was discussed. The references are for 1954 and the first part of 1955.

183. The structure of the MCE and the existing directions in the ministry can be found in appendix IV.

184. ACNSAS, P179/Vol. 4/p. 213.

185. ACNSAS, P179/Vol. 33/p. 569, the volume of the second financial assessment.

186. ACNSAS, P179/Vol. 34/p. 12

187. These were not the only false data in the assessment. I have exclusively referred to the C120 contract analyzed earlier.

188. Sidonia Grigoriu' s testimony ACNSAS, P179/V34/p. 123v.

189. Adalbert Rosinger's testimony, ACNSAS, P179/V34/p. 69v.

190. After its nationalization, following 1956 events in Egypt, Toriel was renamed Cofiltra, but throughout this document, the name Toriel will be preserved.

191. ACNSAS, P179/Vol. 34/p. 125v, p. 127v.

192. ACNSAS, P179/Vol. 4/p .225.

193. The statement was already made earlier, when it came to problems that arose after the signing of C120. The problem created by the exaggerated demand for transport vessels had ultimately led to raising the shipping costs.

194. ACNSAS, P179/Vol. 31/p. 3, Ciobanu's testimony.

195. ACNSAS, P179/Vol. 24/pp. 79–80.

196. ACNSAS, P179/Vol. 4/p. 274.

197. Under the leadership of Gamal Abdel Nasser (1918–1970) along with Mohamed Naguib (1901–1984), who would become the first President of the Republic of Egypt, the Egyptian monarchy was overthrown in 1952. Shortly afterward, Naguib was put under house arrest and G. A. Nasser was elected as the second president of Egypt starting in 1956.

198. ACNSAS, P179/V34/p. 135, Angelo Chinzbrunner's testimony in court.

199. ACNSAS, P179/V34/p. 92v, Paul Sefanescu's testimony in court.

200. ACNSAS, P179/V34/p. 113v.

201. The *Journal of the Chamber of Commerce of Romania* periodically published lists of the companies with which Romania had commercial connections, including the products sold and the suppliers. On certain occasions, the existing conditions on the world market in certain areas of foreign trade were also published. This type of information on the import plans of some countries was mentioned in specialized publications. Commercial information regarding products and quantities used to be published, as Gheorghe (Gyuri) Leuchter, who had worked in both MCE and RE, explained to me during our September 2010 meeting in Düsseldorf, Germany. He served as a witness for the prosecution in the RE trial, and was also mentioned in the previous subchapter. Leuchter was a textile engineer and after leaving Romania (1974), he moved to Germany where he continued to live until his death in 2012.

202. ACNSAS, P179/Vol. 4/p. 274, the last pages of Sidonia Grigoriu's investigation on February 10, 1964.

203. ACNSAS, P179/Vol. 2, p. 226.

204. This refers to cigarettes, hand watches, pens, nylon stockings or various textiles, as well as medicines. These items could be purchased from a daily allowance paid to officials who went abroad.

205. ACNSAS, P179/V4/pp. 204–237.

206. This information was received following a request addressed to the current public company, Romănoexport SA, to study the archive of the former RE enterprise. The enterprise, whose old headquarters was located in Rosetti Square, is located today in Doamnei Street number 13-15, Bucharest.

207. Referring to the last chapter of the financial assessment, in its first version, it can be seen how the Securitate made use of various exchange rates for currency, according to unclear criteria, apparently related to the traded goods. For example, according to ACNSAS, P179/Vol. 33/pp. 379–380, the dollar exchange rate in cotton sales-purchases was calculated at 31 lei/dollar, for cotton yarns 36 lei/dollar, for fabrics 57.9 lei/dollar, for cement 52.6 lei/dollar.

208. According to the tables 6.1 and 6.2, the conversions rates for the first evaluation was 1 leu = $54, for the second evaluation was 1 leu = $51, so making an average of these two, in the final evaluation can be considered that 1 leu = $52.

209. ACNSAS, P179/Vol. 36/p. 240, a document that is an annex to the appeal request made by Adalbert Rosinger on August 8, 1964.

210. See chapter 1.

211. Both in the PE 1 and the RE trials, the prosecutor requested the death penalty for some of the accused, according to CP-1960, Art. 209[1], paragraph 2, as punishment for a particularly serious crime.

212. For example, Iosif Bistran, who was deeply involved in the arrest and investigation of economic trials officials (chapters 5 and 6), and who benefited from priority conditions, many years after the overthrow of communism, would fall into this category. About Bistran's positions in Securitate, CNSAS archive, at the address http://www.cnsas.ro/documente/cadrele_securitatii/BISTRAN_IOSIF.

Conclusion

> When justice does not succeed in being a form of memory, memory alone can become a form of justice.
>
> Ana Blandiana[1]

The progression of actions and events presented in this book takes place between two worlds. One is that of law and transitional justice, the other is the world of history, telling the story of characters from Romania in the 1960s. The continuity of some manifestations of anti-Semitism was evident at that time in Romania, reminiscent of those that had taken place in the nineteenth century, or even up to the first part of the twentieth century. The existence of such attitudes had generated various movements against the Jews over the years. The past accusations against the Jews, many of them with religious connotations, had been replaced by another type of slander in modern times, like the foreign trade economic trials. They retained the defining element of the incrimination of people belonging to Jewish ethnicity, changing the setting, scenario, and human typology.

It should be mentioned that a certain kind of political openness, perhaps liberalization, was felt around 1964, as a pertinent conclusion to what happened in Gheorghiu-Dej's Romania. Although nearly all political prisoners were released at the time, none of the foreign trade prisoners (at that moment, all except those from RE, were already condemned) enjoyed this measure.

The reason was likely to be connected to both the fact they were condemned not such as "simple" enemies of the regime, but as people who had produced significant damages to the national economy, which represented the main reason for their being judged and imprisoned. As I have explained, those trials were unique, mainly because of this specific feature. But more than that, I considered the fact that they remained in prison, even at that specific moment, was also an expression of the original anti-Semitic intention of their being dismissed from their positions. It was also known that part of those people had, at times, expressed their will to emigrate.

The economic trials that took place in Romania between 1960 and 1965, at the end of Gheorghiu-Dej's leadership, remained unique for other reasons as well, as compared to the staged political trials in other satellite countries of the Soviet Union. The trials were kept secret and were not commented on by the press. They were held at a military court, the allegations being political in nature, and the Securitate was the body in charge of the investigation. Most of the defendants were Jews, but not all Jewish foreign trade officials who held senior positions at the time were removed from office. However, the gradual elimination of Jews from foreign trade was a trend that began in 1958 and did not stop even with the death of Gheorghiu-Dej.

Though chapter 2 of this book argues about the uniqueness of the foreign trade trials within the East European bloc, with the possible exception of the Soviet Union, it neither can be concluded that their organization was determined by the influence of Moscow, nor it was under this influence, the senior officials were eliminated from foreign trade. Neither were significant similarities found between the various economic trials in the Soviet Union and those that took place in Romanian foreign trade.

As shown in chapter 1, this time period coincided with the strengthening of the nationalistic tendencies of the party's policy, led by Gheorghiu-Dej. The legal expression of the harshening of the repressive tactics employed by the Romanian political bodies from the 1950s was the widespread application of exaggerated accusations according to the Criminal Code, among which were "attack and conspiracy against the social and constitutional order in the Romanian People's Republic," "undermining the national economy," and "counter-revolutionary sabotage." I have also mentioned before that following 1964, in several cases, defendants of the first trials (PE, AE) had their prison terms reduced by half, as a consequence of decisions made by the High Court of Romania. This might have also been a result of the large number of amnesty decrees issued in that year and previous ones for other political prisoners, among whom the foreign trade defendants were not included.

Regarding the order and the exact date of the initiation of these trials, we were not able to access documents that could have served as a direct testimony. In their absence, the conclusion of the paper is that the protocol of the Working Meeting of the Workers of the Ministry of Commerce of October 1958 was the defining moment of the decision to incriminate the Jewish officials in the ministry. During this meeting, the members of the party, led by Florian Danalache, underlined their dissatisfaction with the way in which these officials performed their tasks, as well as spotlighting the intention of some of them to leave the country and emigrate to Israel. Romanian historiography only mentions the existence of these trials sporadically.

The extensive documentation prepared to complete the investigation and prosecution of foreign trade officials was the result of a meticulous and long-lasting effort by the Securitate's intelligence network, which formed the basis of the serious accusations against those arrested.

> Despite their apparent authenticity, the files must be read with great caution: they mirror countless details, but unscrupulously fictionalize the overall reality.[2]

This statement, even if it was made in the context of another staged trial, refers to the reality of any of the trials initiated by the party through its executive arm, the Securitate, which managed to procure information with the help of tens, hundreds, or even thousands of informants or agents, professionals or amateurs, with deliberate or accidental positions. There have been cases in which the Securitate's own members admitted the falsity of their own testimonies.[3]

But we must not forget that these criminal cases, the foreign trade trials, lack any original material that could represent the accused party. After careful, serious study of the economic trials, it cannot be completely ruled out that some foreign trade officials may have abused their position in order to gain some personal material advantages or certain favors for some family members or friends. This could have been achieved by obtaining special products, or by a currency transfer from which they could have benefited, through the relationships they had. Could these deeds be considered political crimes or attempts to betray the Romanian state? Could they be considered a conspiracy against the social order in the country or undermining the national economy? There is no single answer to this question. But even if some of those accused of serious political crimes, as we have seen, committed some deeds prohibited by the Romanian law of the 1950s and 1960s, they were minor in relation to the significance and gravity of the Military Court's decisions and sentencing, stated at the end of each trial. The Securitate, little by little, but skillfully and persistently, wove the web of accusations that enveloped the senior foreign trade officials.

From the moment of their arrest, each defendant was overwhelmed with a torrent of serious accusations, mostly unrealistic, but under the influence of the violent physical and verbal attacks they were subjected to, each of these persons eventually turned into a puppet controlled by others. Unable to cope with the pressures and the humiliations to which they were subjected every day, with the threats, beatings, insults, and venomous harangues that were hurled at them every step of the way, the arrested men reached the point of a blurring of their identity, and under the pressure of the Securitate investigators, were forced to accept their new identity as political criminals, taking on the accusations brought against them. The change in personality induced by long years of incarceration didn't stop even after release from prison. These people, who had experienced the communist prison for so many years, had almost completely lost all desire to try to prove their innocence, even belatedly, and to expose the truth behind the criminal charges against them. And yet, a small minority of former defendants continued to fight the authorities, even after Gheorghe Gheorghiu-Dej's death in March 1965, and to try to prove their innocence.

The accusations that led to the whole course of the trials were the consequence of Securitate investigators' consultation of some documents through which they tried to prove the strategic mistakes made at that time by the Jewish officials in the policy of both sale and purchase under the control of the Foreign Trade Ministry. The allegations involved a lack of timeliness of the decisions made by the accused officials and their preference for certain businesses or sales agents of some Western states. The cited documentation could not prove in any way any bribery or receipt of personal commissions or the appropriation of money for their own interests. All the damages designated by the appointed expert commissions were basically presumptive damages. They were based on statements claiming that the prices for the sales of Romanian products were too low, while the prices for purchases of foreign products were overestimated. The differences between the real prices and those determined arbitrarily by the expert commissions were the basis for calculating the damages that led to the decision to accuse the officials of the four enterprises of undermining the national economy. All these accusations, as well as the evidence brought by the investigators, came exclusively from the documentation found in the files of the foreign trade enterprises, which are irrecoverable because the archives of these enterprises were destroyed. Another source was the malicious information of Securitate collaborators and informants. Many of the accused admitted their guilt, but this occurred in the context of terror and unrelenting pressure carried out by the Securitate.

Along with the serious accusations brought against the foreign trade officials, their contribution to the development of the Romanian economy was deliberately disregarded. During the decade in question, they had succeeded in concluding numerous commercial contracts, whose volume of purchase and sale was hundreds of millions of dollars.

During my investigations for the purpose of writing this book, the primary historical sources that were available to me were combined with a personal point of view regarding the accused individuals and what happened during the trials. My personal connection with one of the defendants in the RE case study trial may have weakened the objectivity with which I endeavored to analyze the course of these events. My hope is that I have managed to demonstrate that the personal story has been reinforced by a rational analysis of the situations, in my effort to observe the events and phenomena described here from a certain distance, at least that created by the elapse of time.

After his release in August 1969, the last inmate of the foreign trade lawsuit, my father, Rosinger Adalbert, repeatedly tried to get the relevant hearings and a judicial review of the RE trial, and thus to be exonerated. These attempts received only the blunt refusal of all the authorities involved, and his life, as well as the lives of most of the convicts in the economic trials, ended without the sense of justice having been done. It is worth noting, however, that a few of the convicts were relieved of their pecuniary debts to the state in the late 1970s, allowing them to leave the country and immigrate abroad.

In recent years, in Romania, the implementation to some extent of transitional justice procedures was the main reason that access to the documents and to basic archival information used in researching this book was allowed. The change in totalitarian power and the gradual implementation of transitional justice[4] has resulted in the opening of archives to researchers and the general public. After the opening of the archives, made possible by the Romanian Parliament's legislation regarding access to personal files and disclosure of the Securitate,[5] 10 years after the fall of the Ceauşescu[6] regime, each person was granted the right to inspect his or her personal file or, as the case may be, the files of relatives who had been interrogated or arrested during the communist years. The political change that occurred in Romania allowed access to primary sources and facilitated the research whose results are presented throughout this book. There were, however, certain restrictions regarding access to the various files.

As a natural consequence of the procedures imposed by transitional justice, Romania issued Law 221/2009,[7] unfortunately carried out with an irresponsible delay. This significantly delayed law had already been initiated in 2007, following the sustained effort of three people, Marius Oprea, director of the Institute for the Investigation of Communist Crimes, former senator Constantin Ticu Dumitrescu, head of the Association of Former Political Prisoners,[8] and Minister of Justice at the time, Monica Macovei.[9] This initiative encountered strong opposition on the grounds that the compensation that could be claimed by the applicants might have totaled as much as 15% of the gross domestic product.[10]

Article #2 of this law totally cancels all the political accusations pronounced by any of the communist courts in the period between 1945 and 1989, as well as those based on the administrative measures taken at that time. The basis is made of a list of articles, which had belonged to the various Criminal Codes, which had changed during the communist decades and are listed in the Article #1 of the same law. Article #2 also provides for the application of these measures without a review of the old sentences.

One of the Law 221/2009 articles, in its original form, Article #5, allowed victims, or their families, to claim compensation from the Romanian state. This article can be identified with the implementation of Compensatory Justice, a characteristic element of transitional justice procedures. Shortly afterward, in fact, about one year after its publication, the law was deprived of any capacity for compensation, which would have been one of its essential functions. This is because the law, through its Article #5, was to grant financial compensation either to those who had been victims of the legal system during the communist period, or to their descendants, so insuring some compensation, both for physical and moral damages.

Within three years of its enactment, Law 221/2009 lost most of the purpose for which it had apparently been drawn up.

I hope that this work has succeeded in eliminating some of the mystique created around the foreign trade economic trials of the 1960s, thus making an important contribution to their research, while emphasizing two issues with a double significance that goes beyond the context of Eastern European communist societies:

First, the way in which the state, any state, is able to make use of its legal system, not to allow a life of security and well-being for its citizens, but on the contrary, to establish an oppressive regime with the help of its subordinate bodies. Second, the way in which a communist regime that claimed from the beginning to be an anti-religious regime, made use of the image of the Jew, according to perceptions existing since the Middle Ages, as a pariah,[11] who maintains connections with his brothers of the same religion spread throughout the world. These conceptions seem to have remained unchanged until the middle of the twentieth century, preserving the image of the Jew as the one who continues to take advantage of the relationships created to his personal advantage and to the detriment of the state in which he lives. These attitudes and beliefs were not explicitly written anywhere. There was no need for them to be written or spoken. They were simply perceived as natural. The economic trials studied in this work served as a living proof of those prejudices that had remained intact and unchanged throughout history.

NOTES

1. Ana Blandiana, one of the most famous Romanian poets, was born in 1942, under the name of Otilia Valeria Coman. She wrote not only poems but prose and essays as well. After the 1989 change of power in Romania, she also performed a political function. In 1994, she set up with other people, including her husband Romulus Rusan (b.1935–d.2016) a public foundation (the Civic Academic

Foundation) of which she is president. The foundation aimed to reconstruct the history of Romania, falsified during the communist power.

2. Stelian Tănase, "Acasă se vorbeşte în şoaptă," *Dosar & Jurnal din anii târzii ai dictaturii*

(Bucureşti: Compania, 11, 2002), in English, "There is whispering at home."

3. Florian Banu, "Adevăr si Fictiune în Dosarele Securitatii,"

in English "Truth and Fiction in Security Records," 5, accessed November 3, 2020, http://www.cnsas.ro/documente/istoria_comunism/studii_articole/arhiva_securitatii/Adevar%20si%20fictiune.pdf.

4. Romania belongs to the former eastern socialist countries, where this process was not accomplished. The main reason is the fact that no Lustration law has ever been approved in the Romanian Parliament. Lustration is a kind of political purification of a country's leadership when changing its political system from a totalitarian to a democratic one, ensuring that leaders aligned with the old regime are replaced. The word lustration comes from the latin "lustratio," that is, purification rituals.

5. Law number 187/1999 originally published in the M.O., nr. 603 of December 9, 1999.

6. December 1989.

7. http://legeaz.net/legea-221-2009/ published in the M.O. no. 396 of June 10, 2009, accessed on July 11, 2021.

8. Site of the organization at http://afdpr.ro/, accessed on July 11, 2021.

9. Monica Macovei (b. 1969) is a Romanian jurist and politician who held the position of Romanian Minister of Justice between 2004 and 2007.

10. Lavinia Stan, *Transitional Justice in Post Communist Romania* (chapter 7, Compensation and Rehabilitation).

11. A word coming from India, a person who doesn't belong to any caste and figuratively a despised person or community, to whom no right is recognized.

Appendix I

Glossary of Legal Terms

In this work, we refer to the Criminal (Penal) Code using the abbreviation "CP" and the Code of Criminal Procedure using "CPP." In the same vein, we refer to the Penal Code and the Code of Criminal Procedure in effect at a certain year, say 1960, with the abbreviations CP-1960 and CPP-1960, respectively.

Actus Reus—Also known as the external element or the objective element of a crime, is the Latin term for the "guilty act," which, when proved beyond a reasonable doubt in combination with the mens rea, "guilty mind," produces criminal liability in Common Law.

Common Law/English Law—Also known as judicial precedent law, is a legal system developed mostly through the rulings of judicial instances, as opposed to systems of Civil Law, which is developed mainly through actions of the state's legislative and executive branches.

Continental Law/Corpus Juris Civilis—Known also as Romano-German, German-French, or Civil Law, this is a model legal system of notable use in Western Europe, but also in other parts of the world, whose core principles are codified into a referable system, which serves as the primary source of law. Such legal systems stand in contrast with Common Law, practiced in English-speaking countries, which prioritizes previous decisions by judges: a Continental Law outlook would find it objectionable that different judges may be able to adopt contradictory decisions in cases with similar facts.

Habeas Corpus—Literally, "that you have the body" in Latin. This expression is used in a Common Law request of a judge, to order the authorities holding a person to present them before the court, so that the legality of the custody or detention may be determined.

Jurisprudence—The theory and philosophy of law. Scholars of jurisprudence seek to deepen the understanding of the nature of law, legal reasoning, legal systems, and legal institutions.

Intent—A conscious internal initiative, accompanied by a volitional effort toward some purpose, expecting to realize it by committing some act.

Legalism—Preoccupation with observing the details and minutia of the letter of the law; a legalist mindset. Also, an approach to the analysis of legal issues through abstract logical reasoning, focusing on the applicable legal texts—such as a constitution, legislation, and jurisprudential writing—rather than on the social, economic, or political context.

Mens Rea—Is the Latin term for the mental component of a criminal action or the intention to commit a crime. A person's intention is a necessary element of a crime in Common Law systems. The test of Common Law criminal liability is expressed in the phrase "Actus reus non facit Reum nisi mens sit rea": the act itself does not render the accused guilty, except when he has had the mental element of guilt, that is, criminal intent.

Inquisitorial Method—A method of adjudication in which the control of the process lays with the judge, playing an active role. In addition to whatever the opposing parties present, a judge engaging in this method will look for evidence themselves.

Adversarial Method—A method of adjudication whose rules are based on action only by the parties to the legal dispute. Thus, a prosecutor and a defendant, or their representatives, are responsible for presenting their point of view and of convincing the judge or jury of the merit of their case. Trials in this method are conducted by a judge, who must arbitrate the dispute in a state of impartiality—as opposed to the inquisitorial method, in which the judge takes an active role.

Due Process—This phrase refers to the right of every person to be duly and publicly heard by an independent and impartial tribunal for the determination of their rights and obligations and in any accusation against them of having committed a crime. This principle is enshrined in the Universal Declaration of Human Rights.[1] In particular, it is considered to include the principle of presumption of innocence, a legal custom used in most civilized states, being the assumption that a person is considered innocent until proven otherwise through evidence.

The Rule of Law—A political regime in which state power is framed and constrained by law. This concept was developed in continental Europe at the end of the nineteenth century in German jurisprudence. The very expression—"rule of law" (or "state of law", "Rechtsstaat")—first appears in German legal terminology in the nineteenth century, then in French doctrine ("État du droit"). It is believed that the concept originates in Kantian philosophical conception of civil society, in which the individual's natural rights are guaranteed.

Attempt—The beginning of execution of an intent to commit a crime, which is interrupted or otherwise fails to produce its intended effect.

NOTE

1. Art.9 of the Declaration of the Rights of Man and of the Citizen (in Romanian, Declarația Drepturilor Omului şi Cetățeanului).

Appendix II

Intelligence Institutions in Romania

SSI[1]—the Romanian state's intelligence service—had two different designations, with a change during the long period of its operation, but they both had the same acronym: prior to the communization of Romania, it was called the Secret Intelligence Service and played the role of an internal security body during World War II. It was founded by King Carol II in 1938 and dealt mainly with the collection of internal intelligence, especially against the Iron Guard politicians and dissidents. In November 1940, Order No. 3919 was issued, which changed its name to the Special Intelligence Service.[2] Later, after the communists took over the political power, and the fall of the Antonescu government in 1944, this service became the Intelligence Service[3] again, by Order no. 1695 being subordinated to the Ministry of War. Shortly afterward, in April 1945, Decree no. 79, issued by the Council of Ministers, returned the service to the subordination of the Council of Ministers.

The Securitate, officially established by Decree no. 221, issued by the Presidium of the Grand National Assembly on August 28, 1948, was originally called the General Directorate of People's Security (DGSP).[4]

The original structure was composed of the following Divisions after 1948:

- Division I: Internal Intelligence
- Division II: Sabotage prevention
- Division III: Prison and Militia[5] counterintelligence
- Division IV: Military counterintelligence
- Division V: Criminal investigations
- Division VI: Office for the protection of ministries
- Division VII: Technical
- Division VIII: Personnel

- Division IX: Political Division of the Romanian Workers' Party
- Division X: Administration and accounting

This structure was maintained until the transformation of DGSP, by Decree no. 50 of March 30, 1951, to the General Directorate of State Security (DGSS).

By Decree 264 of April 1951, the SSI (Special Intelligence Service), which after 1945 was subordinated by the Council of Ministers,[6] was abolished as a special service and became itself a part of the DGSS. The new DGSS structure consisted of 12 Divisions:[7]

- Division A: Foreign Intelligence Service, SIE (Foreign Intelligence)
- Division B: Counterintelligence
- Division C: Sabotage prevention
- Division D: Trucks (Transportation)
- Division E: Militia counterintelligence
- Division F: Surveillance and investigations
- Division G: Criminal investigations
- Division H: Military Counterintelligence
- Division I: Dignitary Personal Security
- Division J: Personnel and training schools
- Division K: Administration
- Division L: Political

By Decree 324 of September 20, 1952, the Ministry of State Security (MSS) was established as a central body, distinct from Ministry of Internal Affairs (MAI), but on September 7, 1953, by Decree 365, merged with MAI.

A new decision, this time issued by the Council of Ministers (HCM[8] 1361) as of July 11, 1956,[9] established a new change in the MAI structure. It was now made up of two departments, the Department of State Security (Securitate) and the Department of Internal Affairs. This structure remained the same when the Foreign Trade trials took place. Each of the departments had a substructure that of the Securitate being nearly identical to those previously presented.[10]

NOTES

1. In Romanian Serviciul Secret de Informaţii active until 1940.
2. In Romanian Serviciul Secret de Informaţii active between 1940 and 1944.
3. In Romanian Serviciul de Informaţii active between 1944 and 1948.

4. Florica Dobre, ed., *Securitatea, Structuri/Cadre, Obiective şi Metode Volumul I 1948-1967*, Documente inedite din arhivele secrete ale comunismului (Bucureşti: Enciclopedica, 2006) henceforth *Securitatea Cadre şi Obiective*, XII.

5. The Romanian Police was called Militia at that time.

6. It is mentioned earlier.

7. Accessed December 6, 2021, http://www.cnsas.ro/documente/cadrele_securitatii/Ministerul%20de%20Interne%20-1948-1978.pdf, p.3.

8. Decision of the Council of Ministers (in Romanian Hotărârea Consiliului de Miniştrii, HCM).

9. Accessed December 6, 2021, http://www.cnsas.ro/documente/cadrele_securitatii/Ministerul%20de%20Interne%20-1948-1978.pdf, p.6.

10. This appendix presents a very concise description of the Securitate's structure from the early days of the RPR, until the unfolding of the Foreign Trade trials analyzed in this volume. Florian Banu and Liviu Ţăranu, ed., *Securitatea 1948–1989, vol. I Monografie* (Târgovişte: Editura Cetatea de Scaun, 2016), Accessed August 5, 2021, http://www.cnsas.ro/documente/publicatii/Securitatea%20vol.%20I.pdf.

Appendix III

Types of Files within CNSAS

Initially, these types of files[1] were according to those held and inventoried by the Securitate archives. Depending on the case or requests, these files were transferred from the offices of the former Securitate, today the Romanian Intelligence Service, SRI, to the CNSAS institution, the National Council for the Study of Security Archives. All files were paginated, renumbered and renamed, so they are identified by a capital letter indicating the type of file, followed by an identification number of the person or group of persons to whom the information contained in the file refers. The information recorded in the various cases was part of the Securitate database, the result of an extensive follow-up activity. People's surveillance was done according to different criteria, and the files were recorded according to the type of pursuit to which the persons were subjected, as shown below:

PRE-SURVEILLANCE FILE

This type of file[2] was intended for storage of information regarding persons who were candidates for further surveillance by the Securitate bodies, in order to open a follow-up surveillance file in the future or to be recruited as an informant or a collaborator. People who were suspected of expressing ideas or having opinions that might be contrary to the official policy of the government or that might pose a danger of any kind to the socialist state could be targeted for such pursuits. The follow-up did not usually last for more than six months, enough time to decide on further surveillance. If the results of the follow-up proved to be of no interest, the file was closed; in the other cases, the surveillance file would be open for further tracking.

SURVEILLANCE FILE

This type of file[3] can be identified by the letter I followed by a five- to six-digit number, for example, I12345. It was intended for the storage of information regarding those persons targeted as having criminal potential, who might be indicted in the future. The surveillance was performed by mounting microphones on home and work phones, wiring, and tracking correspondence in both directions (sending or receiving).

INFORMANT NETWORK FILE

This type of file is identified by the letter R followed by a five- to six-digit number, for example, R12345. The information network consisted of all those people used by the Securitate, as informants or collaborators, each under the supervision of an officer, or a particular unit, for a certain period of time. Each of them had a cover name and had to report to a specific person in the service of the Securitate, responsible for his manipulation.

CRIMINAL CASE FILE

The Criminal Case file[4] is identified by the letter P, followed by a five- to six-digit number, for example, P12345. The criminal file contains the collection of documents related to the events of a criminal trial and begins with the issuance of the warrant to initiate criminal proceedings. The file includes in most cases the motivation for initiating criminal proceedings, the various custody and arrest warrants, investigation procedures, medical documents, and the indictment conclusions, which in the end would be submitted to the Court. All the documents following the events that took place during the Court session (the Appeal included) are also part of this file.

INTELLIGENCE OBJECTIVE FILE

This type of file was intended for the operational investigation of institutions or groups of persons that the Securitate considered suspicious or whose activities it wanted to track. Businesses could be varied, as could be the groups, and they often included people who had a common basis, either cultural, religious, or other, suspected to lead to dissident activities. The archiving of these files, usually done in the past in the Securitate Archives, was cataloged after their transfer to CNSAS in the Documentary Fund.

NOTES

1. List of Terms and Abbreviations used by the Securitate. Accessed on November 9, 2020. http://www.cnsas.ro/documente/arhiva/Dictionar%20termeni.pdf.
2. In Romanian, "Dosar de Verificare" or "Mapă de Verificare."
3. In Romanian, "Dosar de Urmărire Informativă."
4. In Romanian, "Dosar Penal."

Appendix IV

Organizational Scheme of the Ministry of Foreign Trade

Here is a structural scheme of the Ministry of Foreign Trade during the period of time the trials took place (1960–1965):[1]

1. Economic relations directorate I (Socialist countries), shorthand "Relations I"
2. Economic relations directorate II (Western countries), shorthand "Relations II"
3. Economic relations directorate III (Africa and the Middle East), shorthand "Relations III"
4. Economic relations directorate IV (Asia and Oceania), shorthand "Relations IV"
5. Economic relations directorate V (America), shorthand "Relations V"[2]
6. Department for international economic cooperation:
   a. Directorate for Import of complex systems and technical services
   b. Directorate for cooperatives and joint-ownership companies
7. Directorate of economic planning in foreign trade
   a. Economic transaction planning directorate
   b. Import directorate
   c. Export directorate
   d. Planning directorate
   e. Statistical directorate and computation center
   f. Financial planning and accounting directorate
   g. Cooperation and economic planning directorate
8. Legal agreements directorate
9. Monetary directorate
10. Directorate for price determination and trade efficiency
11. Directorate of organization and control

12. Directorate of personnel and guidance
13. Economic directorate
    a. Customs directorate
    b. Transport directorate
    c. Interior trade directorate
    d. Secretarial and administrative service
    e. Special chamber directorate[3]

NOTES

1. This scheme was prepared by Mrs. Monica Mureşan, archivist in the Economic Section of the Romanian National Archives (ANR).
2. The Relations V department did not exist during the 1960s.
3. The MCE structure has meanwhile changed and the new structures can be viewed. Accessed November 9, 2020.

http://lege5.ro/en/Gratuit/g43tsoby/decretul-nr-622-1969-privind-organizarea-si-functionarea-ministerului-comertului-exterior/2, or http://lege5.ro/en/Gratuit/g43tsoby/decretul-nr-622-1969-privind-organizarea-si-functionarea-ministerului-comertului-exterior/2.

Appendix V
INCOTERMS

INCOTERMS is an acronym for International Commercial Terms,[1] which means International Trade Clauses. In any contract of sale, there is the issue of establishing the delivery conditions, the transfer of risks and the distribution of expenses related to the transport of goods (expenses for insurance of goods, the value of transport, etc.) between the seller and the buyer.

The sale and delivery of goods in international trade can be done in several ways. The main differences between the various conditions of delivery of the goods involve establishing the responsibility of the seller or the buyer on transport costs (freight), on the guarantee of the delivery of the goods, from departure to arrival at the delivery address, that of the exporter (seller), the importer (buyer), or any intermediary.

These issues are resolved by inserting in the contract some detailed clauses, including the regulation of all these aspects, clauses that of course must be negotiated with the contract itself. In this sense, a series of terms used by the International Trade has been defined, both in the field of land and maritime transport, regarding the expenses of transport and insurance of goods, as well as the party that is responsible.

The terms or concepts that define the types of contracts in international trade have existed for many years. International Chamber of Commerce (ICC)[2] has defined these terms as INCOTERMS. Among the delivery methods that were mentioned in this book as concerning Românoexport in its relations with foreign companies, the following terms can be listed regarding the conditions of delivery of goods:

Free on Board (FOB) represents the condition of delivery of the goods from the seller to the buyer, so that the transport from the factory yard to the loading onto the transport ship (or land means), in the port of departure, is done by and with the responsibility of the seller. All subsequent expenses, formalities, and risks, from the moment the goods have passed the railing (cover) of the vessel, are borne by the buyer.

The cost of transport from the point of origin to the port of destination, storage of goods and transport insurance are to be borne by the importer. In this case, the buyer has control over the transport (sea or land costs) and insurance prices from the port of origin. According to this FOB model of delivery of goods, it can be said that the seller prefers to sell according to this delivery condition, because it is independent of possible changes in the price of transport, the seller's obligation ending after the arrival of the goods in the port of loading, including their loading on the transport means (sea or land ones).

Cost Insurance and Freight (CIF) represents the condition of delivery of the goods from the seller to the buyer so that the seller (exporter) is responsible for all transport costs (freight) and insurance against maritime risks of damage or loss of goods during transport to the port destination. The buyer is only responsible for unloading and transporting the cargo from its release at the port of arrival to its final destination.

Cost and Freight (C&F) is the condition of delivery of the goods under which the seller (exporter) is responsible for all transport costs (freight) to the agreed port of destination. It is the responsibility of the exporter to carry out customs procedures from the port of departure to the port or point of arrival. Its responsibility ends with the unloading of the goods from the ship, or from the means of transport of the goods, to the destination. After unloading the goods, the responsibility for transport costs to the destination falls on the buyer. Also, the costs of insuring the goods are paid by the buyer. The difference between the C&F and CIF methods is related to the payment of the insurance during the transport.

Currency conversion used in the RE cement contracts:

Value of 1 pound sterling was equivalent to either 20 shillings or 2.8 dollars.
Value of 1 dollar was equivalent to either 7.1428 shillings or 0.35714 pound sterling.
Value of 1 shilling was equivalent to either 0.14 dollars or 0.05 pound sterling.

NOTES

1. International Commercial Terms, accessed July 19, 2021, http://www.incotermsexplained.com/the-incoterms-rules/the-eleven-rules-in-brief/delivered-place/.
2. Accessed July 19, 2021, http://www.iccwbo.org/.

Appendix VI

Accused and Accusers of the RE Trial

DEFENDANTS

Name	*Religion*	*Date of Birth*	*Place of Birth*	*Function at Time of Arrest*	*Date of Arrest*	*Year of Release*	*Case File/ Reference*
Alexandru Rado	Jewish	17/06/1905	Reşita	Import-export advisor	09/06/1961	12/10/1968	P179/Vol 1&2
Adalbert Rosinger	Jewish	31/07/1909	Oradea	Advisor	9/06/1961	16/08/1969	P179/Vol 2&3
Mihai Crainic	Converted from Jewish to Christian	16/05/1904	Bucharest	Export line manager at a confection factory	24/02/1962	22/02/1966	P179/Vol 3
Sidonia Grigoriu	Jewish	1/04/1916	Bucharest	Advisor on cement exports	28/07/1962	10/1967	P179/Vol 4
Biniamin Schwartz	Jewish	29/05/1909	Bucharest	Service manager in cotton imports	14/02/1063	31/01/1969	P179/Vol 4
Alexandru Samuila Costin	Jewish	19/07/1911	Zabalţi, Lipova	Coordinating manager	14/02/1963	2/07/1968	P179/Vol 30
Angelo Chinsbrunner	Jewish	14/01/1917	Bucharest	Advisor and technical expert	14/02/1063	11/03/1966	P179/Vol 30
Gheorghe Manheim	Jewish	09/09/1924	Poeni, Huedin	Service manager in wool imports	14/02/1963	11/03/1966	P179/Vol 30
Paul Ştefănescu	Jewish	03/10/1915	Tulcea	Import manger in MCE	14/02/1963	30/07/1966	P179/Vol 30

MEMBERS OF THE MILITARY COURT[1]

Name	*Function*
Octavian Cuciureanu	President
Major Valeriu Sitaru	Judge
Colonel Ilies Badea	People's assessors
Lt. Colonel Ioan Matei	
Captain Nicolae Butnaru	Military prosecutor
Captain Constantin Alexandru	
Teodor Petrescu Joiteanu	Secretary
Marin Carstea	

FINANCIAL EXPERTS[2]

Name	*Profession*	*Function/Workplace*	*Comments*
Gheorghe Postolea	Economist, accountant	Deputy director, Ministry of Sustenance	No surveillance or operative files were found at CNSAS about all these individuals.
Traian Bobocea	Textile engineer	Director of cotton spinning, Dacia, Bucharest	
Stelian Dumitrescu	Chemical engineer	Deputy director, Ministry of Light Industry	
Constantin Bărbulescu	Banking specialist	Director at Romanian National Bank	
Petrică Sava	Jurist	Jurist at Prodexport	

NOTES

1. ACNSAS, P179/Vol 35/p.33, the volume includes the sentence of the trial.
2. ACNSAS, P179/Vol 1/p.60, the order for a financial assessment execution was done during Alexandru Rado's investigation, on January 15, 1961. No personal files of the financial experts were found neither at CNSAS nor at SRI.

Bibliography

National Archives of Romania (arhivelenationale.ro)
Central National Historical Archives Service - SANIC
Bucharest Archives - DBAN
National Council for the Study of the Securitate Archives (CNSAS - www.cnsas.ro)
Archives of the Romanian Ministry of Foreign Affairs
National Archive of Israel (www.archives.co.il)
Open Society Archives - Budapest (www.osaarchivum.org)

"Extraits de les produits d'exportaţion de l'entreprise Prodexport", *Journal of the Chamber of Commerce of Romania*, Nr.3(36), 1960.

"Roumanie, exportatrice de produits de l'industrie légère", *Journal of the Chamber of Commerce of Romania*, Nr.2(23), 1957.

"Voyage aux abattoirs de Salonta en train frigorifique, Prodexport", L'activite deployee par les agences Prodexport dans les ports roumains", *Journal of the Chamber of Commerce of Romania*, Nr.1(34), 1960.

Andreescu, A., Nastasă, L., and Varga, A., *Minoritâti etnoculturale : marturii documentare : evreii din România (1945-1965).* Cluj: Centrul de Resurse pentru Diversitate Etnoculturalâ, 2003.

Belknap, Michal R. ed. *American Political Trials.* London: Grenwood Press, 1994.

Benjamin, Lya, *Evreii din România între anii 1940-1944 Vol I Legislaţia Antievreiască.* Bucureşti: Hasefer, 1993.

Berman, Harold J., *Justice în URSS.* New York: Harvard University Press, 1963.

Berman, Harold J. and Spindler, James W., *Soviet Criminal Law and Procedure.* New York: Harvard University Press, 1972.

Betea, Lavinia, *Alexandru Bârlădeanu despre Dej, Ceausescu, Iliescu.* Bucureşti: Evenimentul Românesc, 1997.

Betea, Lavinia, *Lucreţiu Pătrăşcanu, Moartea unui lider comunist.* Bucureşti: Curtea Veche, 2006.

Brucan, Silviu, *The Wasted Generation.* Boulder, CO: Vestview Press, 1993.

Brustein, I. William, *Roots of Hate*. Cambridge: Cambridge University Press, 2003.

Burgess, A. J., "Direct Foreign Investment în Eastern Europe: Problems and Prospects of România's Joint Venture Legislaţion", *Law and Policy în Internaţional Business*, 6, no. 4 (1974), 1059–1104.

Checinski, Michael, *Poland, Communism, Nationalism, Anti-Semitism*. New York: Karz-Cohl, 1982.

Chirot, D., "Social Change în Communist România", *Social Forces*, 57, no. 2, Special Issue (1978), 457–499.

Christenson, Ron, *Political Trials, Gordian Knots în the Law*. New Brunswick, NJ: Transactions Publishers, l994.

Ciobanu, Monica, *Repression, Resistance and Collaboration in Stalinist Romania 1944-1964, Post-communist Remembering*. London: Routledge, 2020.

Cioroianu, Adrian, "Atuurile lui Gheorghiu-Dej", *Dosarele Istoriei*, 3, no. 8 (1997), 20–25.

Cioroianu, Adrian, *Pe Umerii lui Marx, O introducere în istoria comunismului românesc*. Bucureşti: Editura Curtea Veche, 2005.

CNSAS, *Securitatea. Structuri-cadre. Obiective şi metode, cord. Florica Dobre, vol. I-II*. Bucureşti: Enciclopedică, 2006.

Codul de Procedura Penala, Editura Ştiinţifică, Bucureşti, 1960.

Codul Penal, Editura Ştiinţifică, Bucureşti, 1960.

Constantiniu, Florin, *O Istorie Sincera a Poporului, Român*. Bucureşti: Univers Enciclopedic, 2002.

Costin, Alexandru, "Confections et tissus roumains" (entretien avec M.A. Costin, directeur de l'entreprise Românoexport), *Journal of the Chamber of Commerce of Romania,* Nr.1(34), 1960.

Cristureanu, Titu, *Romania Foreign Trade*. Bucureşti: Meridiane Publishing House, 1969.

Cutic, Meir, *The Prague Trial*. New York: Herzl Press, 1987.

Deletant, Dennis, *Communist Terror în România: Gheorghiu-Dej and the Police State, 1948-1965*. New York: St. Martin's, 1999.

Deletant, Dennis, *România sub Regimul Comunist*. Bucureşti: Fundatia Academia Civica, 2010.

Donath, Pavel, "Les produits alimentaires roumains s'affirment de plus en plus sur le marché international ", *Journal of the Chamber of Commerce of Romania*, Nr.3(36), 1960.

Douglas, Laurence, *The Memory of Judgement, Making Law and History în the Trials of the Holocaust*. New Haven, CT: Yale University Press, 2001.

Evel'son, Evgenia, *Судебные процессы по экономическим делам в СССР (Sudebnyie protzessy po economicheskim delam v SSSR*). London: Overseas Publicaţions Interchange, 1986.

Evidența și Analiza Activității Economice a Întreprinderilor de Comerţ Exterior. București: Editura Didactică şi Pedagogică, 1965.

Falk, Barbara, "Making Sense of Political Trials, Causes and Categories", *University of Toronto, Munk Center Occasional Paper*, VIII (2008), 2–72.

Fejtő, François, *Les Juifs et l'antisemitisme dans les pays communistes*. Paris: Plon, 1960.

Florian, Banu. "Adevar şi Fictiune în Dosarele Securitatii", *Analele ştiinţifice ale Universităţii "Alexandru Ioan Cuza" Iaşi, seria Istorie*, 51 (2005), 375–392.

Florian, Banu and Liviu, Ţăranu, ed., *Securitatea 1948-1989, vol. I Monografie*. Târgovişte: Editura Cetatea de Scaun, 2016.

Frunză, Victor, *Istoria Stalinismului Românesc*. Bucureşti: Humanitas, 1990.

Gitelman, Zvi, *A Century of Ambivalence, The Jews of Russia and the Soviet Union, 1881 to the Present*. New York: Schocken Books Inc., 1988.

Grosescu, Raluca, and Ursachi, Raluca, *Justiţia penală de tranziţie - De la Nürnberg la postcomunismul românesc*. Iaşi: Polirom, 2009.

Gross, George, "Rumania: The fruits of Autonomy", *Problems of Communism*, 15 (Jan–Feb 1966), 16–28.

Hodos, H. George, *Show Trials*. New York: Praeger, 1986.

http://bibliotecatest.ase.ro/resurse/resurse_electronice/teza_capitole.php?tid=977&qs=sort%3Dtitlu%26dir%3Dup%26pagina%3D11 .

http://old.clujeanul.ro/general/afisare_articol.php?id_obiect=148&cat=50.

http://www.cnsas.ro/documente .

http://www.cnsas.ro/documente/arhiva/Dictionar%20termeni.pdf.

http://www.cnsas.ro/documente/istoria_comunism/studii_articole/arhiva_securitatii/Informatizarea%20activitatii.pdf,http://armyuser.blogspot.com/2009/06/cazarma-malmaison.html.

http://www.iccwbo.org.

http://www.incotermsexplained.com/the-incoterms-rules/the-eleven-rules-in-brief/delivered-place/.

http://www.observatorcultural.ro.

http://www.presidency.ro/static/ordine/RAPORT_FINAL_CPADCR.pdf.

http://www.Românialibera.com/articole/articol.php?step=articol&id=3136.

http://www.scribd.com/doc/55874512/Comerţul-Exterior.

http://www.time.com/time/magazine/article/0,9171,840966,00.html.

https://www.wilsoncenter.org/sites/default/files/media/documents/publication/ACFAF5.pdf.

http://www.wilsoncenter.org/topics/pubs/ACFAF5.pdf.

http://www.yadvashem.org/odot_pdf/Microsoft%20Word%20-%203128.pdf.

http://www.ziaruldeiasi.ro/files/fstore/z_is/staticpages/Raport.pdf.

Ionescu Ghiţă, *The Breakup of the Soviet Empire in Eastern Europe*. London: Penguin Book, 1965.

Ionescu, Ghiţă, *Communism în România, 1944-1962*. Westport, CT: Greenwood Press, 1976.

Ionescu, Ghiţă, "Communist Rumania and Nonalignment (April 1964-March 1965)", *Slavic Review*, 24, no. 2 (June 1965), 241–257.

Israel, Gerard, *The Jews of Russia*. New York: S't Martin Press, 1975.

Janos C., Andrew, "Modernization and decay in historical perspective: The case of Romania", in *Social Change in Romania*, 1860-1940, ed. Kenneth Jowitt. Berkeley: University of California, Institute of International Studies, 1978, pp. 72–116.

Jowitt, Kenneth, *Revolutionary Breakthrough and Naţional Development: The Case of Romania, 1944-1965*. Oakland, CA: University of California Press, 1971.

Judt, Tony, *Postwar: A History of Europe since 1945*. London, William Heinemann, 2005.

Kaplan, Karek, *Report on the Murder of the General Secretary*. Chicago, IL: Ohio State University Press, 1990.

Kirschheimer, Otto, *Political Justice, The Use of Legal Procedures for Political Ends*. WestPort, CT: Greenwood Press, 1980.

Kirchheimer, Otto, "Politics and Justice", in *Politics, Law and Social Change*, ed. Friederic Surin and Kurt Shell. New York: Columbia University Press, 1969.

Kline, George, "Economic Crime and Punishment", *Survey*, 57, no. 3 (1965), 67–72.

Kline, George, "Philosophy, Ideology and Policy în the Soviet Union", *The Review of Politics*, 26 (1964), 174–187.

Lăcătuşu, Dumitru, "Torţionarii mor în somn: Colonelul Iosef Bistran", Accessed November 11, 2020. https://www.contributors.ro/tortionarii-mor-in-somn-colonelul-iosif-bistran.

London, Arthur, *Confession*. New York: Ballantine Books, 1971.

Manheim, Gheorghe, "L'industrie roumaine de la laine et le commerce de matieres premieres pour l'industrie de la laine", *Journal of the Chamber of Commerce of Romania*, Nr.2(23), 1957.

Medvedeev, Roy, *Let History Judge*. Oxford: Oxford University Press, 1989.

Montias, Michael John, *Economic Development in Communist Romania*. Cambridge, MA: MIT Press, 1967.

Muraru, Andrei, Cucerai, Sorin, Lăcătuşu, Dumitru Mareş, Clara, Petre, Constantin, Roman, Cristina, Marius Stan, *Dictionarul penitenciarelor din România comunistă (1945-1967)*. Institutul de Investigare a Crimelor Comunismului în România, Iaşi: Polirom, 2008.

Murgescu, Costin, *L'economie Socialiste en Roumanie*. Bucureşti: Meridiane, 1974.

Nouveaux produits roumains d'exportaţion : Une merchandise de prix: les plumes", "Des semences de plantes fourageres", *Journal of the Chamber of Commerce of Romania*, Nr. 1(26), 1958.

Oprea, Marius, *Banalitatea Răului, O Istorie a Securităţii în documente, 1949-1989*. Iasi: Polirom, 2002.

Oprea, Marius, Cosmin Budeancă, Sorin Cucerai, Andrei Muraru, and Raluca Grosescu, (ed.), *De ce trebuie condamnat comunismul*. Iasi: Polirom, 2006.

Osterud, Oyvind, "The Uses and Abuses of Geopolitics", *Journal of Peace Research*, (Thousand Oaks, CA: SAGE Publications, 2, 1998), 191.

Pacepa, Ion Mihai, *Cartea Neagra a Securitatii, vol I, II*. Bucureşti : Omega, 1999.

Pătrăşcanu, Lucreţiu, *Sous Trois Dictatures*. Paris: J.Vitiano, 1946.

Pavelescu, Alina, and Dan, Cătănus, *Amurgul Ilegalistilor Plenara C.C. al P.M.R. din 9-13 iunie 1958*. Bucureşti: Vremea, 2000.

Pelikán, Jiří, *The Czechoslovak Political Trials 1950-1954*. Redwood City, CA: Standford University Press, 1971.

Pineles, Marcela, *Memorii personale*, partially in the possession of the author.

Polonsky, Antony, *The Little Dictators, The History of Eastern Europe since 1918*. London and Boston, MA: Routledge & Kegan Paul, 1975.

Posner, Eric, "Les infractions Economiques en Union Sovietique", *Revue de la commission Internaţionale des juristes*, 5, no. 1 (Summer 1964), 3–47.

Posner, Eric, "Political Trials în Domestic and Internaţional Law", *Duke Law Journal* (2005) 75–152.

Potock, Chaim, *The Gates of November*. London: Seckler and Warburg, 1997.

Razi,G.M, "Rumania: Don't Rock the Boat", *Problems of Communism*, 11, no. 3 (May–June, 1962), 18–21.

Rosen, Moses, *Dangers, Tests and Miracles*. London: Weidenfeld & Nicolson: 1993.

Rosinger Adalbert, *Cartea Neagră a Comerţului Românesc din România*, A detailed Summary of 34 chapters and another written 12 chapters, Israel 1979, in the possession of the author

Rusan, Romulus, *Cronologia şi geografia represiunii comuniste în România*. Bucureşti: Fundatia Academia Civica, 2007.

Schöpflin, George, "Românian Nationalism", *Survey*, 20, no. 2–3 (Spring-Summer 1974), 77–100.

Schwartz, Charles, "Economic Crime in the USSR: comparison of the Khrushchev and Brezhnev eras", *International and Comparative Law Quarterly*, 30 (1981), 283.

Simon, Titus, *Pacepa : Quo vadis ? Din culisele Serviciilor Secrete Româneşti*. Bucureşti: Editura Ştefan, 2009.

Solomon, Peter H. Jr., *Soviet Criminal Justice under Stalin*. Cambridge: Cambridge University Press, 1996.

Stan, Lavinia, *Transitional Justice in Post-Communist Romania: The Politics of Memory*. Cambridge: Cambridge University Press, 2012.

Stănescu, Mircea, *The Reeducation Trials in Communist Romania (1952-1960)*. New York: Columbia University Press, East European Monographs, 2011.

Tănase, Stelian, *Elite si Societate, Guvernarea Gheorghiu-Dej, 1948-1965*. Bucureşti: Humanitas, 1998.

Teitel, Ruti, *Transitional Justice*. London: Oxford University Press, 2000.

Tismăneanu, Vladimir, "The Ambiguity of Romanian Communism", *Telos*, 60 (summer 1984), 65–80.

Tismăneanu, Vladimir, *Fantoma lui Gheorghiu Dej*. Bucureşti: Humanitas, 2008.

Tismăneanu, Vladimir, "Gheorghiu-Dej and the Romanian Workers' Party: From De-Sovietization to the Emergence of National Communism", *Woodrow Wilson International Center for Scholars* (May 2002).

Tismăneanu, Vladimir, *Stalinism pentru Eternitate*. Iasi: Polirom, 2005.

Toma, Sorin, *Privind înapoi - din amintirile unui fost jurnalist comunist*. Bucharest: Compania, 2004.

Treptow, W, Kurt, "Alegerile din decembrie 1937 şi instaurarea dictaturii regale", *România şi Al doilea Razboi Mondial, Iasi, Centrul de Studii Românesti*, (1996), 42–43.

Tsantis, Andrea C., and Pepper, Roy, *România, The Industrialization of an Agrarian Economy under Socialist Planning* (Report of a Mission sent to România by the World Bank). Washington, DC: World Bank, 1979.

Tudor-Pavelescu, Alina, "Avatarurile antisemitismului Românesc", *Sfera Politicii* no. 60, (mai 1998), 44–45.

Văsioiu, Oana H., *Evolutii ale comerţului exterior Românesc în perioada 1950-2000: România de la CAER la UE*. Bucureşti: ASE, 2007.

Verdery, Katherine, *National Ideology under Socialism Identity and Cultural Politics in Ceausescu's Romania*. Berkeley: University of California Press, 1991.

Zilber, Belu, *Actor în Procesul Pătrăşcanu*. Bucureşti: Humanitas, 1997.

Zwick, Peter, "The Marxist Roots of National Communism", *Canadian Review of Studies în Naţionalism,* 3, no.1 (Fall 1975), 127–145.

Zwick, Peter, *The National Communism*. Boulder, CO: Westview Press, 1983.

Index

Italicized pages refer to figures.

About the Author

Dr. Veronica Rozenberg was born in Bucharest, the only daughter of her parents, Malvina and Adalbert Rosinger. She attended primary school and high school in Bucharest, and in 1975, she graduated with a master's degree from the Faculty of Mathematics of the University of Bucharest. In September 1975, she emigrated to Israel. Initially, Veronica and her parents were denied the right to emigrate due to her father's conviction in the Romanian Export trial. Although he had been released from prison in 1969 as a result of Nicolae Ceausescu's amnesties for the 20th anniversary of the proclamation of the Romanian People's Republic (1947-1967), he was still considered liable for the high fines imposed as part of his sentence. The approval of their emigration was obtained only after a chance meeting in Bucharest, in 1974, between Veronica and the American-Jewish lawyer Jacob Mellitz, who intervened on her behalf, with the help of the Connecticut senator, Abraham Ribicoff. Once in Israel, Veronica adapted to the new living conditions, studied computer science, and worked for many years as a programmer in various IT companies, after which she wrote a doctoral thesis in Hebrew at the University of Haifa, with the theme of the present book. In 2006, she was accredited as a researcher at the National Council for the Study of the Securitate Archives (CNSAS) in Bucharest, Romania.

The doctoral thesis became a Romanian book, first published by Mega Publishing House, Cluj-Napoca, in 2018.

In recent years, Veronica has continued writing short stories and travelogues and published the Romanian book *EPPUR SI MUOVE...and yet it continues* at SmartPublishing, in 2019. She also writes, from time to time, for the internet magazine *Revista Baabel* (ISSN 2734-4967). The past two years were dedicated to the translation of her Romanian book regarding the staged economic trials of the Jewish Foreign Trade Officials between 1960 and 1964 into English.

www.ingramcontent.com/pod-product-compliance
Ingram Content Group UK Ltd.
Pitfield, Milton Keynes, MK11 3LW, UK
UKHW021904150926
475560UK00004B/337

9 781793 652843